25,000 Miles to Glory

A Road Trip About Football, Freedom, Friendship, and America

Rhett Grametbauer

25,000 Miles to Glory

ISBN 978-1-48358-214-6

Printed in USA

ACKNOWLEDGEMENTS

It has taken me over forty years to live the experiences needed to write this book, and countless people have been involved in its production at various stages.

I would be a greatly different person if not for my parents and my brother. Growing up with them is the greatest gift a child could receive; the endless games of catch, encouragement, and laughter that was prevalent in our house helped me become the person I am today. I also have been blessed with two truly special sons, Chandler and Roman, who have encouraged and believed in me even when I did not believe in myself. Their support has made me better than I could have ever been on my own, giving me a purpose in life and a meaning to my existence on Earth.

Monique, I cannot thank you enough for everything you have done for me. Let this book be a tribute to your hard work and devotion that made all of this possible.

My long-time friends, Brad Clarkson and Andy Hello have also shaped my life. The only way to convey your importance to me is to say I have experienced the most important parts of my life with you. A lot has changed over the thirty-plus years we have known each other, but nothing has changed among us, and I do not know where I would be without both of you in my life. It is remarkable to find a lifelong friend. I am fortunate to have two.

Steve Sabol, who inspired a generation of young football fans like myself to see the game in a different light, was there with us on our journey. Hopefully, we have made him proud: Life is Good. Football is Better.

I also want to thank everyone involved with the road trip and documentary, *25,000 Miles to Glory*. Grayson Berry and G. Eric Carpenter, without your companionship I would still be on the side of the road in North Carolina or, even worse, still in my driveway. This journey was the greatest adventure of my life and it is my hope that this experience helped each of you find the will to live your dreams.

Patrick Hazlewood, you supported me and saved me countless times in the many years since we met. Your house on Herschel Avenue was witness to some of the best moments of the trip and will forever be a home to me. The editor of the documentary, Douglas Holloway, somehow took four months of my life and a worn out Volkswagen Bus, and made something watchable if not inspiring. My editors for this book, Roger Malespin, Margaret Simon, and Judy Rider: You read the story, understood the vision, and created something better than I could have ever imagined.

To the countless Volkswagen people who helped keep Hail Mary on the road and the NFL fans we met who shared their lives with us: You did not just add to the story, you were the story.

Finally, I would like to thank my VW Bus, Hail Mary. Few will ever understand the devotion to something that is clearly past its prime, temperamental, and prone to let you down from time to time, but you stuck with me despite all of my shortcomings.

CONTENTS

INTRODUCTION

Steve Sabol, Hail Mary, and a Dream

The use of travelling is to regulate imagination by reality, and instead of thinking how things may be, to see them as they are.

– *Samuel Johnson*

There are few things that set my mind at ease and force me to live in the moment more than driving my 1967 VW Bus. I affectionately named her "Hail Mary," and since the first time I ever laid eyes on her she has woven herself into the very fabric of my soul.

Far from my home in Texas, I found myself driving through rural, western New York after experiencing a Buffalo Bills game first-hand. I could not help but let a slight grin invade both my face and spirit as I drove through the rolling hills, which were spotted by livestock that reminded me of the Texas that I missed so much while traveling the country. Driving into a sunset on a simple, two-lane road with a few fellow travelers was the canvas that life had painted for me and I was more content than I had been in a very long time, maybe ever.

Going down a hill, the cars in front of Hail Mary were quickly approaching so I applied the brakes. My idea was to slow down, but she had other plans. The brake pedal got stuck and needed to be pried off the floorboard, but I pressed down on the pedal again hoping to awaken from the nightmare that was quickly becoming my reality. Again, the pedal stuck to the floor. The emergency brake was useless and most likely had been dormant for most of the forty-six years of Hail Mary's existence. I scanned the scenic landscape I had enjoyed just moments before, looking for a place to safely crash her.

What kind of life experience brings someone to the point of driving a nearly fifty-year-old vehicle into a cornfield and hoping for the best crash possible, and how did that someone become me?

I had just turned forty and my life had reached a fork in the road. As the great New York Yankee, Yogi Berra advised: "When you reach a fork in the road, take it." So I did, little knowing that the fork would lead me to my current predicament of racing down a two-lane road in western New York in a 1967 VW Bus without any brakes.

My misery had company in the form of two other football fans, Grayson and Eric who, the month before, joined me as we set out to conquer the National Football League (NFL)—one stadium at a time for seventeen consecutive weeks—while filming a documentary about the entire experience. I had even managed to convince NFL Films to work with us on the project. But now, not even halfway into the adventure, we found ourselves challenging our own mortality, thanks in no small part to Hail Mary.

Driving an automobile without brakes is definitely a unique experience and, ironically, when time is of the essence your mind has the ability to question your entire existence on Earth in just a few seconds: Is this what the road less travelled really looks like? Who thought this was a good idea? Why am I here? Where is here? How did I get here and how can I get out of here alive? I would soon have the answers to all of those questions.

Before buying Hail Mary I was clinging to a monotonous, regimented, mundane existence of being relegated to a nobody. My uninspired life was not what I had signed up for or dreamed about as a child, and I was determined more than ever to do something substantial with my life; to make something happen and to fulfill those promises and dreams I had as a child. I was longing to put miles on my soul. This was supposed to be my moment of glory, but first I had to find a way to stay alive and prevent Hail Mary from careening off the road.

Tom Landry, legendary coach of the Dallas Cowboys, said football is as important to Texas as religion is to a priest. Respectfully, I think he underestimated the importance of football. I grew up in Texas and more than willingly embraced most every aspect of being a Texan, including, and perhaps most of all, being a die-hard football fan. Texans are indoctrinated to football early and often—it has become almost a parental obligation or a birthright in the Lone Star state, where learning to throw a spiral goes hand-in-hand with learning how to walk.

My first recollection and most vivid memory of my room growing up is of the small pennants adorning the walls. Not those of just my team, the Dallas Cowboys, but of every team in the NFL. The five-year-old version of me would drift into a dream while gazing up at the logos emblazoned on the sides of the helmets. I burned up most of my days as a child dreaming of those places and stadiums, even pretending to be a professional football player. The family couch was the offensive line and my living room was the stadium that came alive through my television every Sunday in the fall. Those cities and teams were distant, almost mythological places, and to a young football fan the actual stadiums were little more than ideas to fill an imagination fertile for everything football.

The long street I lived on as a child was more than adequate as a stadium, and the other kids in the neighborhood consistently provided enough players to competitively field two teams. Most of the time there was a clear demarcation of who was on which team and the teams rarely changed, allowing me to build up a significant animosity toward the players of the opposing team. As a Cowboys fan, I dismissed the other team's players as being on the Philadelphia Eagles, New York Giants or, perhaps worst of all, the Washington Redskins. They simply were on the wrong side of the fence and I was determined to push them through the fence if the score of the game necessitated such action.

The games and players I saw on television were emulated in the neighborhood contests fought on my street and in various backyards. Because Austin, Texas, rarely had a significant amount of snowfall at any one time, the legendary cold-weather games in places like Denver, New England, Cleveland, Pittsburgh, and Cincinnati were difficult for us to emulate. In January 1985 that changed, if only for a week. We received nearly eight inches of snow over a few days, but making a snowman or snow angels never entered my thought process. It was all about football and, finally, we would get to play in the snow. Our overzealous parents, who insisted several coats be worn, provided the best defense that had been played in years. Although points were at a premium, we had our snow game and it would be talked about in our neighborhood with the same reverence and conviction as the Ice Bowl.

Most of my school pictures in the elementary years, or at least the ones I could control, were taken of me wearing some sort of football uniform. My lunchbox was metal with the helmet of every NFL team on it. Tony Dorsett, the Hall of Fame running back for the Dallas Cowboys, was there to open the new mall in Austin and so was I. My brother and I waited in line for what seemed like an eternity to a young football fan for him to sign our photo. "You look tired," he said when we got to him. "Anything for you, Mr. Dorsett," I said, in shock that this was *The* Tony Dorsett and he was talking to me.

I learned to add, subtract, multiply, and divide using the number seven first because touchdowns were easy for me to calculate. The number three was next because of field goals and was followed by six, which were touchdowns without the extra point. I gambled on my first football game in sixth grade, picking the Dolphins to beat the Bears because I could not bring myself to bet against Dan Marino on *Monday Night Football*. It was the only game the Bears lost that year.

Somewhere along the way my life had subconsciously become more about football than anything else. I would not have stopped it even had I been aware of my obsession that sometimes teetered on being completely irrational. At first I was only irrational during Dallas Cowboys games. Then, with the advent of fantasy football and having to watch my players as well as all the players on the opposing team, I became irrational during every NFL game. Actually, delusional may be a better word for it: I truly believed that I had an impact on the players and games, or the success or failure of my fantasy football team. During the football season I would often leave my office in downtown Austin and walk the five blocks to Fed-Ex Kinko's to change my fantasy lineup only to return a few hours later to change it back.

My inability—or unwillingness—to conform to what society expected from adulthood, my delusional sense of self-importance within the world of football, and that youth who grew up wanting to go to football games in far-away places got me dreaming. Not just dreaming, but believing that I could go to every NFL stadium. While sanity would dictate I needed to spread out the thirty-one stadiums over years and travel largely by air, dreams are not usually sane. If you have a dream, why not go big?

With that in mind, it was clear that I needed to do all thirty-one stadiums in one year—not ten—and not use a plane to get from game to game. The appropriate vehicle for the trip of a lifetime needed to have extraordinary character to match the size of the dream in my heart. An RV is cliché, and using a modern automobile would dilute the challenge to a large extent. If this was going to happen I needed to include a flair for the dramatic, add some panache, and an element of danger to my circumventing the country in the name of football. This dream would require the services of an air-cooled, 1967 Volkswagen Bus.

CHAPTER 1

A Leprechaun and a King

Denver, San Francisco and San Diego (Three stadiums and 2,683 miles)

If all difficulties were known at the outset of a long journey, most of us would never start out at all.

– Dan Rather

My friend and co-dreamer, Grayson, found a camera guy who was willing to take the adventure with us. He had worked with him before, but it was not the same crew I hired to film us at the Super Bowl. Actually, it was not a crew at all, rather it was a single guy who needed to work audio, video, and anything else that might come up on the road. The new camera guy was young and somewhat experienced, and had a very expensive Red camera—easily the most expensive piece of equipment in use for the documentary, including Hail Mary. As great as having a high-end camera was, the man behind the camera was not as reliable as we needed for such a production.

Three days before we left, Grayson decided a change was necessary. I told him it was his call and if he wanted to go a different direction to just lead the way. I was not as convinced as he was that we would be able find someone willing to leave their current life in three days to ride in a forty-five-year-old vehicle for four months with little in the way of creature comforts, including pay. Before I could figure out how to film a documentary without a cameraman Grayson managed to find someone else.

That someone was Eric. He lived in Conroe, Texas, which is just outside of Houston. After making the two-hour drive to Austin, Eric landed on my doorstep with his wife and mother who turned around and headed back to Conroe after meeting Grayson and me and saying goodbye to Eric.

He had quit his full-time job to go on this trip. His willingness to fulfill his dream of producing a documentary by leaving behind the structure that a job, house, wife, and dog provided, was a positive sign to me. He was friendly with a nervous energy surrounding him. That was understandable—we all had a nervous energy about us, including our wives, mothers, and significant others. He also wore a New York Giants cap, but he was originally from New Jersey, making the cap excusable. He was quite a bit larger than Grayson and me, which made riding in Hail Mary a challenge for him, but he never balked at the idea of spending four months in tight quarters. Eric was opinionated and proud of being from New Jersey, but I was equally as proud to point out that he moved to Texas as quickly as he could. I also shared my take on the Giants quarterback, Eli Manning, less than fifteen minutes into the trip. Eric did not share my assessment of Manning being finished as a good quarterback in the NFL, and was just as eager to express his thoughts on the Dallas quarterback, Tony Romo, and the Cowboys. The Giants and Manning would prove me right as their season was over before the calendar reached the end of October. The Cowboys and Romo waited until December to prove Eric right.

My imagination, which often pushes the boundaries of reality, was fertile with ideas of how the documentary of our trip would look and feel, but there was never any hesitation that Hail Mary would be front and center. I believed she would help people identify with us and what we hoped to accomplish. I figured it should be obvious that we were just like millions of NFL fans: Just three ordinary guys traveling the country to every NFL stadium.

Who could not relate to us or, at the very least, relate to having a dream and actually living it? Being relatable was important to me because I wanted to make a film that inspired others and in some small way make the world a better place through the realizations of their dreams. I saw Hail Mary as possibly being the main character, because, although she has many flaws, she also has as many, if not more, endearing qualities. For reasons unknown to me, people are enamored with a split-window VW Bus. To put it simply Hail Mary has IT—whatever IT is.

One day when I was a teenager I jumped into our backyard swimming pool while snow was falling. As soon as I hit the water, I started moving with the desperation of a fugitive to get out. I guess at that age our brains have not fully developed and, after considering everything we can consider, we think to ourselves, "this should work." That is exactly what happened the previous Halloween when I purchased a smoke machine because, if for no other reason, on Dallas Cowboys game days I could start it up outside the living room doorway and, wearing my Troy Aikman jersey, run through the smoke to my seat. I believed the smoke machine would take my game watching to the next level. Once again, I considered everything I could and thought "this should work." Funny thing about a smoke machine is that even though it is not real smoke it will set off a smoke detector. Regardless, I was undeterred in making ample use of the smoke machine throughout the year.

I envisioned the opening scene of the documentary as a tight shot of the VW logo on the front of Hail Mary with smoke rising, then a wide shot of her emerging from a plume of smoke—like Darth Vader at the beginning of *Star Wars.* We loaded Hail Mary with all the essentials needed to live on the road for the next seventeen weeks and placed the smoke machine directly underneath. With both garage doors closed, I pressed the red button on the remote and smoke began to fill the garage. My only thought was that this must look totally awesome and will be even better on camera. The dream of creating a documentary was about to begin and we were about to launch Hail Mary into the world! We raised the garage door, but before it could open enough for her to see the light of day all of the smoke escaped. Despite our best efforts and a less than well-thought-out tactical plan, we would not be launching Hail Mary into the world—at least not through a cloud of smoke.

We did not even make it out of my driveway before having our first issue with Hail Mary. The back would not close, so we quickly took ourselves to Vintage Wizards to see our mechanic, John. As he was fixing the latch on the back, Grayson asked him the worst thing he had ever seen happen to a VW Bus. John smiled and started to laugh under his breath, almost in disbelief of the question. He repeated the question back to us to verify that his ears had not betrayed him and that Grayson had indeed asked the worst thing he had ever seen happen to a VW Bus. His answer struck fear into the hearts of us all and made a childhood episode of a VW Bug catching fire an indelible episode in my life.

John, with a slight grin, told us the worst thing he had seen happen to a VW Bus was that it had caught on fire. Before we could respond to his initial comment, he warned us that if Hail Mary did catch fire we should grab all of our stuff while we could because we were not going to be able to put it out. "... catch on fire and it's gone," John's exact words would haunt me for the next four months.

The other piece of advice John gave us was to take it slow, try to drive at night, and do not push it too hard. Being that we were already behind schedule on Day One because of the ninety-minute detour we had to make for our first issue with Hail Mary, we were going to have to push it to stay on schedule. I would learn later in the trip that sometimes in life you are forced to push your VW Bus to get it started, but to make a VW Bus do something it does not want to do or that exceeds its capabilities is an exercise in futility.

I also learned that the efficiency of travel is inversely related to the ability to connect with people. Evidently, Hail Mary liked to connect with people, because she was anything but efficient.

John's advice was counterintuitive. The last thing I wanted to do was break down at night and have to sleep in Hail Mary until morning when, hopefully, we could find help to get us back on the road. On our way out of Austin we stopped at a grocery store to pick up some food for the road, since being already behind meant skipping a meal or two to stay on schedule.

About fifteen miles outside of Austin we were greeted with a light drizzle that served to cool us off in the otherwise unforgiving Texas heat. Not a storm, but enough to get the ground wet and form the occasional puddle on the road. Along with the drizzle came a peculiar noise emanating from the front passenger tire, or maybe it was the windshield wipers, or really God knows where. My heart sank and I alerted my passengers that fifteen miles into the trip we had an issue. The mood in Hail Mary became more serious, but not dire. At least we were not on fire.

I turned off the windshield wipers and waited to hear the noise. The noise waited, toying with our emotions before returning with the wipers off. Since it was not the wipers, it must be the tire, so I pulled over to the side of the road. Everyone emerged from Hail Mary and gave their certified approval that the tire met the standards of three people who had no clue about vehicles, much less the tires on a '67 VW Bus. With all of us in agreement, we reclaimed our places in Hail Mary and began making our way to what we hoped was Denver.

We drove as far as we could the first day, which was Lubbock, Texas. The 373-mile drive had been filled with disappointment and not much else. The food we brought with us was already gone, so we agreed to stop at the Chic-Fil-A across from the Texas Tech football stadium. College kids do not have the same appreciation for a VW Bus as the rest of the population, so we went largely unnoticed. I remember sitting in a booth and gazing out the window at Hail Mary who was looking as exhausted as her crew. Seeing the thousands of bugs that now lay silent across her nose, I thought to myself, "This is going to be a long trip." From the looks of her, she seemed to share the sentiment.

As glamorous as people may make this trip out to be, our hotels and overnight accommodations were anything but glamorous. The Best Western in Lubbock provided temporary shelter from the harsh elements of a Texas summer as well as a calmness that was a welcome relief from the constant movement a VW Bus generously provides. The room had little else in the way of creature comforts, but we were grateful to be on the road to meeting our destiny. The Best Western may have been the most expensive and nicest motel we stayed at the entire trip, but we needed the best accommodations we could afford since that may have prevented any one of us from suggesting driving back to Austin and forgetting this whole thing ever happened, and another one of us agreeing with him.

Making up time in a VW Bus is like driving in reverse to take miles off an odometer—it just does not happen. Despite our best efforts, we were still about two hours behind schedule, and because the September heat in Texas is debilitating, I honestly did not know if Hail Mary and her passengers were going to make it out of the state. While each of us was experiencing his own degree of discomfort, Hail Mary was suffering the most, which led to a side benefit to having to stop often to let a VW Bus cool down; getting to see more of where you are.

At first it was a frustrating necessity, but eventually provided some unforgettable experiences. Then the days either began to get shorter or the miles began to get longer, because soon enough we found ourselves in Colorado, driving at night, just like our mechanic John had suggested.

We have hills in Central Texas, not mountains, and other than skiing in New Mexico, my time spent in mountains was sparse at best. I definitely do not remember anything that would have prepared me to drive a vehicle that struggles to go sixty miles an hour on a straightaway into the heart of some of the highest mountain ranges in the United States.

Our inability to efficiently climb mountains provided adequate time to not only enjoy the view but to read the road signs. I began to notice that one sign, in particular, made a frequent appearance along the roadside. To me it read in an ominous tone that, come late December, snow chains would be required on our heroic trip from Seattle to Dallas. Not optional—mandatory. The signs muffled the grandiose dream I had of leading a parade at a Cowboys game to finish the tour around the NFL. We would need to address the schedule as soon as we could because putting chains on Hail Mary in hopes of not sliding off the mountain was not a particularly appealing way to spend the last days of our trip, or even perhaps the last few moments of our lives. For now, Denver was calling, so the schedule and tire chains would have to wait.

During the first two days of the trip the road won. If our travels had been a football game we would have lost 63-0. I do not think any of us had signed up for a trip like our first couple of days—I know I had not.

The toll riding in a VW Bus takes on a body is something I had not fully experienced or was anticipating, so I know it came to the other two as an extreme shock. Down, but not out, we saw the lights of Denver, Colorado, on the horizon and, just like a thoroughbred at the Kentucky Derby going down the backstretch, we began to give Hail Mary a little extra push.

The *Today* show crew was in Denver for the kickoff of the season and our cameraman Eric had a contact. “Al Roker likes your story and wants to meet you guys tomorrow at four o’clock in the morning at Sports Authority Field,” was the reply to the message he had sent the contact. In hindsight, the likelihood of Al even knowing about us was like expecting Hail Mary to win the Indy 500. Nevertheless, we got a huge boost to our morale when we needed it most, which made the inevitable letdown of the *Today* show worth it.

I had obviously never been on *Today* and was more than a little excited. Our perceived good fortune was proof that if you dare to live your dreams, great things will happen! We called everyone we knew to tell them to watch the *Today* show the next morning. The VW Bus was buzzing with excitement and we could feel the energy from everyone back home who were rightfully concerned that things might not work out in our favor. Being on the *Today* show would be as much validation to them as it would be to us.

We strolled into our budget motel early Thursday morning. Since we would be meeting Al Roker in a few short hours, sleep did not come easy. After a couple hours of silence, everyone was ecstatic to get back into Hail Mary. Tired from the lack of sleep and weary from two days battling our four-wheeled traveling companion to even get here, the excitement surrounding our first game provided all the energy we needed. We had every intention of getting on the *Today* show, but not as some fans of the Broncos only seen in the background. We had more lofty expectations of how things were going to transpire for us and the *Today* show. Our intent was not to interview Al Roker, but for him to interview us. After all, we saw no other reason to get up at four in the morning after driving the past two days to simply be bystanders—atmosphere for their production. We were the production and destined for big things, which were about to begin with our meeting with Al Roker.

After circling the stadium for several minutes, we found the only open gate. As you can imagine, fifteen hours before kickoff there is ample parking, so we put Hail Mary as close to the stadium as possible. Fans decorated in orange and blue dotted the parking lot and milled about outside the stadium. Although it was hard to imagine what sane people were doing at a football stadium fifteen hours before kickoff, I knew why we were there, and after spending two days on the road in Hail Mary we had effectively put all doubt about our sanity to rest.

I like to have everything planned and arrive fifteen minutes early everywhere I go or I feel like I am late. I had read the biography of the legendary Green Bay Packers coach, Vince Lombardi. The book explains the coach's near-obsession with being on time—if you were not fifteen minutes early, you were late. I figured if it worked for the Packers it would work for our trip. Hail Mary, however, did not adhere to that philosophy, so we were late everywhere we went. Obviously, Vince Lombardi never drove a Volkswagen, at least not one like Hail Mary.

My desire to plan everything included researching Broncos fans on the web. If you Google "Denver Broncos Super Fans" and search for images you will soon discover there is no shortage of face-painting, jersey-wearing Broncos fans. There also is no shortage of young, attractive females wearing as little of the required team uniform as possible. As much as we would have appreciated an interview with them, however, that would have made it a different type of documentary.

Google told us that Barrel Man may be the most famous Broncos fan in history. He wore the equivalent of a large Broncos metal trash can held up by suspenders, a Broncos cowboy hat, and little else to the games. Despite sharing a lack of clothing he was the polar opposite of the female Broncos fans we found online. I remember seeing Barrel Man on television during Broncos games when I was a kid. He, unfortunately, passed away in 2009, but has not been forgotten and even has his own bobble-head doll. Your life has been a success when you have reached bobble-head doll status—I hope to get there someday.

Farther down the Google search, there was another fan who stood out, despite not standing very tall. Rocky the Colorado Leprechaun was ornately dressed in orange and blue, and looking like someone you would expect to find at the end of a rainbow. Rocky embraces the role of leading the fans during Broncos games and is a fixture in the Denver community. With his finger on the pulse of everything in Colorado, he was the one who let us know the *Today* show would be at the stadium.

Rocky was our first interview of the day as well as the first for the documentary. When we got to the stadium, however, Rocky was nowhere to be found. We began to make our way inside, hoping he was already there. We figured that leprechauns wake up early, especially for the *Today* show, so we thought if we found a camera we would likely find Rocky. While the security crew gave us the obligatory grief about bringing our camera bag inside, we convinced them that we were members of the press, and may or may not have mentioned working with NFL Films. They relented, giving us a tag for the bag and allowing us to walk onto the field.

It was overwhelming and breathtaking to walk onto the Broncos field—the lights, the grass perfectly manicured and painted, and thousands of empty seats staring back at me. Few people get that kind of opportunity, and those who do probably do not appreciate it or become so acclimated to it that the aura of stadiums does not impact them the way it does me.

I remember my first time entering the Astrodome as a child for an Astros game. Walking with my parents and brother around to our section seemed like it was going to take forever. Eventually, my excitement got the better of me; I had to see the field! I stepped into the next section just to take it all in. My parents kept walking and looked back to tell me I was in the wrong section. They did not understand why I had to break off from the pack to just see the field.

Few people would actually understand, but from that moment on sports stadiums have had a hypnotic effect on me. The stadium experience for me is ineffable—words fail me when I try to explain the feeling of the first glimpse of a stadium or a field, especially one I have never been to. I have been fortunate enough to see many stadiums, but I will never forget looking at the green turf of the Astrodome for the first time. My childish exuberance for being at a game in a stadium has never worn off, and I doubt it ever will.

As soon as we walked out onto the Broncos field we could clearly see Al Roker. He was under the bright lights of the *Today* show facing the stands packed with fans dressed in their best Broncos attire—one outfit more outlandish than the next. All of them were jockeying for position, yelling and screaming incoherent babble in hopes of gaining that coveted pixel of immortality on their friends' television screens. In that sea of insanity, just as we had suspected, was our friend Rocky the Colorado Leprechaun. He was leading the cheers and pulling attention away from the more modestly dressed fans and projecting it onto himself. I am sure he secured his pixel of immortality for the day.

Eric also had managed to get us an on-site contact for Al Roker, but we had nothing to go on but a name—that was all. Grayson started asking people if they were or knew our contact.

In the end zone opposite from Al Roker, I saw a woman I recognized, even with her eyes buried in the notes undoubtedly for her next segment. She was semi-famous within football circles as a sideline reporter. I need to emphasize semi-famous, because Grayson apparently had no idea who she was and approached her to inquire if she was our *Today* show contact. Her expression was one that I can only imagine is the same a celebrity has right before asking,

"Do you know who I am?" to a member of the local police force who either does not know or does not care.

"I'm about to go live!" she quickly sneered, as Grayson hastily retreated to our group like a scorned dog who had just made a week's worth of trash its latest meal.

We eventually found our contact for the *Today* show without insulting any more sideline reporters, but she just stared blankly at us, as if she had never heard of us or our story. Her ignorance came as a somewhat expected shock, if there is such a thing. Dumbfounded that she had never heard of the legend of Hail Mary, Grayson began to negotiate with her. "What is it that you want with Al?" she finally asked.

We knew at that point that things were not exactly going in the direction we wanted, so Grayson simply requested an interview with him. Us interviewing him meant we were not going to be on the *Today* show, and unless he signed a waiver for the documentary the interview would likely land on the cutting-room floor. Our contact was kind enough to make it happen, though, and Al graciously spoke to us on camera for a few minutes.

"Every NFL stadium, in seventeen weeks, in a 1967 VW Bus," Grayson explained to him. Al glanced up at the lights of the stadium as if pondering the sanity of him joining us on our adventure. "Does that have air conditioning?" he knowingly asked.

"It doesn't have air conditioning," Grayson responded like a used-car salesman selling someone a certified lemon, "but I think you can handle it."

After hearing the news that Hail Mary was not climate controlled Al responded as if the lack of air conditioning was a deal breaker. "Nah, I don't think so," he said. Then, as if he needed to convince himself, he repeated it. "I don't think so."

While it was a great interview, us being on the wrong end of the camera was like wanting to see a great white shark in the ocean and settling for a goldfish in a plastic bag. It was definitely not the victory that our tired, road-weary brains pictured when we decided to try to make it to the stadium to actually be on the *Today* show.

We also decided early in the trip that a perfect business for a VW Bus would be a lemonade stand, because it forces you to learn to make the most of what you have been given. A road trip in a VW Bus provides lots of lemons, so having enough product would not be an issue. Since we had left Austin three days earlier, we had become pretty accustomed to making lemonade with the lemons life on the road had given us. The extra trip to see John and the Texas heat causing us to have to stop periodically to keep Hail Mary cool were all lemons of the trip, and although the *Today* show debacle was no different, at least we got to meet Al Roker.

The day was really just beginning, so we made our way back to the parking lot for our highly anticipated interview with Rocky the Colorado

Leprechaun. I did not study journalism in school, but I am pretty sure they do not cover how to interview a leprechaun. Rocky, our first indoctrination into the world of "these people really exist," apparently never met a camera he did not like and thoroughly enjoyed the benefits of portraying a leprechaun in Denver.

We had just started our interview when a local news crew began to feature the posse of decorated fans congregated at the stadium for the *Today* show. Rocky quickly excused himself to navigate his way into the heart of the action of the news crew.

Flashing a smile for the camera, he began to walk back to us and, with a fatigued looked on his face, started to relay the hardships a leprechaun faces on a day like today.

Playing into his persona I started the interview. "Your story is fantastic, born in Ireland," I said. "Oh sure, born in Ireland, brought the luck here. After all, this is where the pot of gold is," Rocky, in his best leprechaun accent, said without missing a beat.

It was still early morning, and having to lead the Broncos cheers— as he has since 1982—later that night was an exhausting experience, he groused. But the people demanded it of him, he said. Although he complained about the long day ahead of him I got the sense he would not have it any other way. Our interview lasted a few minutes and we made our way back to Hail Mary knowing we had made the most of that morning's lemons.

We hurried back to our economy accommodations for some much-needed rest, a conference call with NFL Films, and packing our bags for the game that night. Denver was our first game, which was exciting, but so was our first conference call with NFL Films.

I had met with NFL Films back in April at its headquarters in Mount Laurel, New Jersey. I was actually more nervous that day because I thought I was selling them on the idea of following us around and doing a feature on our trip. That was an exciting day for me even though I had no idea what to wear, who I was meeting with, how long it was going to take, and what they were expecting from me.

I decided to wear my best suit for the occasion and proceeded out of my hotel room in downtown Philadelphia to hail a cab for the fifty-dollar journey to NFL Films. I did not want to come off as someone with an inflated sense of self-worth because I was going to the mecca of the NFL, so I simply gave the driver the address without explicitly saying NFL Films.

He had no idea where I wanted to go and in broken English explained how Garmin could not find the address either. Different scenarios began to enter my thought process: Am I going to be late or even miss the most important meeting of my life? How does this guy not know where NFL Films is located? Maybe I should act like someone important, a sideline reporter or something, and hope it gets me somewhere—that always seemed to work for important people.

Instead, I remembered that the address had changed from 1 NFL Way to 1 Steve Sabol Way after Sabol's death. Maybe the Garmin did not have the updated address. I almost apologetically told the driver I needed to go to NFL Films, and that the address could be 1 NFL Way. He was still puzzled by NFL.

"You know, FOOTBALL!" I told him in the slowest, simplest voice—as if speaking slower would actually help—but my recently found inflated self-worth seemed to do the trick, and we were on our way to NFL Films. It did occur to me that the driver still may not know where he was going, but even if he did I was pretty confident that he did not share my appreciation for our destination.

I always imagined NFL Films to be similar to heaven: Big pearly gates outside, a soft white glow surrounding the buildings that appear to be immersed in clouds that part as you approach them, the lights become brighter, and there is an angelic chorus signifying your arrival. Or maybe, instead of a chorus, it is an original NFL Films score or, instead of angels, it is the great narrator of NFL Films and the "Voice of God," John Facenda, describing your path to NFL Films in a way that only his baritone voice can capture, commanding you to move in slow motion to make your entrance that much more dramatic.

My vision of NFL Films was slightly off. The reality was a nondescript set of grayish buildings. Unbeknownst to me, we had actually used the back entrance, probably bypassing the pearly gates, and failing to alert the angels to sing or John Facenda to begin his narration. I was worried we had actually been led astray by the driver's Garmin or that NFL Films did not really exist, that it was simply a mythical place, a figment of my imagination never to be actually seen.

My eyes canvassed the parking lot and I saw two large utility vans with NFL Films on the back doors. While it was not the heaven I imagined, this was definitely the place.

I paid the cab driver and sent him on his way. Destiny was calling, and I could wait no longer to see the beauty few football fans ever get to experience. I was moving at a pace that would give John Facenda difficulty.

In my exuberant haste, I managed to walk across the nest of a gray goose, which charged at me, so I started to walk with even more of a purpose. As I did, the goose also started to walk with more of a purpose and began flapping its wings like a jet fighter starting its engine preparing to take off. I had heard that some animals only run in a straight line, so I began to serpentine in an attempt to lose my predator. It was possible that all of NFL Films could be watching this idiot in the parking lot get attacked by a harmless goose, and thinking there is no way we can follow this guy around and do a feature on him. Eventually I escaped the no-fly zone, and the goose gave up his chase. I made my way to the buzzer to be let into NFL Films with a disheveled presence that I did my best to conceal.

Steve Sabol's secretary greeted me with tears in her eyes and a warm hug. It was almost as if she saw Steve in me or I had somehow magically brought him back to life and he was going to walk through the door again. Unfortunately, for her, myself, and all football fans, this was not the case. She gave me a quick tour of the wall of Emmy awards that Steve and NFL Films had won over the years. Behind the front desk was an enormous picture of Steve and his father, Ed, receiving one of those Emmy statuettes. The message on the picture was "Life is Great. Football is Better." To me it served as a reminder that life is too short to not pursue your dreams. That was what I was chasing all through the scheduled trip: The dream that Steve Sabol instilled in me as a young football fan; a dream so eloquently created that reality could not possibly live up to what NFL Films had placed in my heart.

After the tour, I was ushered away to meet with an executive producer. I had been in pitch meetings with networks before, which—if they had gone well—I would be out filming my own show for a different network, instead of at NFL Films.

It is interesting how life turns out, since what was a disappointment had turned into a blessing—there is no other place I would rather have been than right where I was.

I walked into the executive producer's office to find a man wearing jeans and a collared shirt. He also was wearing a big smile that was either from my overdressing for the occasion, witnessing the mayhem of "gray goosegate," or he was simply thinking to himself, "So this is the guy who thinks he can travel to every NFL stadium in seventeen weeks in a '67 VW Bus."

I expect Christopher Columbus got a similar reaction when pitching his voyages, and that ended up working out pretty well for him—he even got a holiday named after him. Not quite bobble-head status, but a holiday is validation of a fruitful existence nonetheless.

Different artifacts of the NFL littered the executive's office, and next to me was a big board with a series of dates representing each week of the upcoming NFL season. Under each date was a series of postcards, each with something written on it. They were all story ideas, a player's name, a team, or an idea.

I sat down across from the under-dressed executive producer and next to the big board. I remember seeing Adrian Peterson on the list and wondering if I had just read a major national secret—like the recipe for Kentucky Fried Chicken. My eyes kept moving around the board, and I read the card "Around the NFL in a '67 VW Bus." My heart sang and a smile began to invade my face. Our meeting was not a pitch and I did not have to dress in a suit. The project was a done deal and I was simply on a vacation to NFL Films.

The executive producer asked me a few questions about our plans, what kind of cameras we were going to use, and what we wanted to get out of the trip. After a few short moments, we were walking the hallways of NFL Films. The artwork of Steve Sabol and NFL Films made the football players both brilliant and flawed. Walking through the halls was like taking a trip through my childhood. My gaze of spirit and awe was undoubtedly obvious to the executive producer, but I did not care. The thought that I was going to be part of the history on the walls as a piece of NFL Films soon crept from the far recesses of my mind to my conscience and with it a feeling that I had met my destiny.

Now, months later, I found myself in a budget motel outside of Denver, sitting on a couch with a microphone attached to my shirt and a camera filming me. I was taken back to that day in April at NFL Films, back to that gray goose chasing me around the parking lot, and back to the first time I saw that index card that confirmed *The* NFL Films was interested in our story, interested in Hail Mary—the very VW Bus I had refused to sell on my father's advice.

I placed my phone on the coffee table in front of me, but it did not ring. It was two minutes past the time of the conference call and, considering the Vince Lombardi feelings I have about time, those two minutes made me question if it was actually going to happen. I had one of the other guys call my phone just to make sure it was working—it was—so I hurriedly canceled the incoming call fearing that I would miss the call from NFL Films.

A few minutes later the phone rang and, with all the giddiness of Ralphie finally getting his Red Ryder BB Gun, I answered the phone to find our producer at NFL Films on the other end. We exchanged pleasantries, and he introduced himself to everyone in the room. We began to go over everyone's role on the team, our equipment, and how we were going to get the footage we filmed to him, as well as the different locations along the tour where NFL Films would meet us.

The doubt I had when my phone did not ring at the exact meeting time was quickly replaced with a feeling of belonging. Our journey was supposed to happen, so why should I feel any trepidation about how everything with NFL Films was going to turn out? For the past few weeks I had kept saying that this was going to happen with NFL Films. I do not know if there was doubt in the minds of the other two, but if there was they were playing it off very well.

Sometimes in life it is better not to know enough to be scared or doubtful, and this was one of those times. Grayson knew a little more, but Eric had no idea what I had sacrificed to make this moment happen. It was not as easy as drawing up a schedule and buying a VW Bus on a whim. This whim was years, if not decades, in the making.

I explained to the producer why I was going on the trip and how I made the choice between finishing a Ph.D. on some uninteresting, insignificant, and probably unrealistic subject, and football. As anyone who is a football fan, or someone who has a dream, or anyone who has been on the business end of being a Ph.D. student knows, there really was not a decision to be made. It was football, just like it had always been.

After the conference call with NFL Films, we packed our gear into Hail Mary and began our second trip of the day to Sports Authority Field. Our early-morning trek to the stadium did very little for us in the way of finding out where to park because at 4 o'clock in the morning all of the parking was free, and none of it was reserved.

Since we were better equipped to walk than to pay the absurd ransom that invariably every professional and collegiate stadium charges for parking, I immediately turned Hail Mary away from the stadium as soon as we saw the first man waving an orange safety flag next to a sign reading "Parking $50." These signs were a reminder that all the sports we treasured as children growing up are going away, well, not going away but changing in the name of profit, sacrificing what made them great.

The sign at NFL Films had read "Life is Great. Football is Better." I wonder if it is really better or if it is referring to the NFL that used to be: the NFL I grew up on, and the Denver Broncos that played all of those memorable games with No. 7, John Elway, under center.

Mile High Stadium was the original home of the Denver Broncos and always an annoyingly loud stadium for opposing teams. If the altitude did not get to their opponents, Broncos fans created a home-field advantage that few NFL teams were fortunate enough to have. The team last played in Mile High Stadium in 2000, and the new stadium, Sports Authority Field at Mile High Stadium, by all accounts is one of the nicest in the league.

While the altitude and Broncos fans still create an almost insurmountable advantage for the home team, it is not the Mile High Stadium I grew up watching. In those days, to hear the announcers describe the altitude of the stadium while showing a player on the opponent's team sucking air through an oxygen mask, or seeing the camera shake from the crowd noise, made Mile High Stadium seem like Mount Olympus. Unfortunately, that had all been replaced with a modern version that begged the question: Is football better or was football better?

Regardless, we had thirty-one more games after this one and were not about to pay for stadium parking for the entire trip, which would come out to about $1,600.

We were hungry and managed to find a Thai restaurant, which also offered parking for the games. While it was a significant distance from the stadium, it only cost twenty dollars, so we had found Hail Mary's home for the game. We got to the game early enough to hopefully get interviews with some fans. Our only scheduled interview in Denver, other than Rocky, was the next morning with someone who started a fan website for the Broncos. Not knowing what that interview would bring, and not really remembering what Rocky had said earlier in the morning, other than promising us a pot of gold, we set out to meet more fans.

The atmosphere around the stadium resembled that of the Fourth of July without the fireworks, or Mardi Gras without the high per capita public drunkenness or females pulling up their shirts. In fact, none of those scantily clad female Broncos fans we found so prominently in our Google search were anywhere near the stadium. However, the excitement in the air was palpable.

We met two female Baltimore Ravens fans wearing hats that resembled the Super Bowl ring their team had won the year before, their faces intricately painted to resemble the Ravens logo. With their head-to-toe purple ensemble to support the Ravens in a primarily orange world of Broncos fans, these two ladies were like a beacon in the night and quickly caught our attention. This was the first of many things I learned while on this trip: I did not give female football fans enough credit; and I did not realize how prominent drum lines are at professional football games.

We soon found ourselves in the middle of the carnival-like atmosphere that was the stadium parking lot before the kickoff of the NFL season. The unmistakable sound of a well-choreographed drum line was fast approaching, there was smoked meat on the grills, and every few feet there was a cooler full of adult beverages—all on a Thursday afternoon, all in the name of football, and all heaven on Earth to me. The excitement for the game was contagious, and I had the fever.

Our seats, indicative of our budget, were about as high up as you could get in the end zone. If the players were going to suffer from the lack of oxygen in the thin air on the field, we would definitely have trouble breathing at the extended altitude of our seats, seats that could not be purchased when single-game tickets went on sale to the general public.

All Broncos games were sold out, because with future Hall of Fame quarterback Peyton Manning throwing passes, Denver had Super Bowl expectations of their team and expressed it by making any Broncos game a difficult ticket to get—expensive—at the very least. It did not matter to us, we were just happy to be there, happy to be on the road, and happy to have football back.

We exchanged a few words with the couple next to us, and it turns out our seats were two of their four season tickets. The couple lives in Nashville, but fly back for a few games a year, so they saw no reason to give up their tickets despite the geographic challenges of being Broncos fans living in Tennessee.

There are some things that I really like about being at the games, and seeing the American flag spread across the majority of the field is one of them. There is just something truly beautiful about the flag, someone singing "The Star-Spangled Banner," and everyone anticipating "... home of the brave" so the game can start. During every performance of the National Anthem, I would wait for "and the rockets' red glare" to see if the stadium did anything pyrotechnic for that verse. I would be disappointed if they did not, making the stadium and the team seem somehow less patriotic.

In Denver they have an official parachute team called Team Thunderstorm, which parachutes in before the game, and once they reach a certain height above the stadium, begin an almost free fall to the field. The skydivers come in a few seconds after each other, so the crowd cheers each one separately. They ooooh and aaaaah over them when the free fall begins and cheer vigorously when each skydiver makes a safe landing. To this day I am amazed by Team Thunderstorm and do not understand how they can fall from so high and not be injured. I am not a big fan of heights, as you might imagine of someone who prefers taking a bus, specifically a VW Bus, around the country instead of flying, so the pre-game in Denver was truly edge-of-your-seat excitement for me.

The Ravens had beaten the Broncos in the playoffs the previous year on their way to winning the Super Bowl. That game, known as the "Mile High Miracle" featured a Hail Mary of sorts. With under a minute left, the Ravens quarterback, Joe Flacco, connected with Jacoby Jones for a seventy-yard touchdown pass made possible by a blown coverage in the Broncos secondary. NFL.com selected it as the best game of the year and *Sports Illustrated* described it as one of the most exciting in NFL playoff history. Although the Broncos were heavily favored that day, they failed to finish, which may have given Peyton Manning some extra incentive to make sure the Ravens started the new season off with a loss.

We could not have picked a better game to start our trip, and for the first half it did not disappoint. The Ravens held a 17-14 lead after two quarters, but then Peyton Manning showed us why he is one of the greatest quarterbacks in NFL history. He threw for five touchdowns in the second half as the Broncos took control of the game and beat the defending Super Bowl champion Ravens 49-27.

With the Broncos impressive second half, and Manning's two touchdown passes in the first half, he became the first quarterback in the NFL since Joe Kapp in 1969 to throw for seven touchdowns in one game. I left the stadium that night thinking we had just seen the best team in the American Football Conference (AFC). Turns out I was right: The Broncos won the AFC and would play in the Super Bowl.

Taking a trip like this, while also filming a documentary, on our miniscule budget required us to take a few risks. In order to save money, we would call on family, friends, friends of friends, or anyone who had ever heard of us to give us a place to sleep at night. My original idea was to either sleep in Hail Mary or pitch a tent at campgrounds along the way. I figured we could buy gym memberships to a national chain, work out and shower. Not only would we stay fit, I figured, but we would get a shower. Eric did not share the same excitement for the idea that Grayson and I did, so family and friends became important to our financial well-being and Eric's sanity.

A cousin of Grayson's girlfriend lives in a suburb of Denver and offered us a clean, comfortable room for the night. What made these moments awkward was the fact that we usually arrived at the homes of strangers late at night after a football game. What made this particular experience unique is that our hosts were of Vietnamese descent, and while they spoke English it was at times broken. Actually, most of the time it was broken.

Grayson had never met them, but I did not realize that until we found the house. I was better off not knowing everything beforehand, because I may have balked at the idea and would have missed out on meeting a lot of great people while spending a small fortune for budget motels. When we got to the house, we were offered hot pizza and a warm shower, and gladly accepted both as our reward for conquering Denver. I found my way to the floor in the bedroom where I could get some much-needed sleep, knowing the road to San Francisco would immediately follow our early-morning appointment with the Broncos fan who had started a website devoted entirely to his team.

The Broncos fan insisted we meet him at his office and we were happy to accommodate anyone willing to give us an interview. The building was nondescript, like those found in a suburb of any major metropolitan area in the United States. We grabbed our camera equipment and walked in the front door to find several business cards loitering on a front desk that was clearly not occupied by a human.

There was not a building directory or even suite numbers next to the different doors. One of the business cards, however, radiated orange and reflected someone who had devoted his entire life to being a Broncos fan—the only clue that we were in the right building for our interview. We started going into various suites, explaining our situation.

"You mean the Broncos guy?" one guy grunted, as if annoyed not by our question but by the fact that our interviewee even existed. Knowing the answer before we could respond, he directed us to the suite where the season never ends for the Denver Broncos.

As we walked down the hall toward an open door filled with an orange light that seemed to be glowing, seeping out, and permeating the exterior walls, it was apparent that we had found our next interview.

We peeked in the doorway and were enthusiastically greeted by a guy in a well-worn orange Broncos cap, a blue Broncos V-neck sweater with the vintage Broncos D logo, and orange pants. The suite was about 300 square feet and held about 500 square feet worth of Denver Broncos memorabilia. There was nothing left to want for a Broncos fan in this fan cave, including what he called the Prize Monkey. Our interviewee told us he also films his own show and explained that the smiling, lifelike chimpanzee sitting behind two chairs holding a tray above his head is the Prize Monkey, which, during the show, holds a prize for a viewer to call in and win. Part comedy and part horror film, the monkey had a lifelike smile and eyes that followed us around the room. It is not a stretch to imagine that when the lights are out and the door is closed, Prize Monkey puts on one of the helmets and jerseys adorning the walls of the suite and pretends to make the game-winning catch at the Super Bowl for the Broncos.

One of the many things this trip was giving me was the ability to put faces on the various teams. Not the faces of the players, but those of the fans. I started to not see the Broncos as the Broncos, but rather as our host this morning, who let us come into his world if only for a moment, or Rocky the Colorado Leprechaun, who got three tired souls and a VW Bus to arrive at the stadium fifteen hours before kickoff. These fans were sharing their team and, consequently, themselves with us.

The first few minutes were spent acclimating ourselves to our newfound surroundings. The collection of Broncos gear was impressive and provided me with a feeling of kinship toward the owner. Not because I am a Broncos fan, but because I had much of the same items growing up—just of a different team.

Grayson took a seat next to our host, who quietly exhaled as if he was just now coming off the high of the game the previous night and referenced the vast collection of Broncos memorabilia.

"Wife keeps asking if we are going to make any money from all this," he said. "I tell her that isn't the point."

That got me thinking: What is the point? While there may be no real point to it, he had been infected with the same almost incurable disease for the Broncos that I had for the Cowboys. He had been a Broncos fan since he was three years old, he said, explaining that his brother was always Craig Morton and he was Haven Moses, or Rick Upchurch if he was catching a punt.

"If this keeps up, I may lose my day job," he joked. For the next thirty minutes he told stories about former players who made it a point to be a big part of the Denver community and some who even appeared on his show. Joyfully, with excitement in his eyes, he described the electricity in the air at Broncos games, and with each passing word we were taken back to the night before when we attended the game as Broncos fans.

He then started naming great Broncos players of the past. To me they had always been just players in the NFL, but to this fan they were football royalty. He talked about Elway, Atwater, Mecklenberg, Sewell, and Mark Jackson with the same tone in his voice and gleam in his eyes that I get when I talk about Staubach, Pearson, Dorsett, Randy White, and Ed "Too Tall" Jones, and for that I could only respect and appreciate him as a football fan.

Our journey west to San Francisco began as soon as our interview with the Broncos fan was over. It was Friday, and we needed to drive as far as we could to be sure we would make it to San Francisco in time for the game on Sunday.

When driving Hail Mary, it is always a good idea to go as long as possible when she is running well because anything could happen: the brakes could go out; she could have a flat tire; her engine could overheat; and parts we do not even know about could break and cause us to miss a game.

Not missing a single game was a very important element to our trip because the NFL is different than other major professional sports leagues in that each team only gets eight home games. Other sports get at least forty-one, so a tour to the country's NBA, NHL or MLB stadiums would be much easier than touring the NFL. Every stadium crossed off the list is a team you do not need to complete the tour, so breaking down close to Denver would not do us any good. The league also stops scheduling games three times a week as the season wears on, meaning there are fewer opportunities to cross off stadiums unless you can go to two games in one day—I have actually done that, gone to a Packers game in Green Bay then driven to Chicago for a Bears game in the same day, but not in a 1967 VW Bus, that would be a near impossibility. So we needed to keep driving in order to not miss any games on our schedule.

With Denver safely in our rearview mirror, so was a Subaru Outback, which was approaching at a high rate of speed. The driver moved to the left lane, as did most vehicles we encountered on the road. It seems the awe and wonder of seeing a VW Bus driving down the road quickly turns lackluster with the need to get to their ultimate destination in their lifetime, so they moved to the left and passed us.

This driver, for some reason, decided to slow down and stay next to us. I could see him in my peripheral vision, but just assumed he was taking a picture of Hail Mary. It is not uncommon for someone to risk their life or, at the very least, risk getting a ticket by exceeding the speed limit just to get a picture of a VW Bus.

The Subaru stayed beside us an exceedingly long time for a picture, so my thoughts quickly considered that maybe this guy wants to tell us about an unknown issue with Hail Mary. I glanced over at the driver, expecting him to be pointing at an area of the bus or urging me to pull over. It was a shorter, bald, bearded man wearing sunglasses with mirror lenses, and he was definitely pointing for me to pull over.

The man driving the Subaru was not just anyone, though, it was Rocky the Colorado Leprechaun. I had not recognized him at first, but it was definitely him. We were not sure what he wanted, but he desperately wanted to speak with us.

It was almost like seeing Santa Claus lying on the beach in the off-season in Bermuda shorts and a tank top sipping on a drink with an umbrella. Rocky was dressed, but it was evident the day before had been a long one for the leprechaun.

Rocky told us he had a place in Moab, Utah, and invited us to spend the night. I tried to imagine what a leprechaun's place in Utah looked like, and pictured all of us sitting outside by a campfire, roasting marshmallows while Rocky, dressed in full leprechaun finery, filled our heads with stories of fairy tale lands and pots of gold.

We entertained the idea, even looking on the map to see if there was any possible way to make it to Moab then to San Francisco in time for the game on Sunday. Eventually, the tour and documentary were placed above our need to see Moab, so even though we politely declined, this tour continued to restore my faith in humanity. Rocky could have just sped past us on his way to Moab, yet he took the time to invite us back into his life.

The purity of his offer revealed a soul that was suddenly clear. We would encounter this type of hospitality throughout our journey. Whether the other people remember their generosity toward strangers or not, I do, and that is a lesson that will be with me for the rest of my life.

We drove through Provo, Utah, that evening. Because of its football team, Brigham Young University (BYU), Provo had always been a mysteriously appealing place to me.

In the '80s I followed BYU because of Jim McMahon, Steve Young and Robbie Bosco. I did not really know much about Bosco except that I liked his name. Robbie Bosco just sounded like a football player—like a blue-chip quarterback with a radiant white smile, perfect hair and a cheerleader under each arm. The fact BYU won a national championship in 1984 with him as quarterback helped, but his name had a nice ring to it, like Kurt Russell's character, Reno Hightower in *The Best of Times*.

The University of Texas was playing against BYU that weekend in Provo and, although I was longing to see something familiar to remind me of home, I did not mention going to the game to the others because if we stayed in Provo an extra day to go to the game, it might jeopardize making it to San

Francisco in time to get the interviews we needed for the documentary.

Not going to the game proved to be a wise decision because it had an almost two-hour weather delay, and once it got started, BYU ran over, around, and through Texas for a 40-21 win. I did not need to see that. I especially did not need to pay to see it while jeopardizing our journey.

Instead we spent the night at a campground outside of Salt Lake City. Grayson and Eric pitched a tent while I slept in the back seat of Hail Mary. I remembered the back seat being a little more comfortable than it was that night. We could have spent a lot of nights in the VW Bus, but, truth be told, it would have aged me considerably. The backseat would never be confused with a Tempurpedic mattress, it was more like a worn out futon.

While the sleeping arrangements were not always the best, we were out there—living the dream and loving every minute of it. I looked at the mountains, thousands of miles from home, and started to realize that we were indeed going to make this happen, and for the first time in a long time—maybe forever—my soul was feeling alive; not because every day we got closer to another football game, but because every mile we drove got me closer to realizing my dream. My refusal to leave my sports childhood behind had led me to sleeping in the back seat of a nearly fifty-year-old vehicle, all in the name of football. With that came the ultimate feeling of accomplishment and a sense of pride that can only come from challenging yourself and overcoming the obstacles that life presents, to rise the next day and continue pursuing your dream.

The next morning we were up when the sun peeked over the horizon. I do not know if it was from being so uncomfortable in the back seat or the thought of having to drive to San Francisco the next day that kept me from gaining restful sleep. Regardless, I was tired and began to realize that I would go to sleep and wake up every day of the trip worrying about whether Hail Mary would run and, if so, would our good fortune last long enough to get us to our next destination? Even stopping at gas stations gave me a bit of anxiety. Hearing the distinctive sound of an air-cooled VW engine starting up was truly music to my ears.

We were staying with the mother of one of Grayson's friends from college, who lived in the Bay Area. She had been expecting us since mid-afternoon but, as often happens when traveling by VW Bus, we were late. The sun had gone down and her patience for waiting on us had expired as well.

"Where have you been? I was expecting you a lot earlier!" she greeted us at the door with a smile, almost as if we were teenagers who had missed curfew.

She told us she had two big chairs in the living room with matching ottomans that would be the resting place of the evening for Eric and me, and an upstairs bedroom for Grayson.

Our conversation gradually moved from the kitchen table to the living room where I sat in one of the surprisingly comfortable big chairs. After I told our host,

Bonnie, that I was from Texas and outed myself as a fan of the Dallas Cowboys, she proceeded to inform me of her hatred of people from Texas and fans of the Cowboys.

Although it is always good to know where you stand right off the bat, Bonnie was not mean-spirited, rather she was heavily opinionated and seemed to speak her mind and consider the consequences later. While changing a person's feelings toward the Dallas Cowboys is like changing the religion of the Pope, I was determined to change her perception of Texans, at the very least.

She wore no 49ers fan clothing and, other than a simple flag that was a giveaway at a game, the house was void of any evidence that a 49ers fan lived there. About the time I put her in the "not a football fan" box, she began to tell stories of going to games at Kezar Stadium, the home of the 49ers until 1971. As she recounted memories of games and players long gone, her eyes began to sparkle, suggesting a much younger spirit lived inside her body.

A smile touched her lips when she talked about one player in particular, Richard Lee "Dickey" Moegle, who had captivated the young, teenage heart of our host and may have been the reason she remained a football fan nearly fifty years later.

I had never heard of Dickey Moegle, but evidently he was quite the player or, at the very least, looked good in tight pants to a teenage girl. Among his other accomplishments, he was a consensus All-American at Rice University in 1954 and was inducted into the College Football Hall of Fame in 1979. He played seven seasons for three different teams in the NFL including the San Francisco 49ers. But, most importantly to me, he was born in Taylor, Texas, about thirty miles outside of Austin, meaning he was a Texan! I thought it ironic that her favorite 49ers player of all-time had been from my state, a state she had publicly professed her hatred of just moments earlier. By the time I claimed victory in California on behalf of the state of Texas we were ready to see how comfortably the oversized chairs would sleep.

Candlestick Park was home to one of the most famous plays in the history of the NFL. The 49ers play "Red Right Tight Sprint Right Option" would be forever known as "The Catch," the single play that broke my ten-year-old Cowboys heart and my dream of seeing my team in a Super Bowl.

During the two previous years, the Cowboys seasons had ended one game shy of the Super Bowl, and as a fan the wins and losses become personal. The aftertaste of three consecutive losses in the NFC Championship was bitter and unbearable. I do not know that I will ever get over Joe Montana, surrounded by Cowboys, throwing the ball in the direction of the end zone where Dwight Clark magically pulled the ball out of the sky, propelling the 49ers on to be Super Bowl champions.

The stadium had played host to many childhood memories of listening to John Madden and Pat Summerall call the late game on CBS or FOX. Countless times I had watched the game being played on a beautifully sun-soaked field affectionately called "The Stick." It was a very distinctive venue and this being the last season of Candlestick Park was partly the reason I had to take this trip.

The character of a stadium and the history that lies between its walls is impossible to quantify, yet is unmistakable in its feel. I wanted to see as much of the NFL that I had grown up with before it was lost forever in the name of "progress," another word for replacing an old stadium that holds the history of the NFL with a new stadium barren of any significance other than using taxpayer money to finance suites and other unnecessary amenities that most fans do not care about and will not experience. Maybe because of that, and maybe because of how Bonnie, our host in San Francisco, recounted her experiences at Kezar Stadium, I was compelled to experience this stadium and this field with my own eyes before it was tragically torn down. Not because I was a fan of the 49ers—they had actually been on the business end of many of my heartaches as a Cowboys fan—but out of respect for the stadium and what it meant to the NFL. In a world of ever-improving stadiums and keeping up, literally, with the Joneses for the sake of capitalism, the ancient jewels of the NFL are dying. Cast off like a sixty-year-old beauty queen for a much younger and more attractive supermodel.

Candlestick Park also was famous for being terribly difficult to get to and from for a 49ers game, as well as not located in a great part of the San Francisco area. Not wanting to fight traffic and pay for parking, we opted to leave Hail Mary behind and take public transportation. Since there was a train station not far from where we were staying, we decided that was our best option to get to the game. The train, we discovered, does not go directly to the stadium, so we ended up spending considerable time looking at the map to determine the best stop in close proximity of the stadium. It was apparent to the others on the train platform that we were lost, so people began to approach us to offer help.

Concord, California, where Bonnie lives, is the second to last stop on the yellow line of the Bay Area Rapid Transit (BART) system. According to the map, there was not a stop for anything remotely describing Candlestick Park and I took offense to there being no reference to one of the greatest NFL stadiums of its generation. How many people would visit San Francisco and not see Candlestick Park? Not many, and not this guy.

It is important to note that in September the Giants baseball team was still playing home games at AT&T Park, which would add not to our confusion but to the confusion of the people trying to help us get to the football game. The next train was not going to arrive for fifteen minutes, so we told people what we were doing, explaining why we had a camera with us and why we were going to the game. In their eagerness to help, they had erroneously told us to get off at the Embarcadero stop and the stadium would be within walking distance.

That seemed simple enough, so I started thinking people had made a big deal about the difficulties of getting to Candlestick Park for apparently no good reason. The locals always seem to want to be the one to help out tourists and believe they know their city better than other locals. Thankfully this was the case, because another person began telling us that we had it all wrong. If we took the stop previously suggested we would be stranded in the middle of San Francisco with no way of getting to the stadium. Our initial tour guides were directing us to the baseball stadium that conveniently had a game at the same time as the football game.

When the train rolled into the station, we got on not knowing for sure which stop to take, but at least we were headed in the right direction. We were forced into exiting the train a stop before our actual stop because the stops closer to the stadium were closed, but BART was offering service from the last stop via a bus that would take us to Candlestick Park.

I suddenly understood why people would rant about the difficulties of getting to the stadium. When getting off the bus to get on another one, I caught a glimpse of the streets in and around the area. While it was not entirely the wrong side of the tracks, it was not a gated community filled with expensive German sedans either. The bus was crowded and expensive for what it was. The 49ers fans began boarding while the Packers fans were just as confused as we had been back at the train station. It appeared to provide them with some comfort knowing we were in a similar situation and that they were indeed on the right bus to get to the game. It seems that if you say something with enough confidence and conviction, the world makes it true. We were on the right bus and, at last, I got to lay my confused, weary eyes on Candlestick Park!

You would be hard pressed to find a postcard of the beautiful façade of Candlestick Park, because all of them are aerial shots looking down on the field—and with good reason. The sun-drenched field I had seen on television all those years was surrounded by aged concrete walls with red letters that let everyone know that they had finally made it to The Stick. The façade lacked character, as well as any of the "appeal" of the new stadiums I despise and believe signifies the end of what sports in general and specifically the NFL used to be.

Candlestick Park provided the continual lesson of this trip that money is held above all else, since merchandise honoring the last year of the stadium was readily available for sale. I imagine the team wanted to squeeze as much out of the old stadium before imploding years of memories, and selling commemorative memorabilia is the team's way of making sure every last cent is collected from the old stadium before commemorative memorabilia for the new stadium is available. Evidently, the ten-dollar beer is not enough profit for ownership.

We waited in a long line to get in the stadium to take an even longer escalator to the second deck where our seats were located. Looking down from the escalator revealed the throbbing masses below. A sea of thousands of others, wearing red and white, who also braved the inconvenience that is part of the Candlestick Park experience to watch a football game. I made it to my seat in the upper end zone. Eric and Grayson had tickets in the opposite end zone, so it was up to me to make friends with those around me.

There was an older gentleman wearing a Packers jersey sitting next to me, and on his right were what appeared to be his son and grandson, both wearing 49ers caps and shirts. I made a comment about his jersey being the wrong color—a sports ice-breaker, on par with talking about the weather or how long a day has been—and it sparked a brief conversation. Sports fans talk about how good or bad a team or player is doing, or even the upcoming schedule, in an attempt to break the awkward silence that happens in a stadium with tens of thousands of screaming fans.

I had taken this trip to talk to fellow football fans regardless of their team, and this Packers fan's story was unique because he and his father had been at "The Ice Bowl" in 1967 when Green Bay beat the Dallas Cowboys in fifteen-below-zero weather for the NFL championship. I told him what I was doing, and we talked about the stadiums he had visited. He then offered his take on his loyalties as a football fan. "My two favorite teams are the Green Bay Packers and whoever is playing the fuckin' Cowboys," he said.

Being a Dallas Cowboys fan I had learned to expect the hatred from fans of other teams. People use the "F" word in front of the name Cowboys so often that, if I did not know better, I would think that was the city in which the Cowboys played. As fans we almost become numb to it and even embrace it to a certain degree because people do not hate historically bad teams—like the Cleveland Browns—they take pity on them. So the hatred toward my Cowboys is almost like celebrating their history of success.

In the same breath he asked who my favorite team was and, after a brief pause to reflect on what I was about to say, I claimed another victory for my state. Maybe not my state maybe just my team, but I was no more backing down from this fan than I had in that big comfy chair back in Concord. I unapologetically declared I was a fan of the Dallas Cowboys. My admittance of being a Cowboys fan, in effect, strangled our brief friendship into silence.

All combined, the circumstances getting to Candlestick Park—the exterior of the stadium, and even the overpriced concessions with their excessively long lines that crowded the narrow corridors—were disappointing, but the actual field and the game were anything but. The field was just as I had seen countless times on television; bursting with life. The gold helmets and red jerseys of the 49ers seemed almost illuminated in the bright sunshine covering the field. I even contemplated the end zone where Dwight Clark had made that spectacular play over thirty years ago. It may have been morbid curiosity for a Dallas Cowboys fan, but you do not go to the Grassy Knoll and not wonder exactly where President Kennedy was when he was assassinated or look for the Book Depository window from which Lee Harvey Oswald took the fatal shot.

Like our first game, this one featured two teams that had met in the playoffs the previous season with the 49ers winning that game on their way to the Super Bowl.

This game was everything you could hope for from two traditional NFL powers with two of the better quarterbacks in the league. Colin Kaepernick threw for over 400 yards and two touchdowns while Aaron Rodgers had three touchdowns and over 300 passing yards. Late in the fourth quarter, 49ers running back Frank Gore crossed the goal line, helping to send San Francisco fans home happy with a 34-28 win.

The game was over, and if we thought it was difficult getting to Candlestick Park, it seemed a lot more challenging to get back to Hail Mary in Concord. The buses were overcrowded and riddled with exhausted fans who had spent the majority of the afternoon in the warm California sun.

I was exhausted, too, but content with finally getting to see Candlestick Park. Last times are one of the most difficult experiences in life, and knowing that this was the last time I would ever see Candlestick Park made me feel as if I was saying my final farewell to part of my childhood. In an age where football teams, players, and even some fans, are more interested in the sizzle of a new stadium versus football lore, this last time had become a too-often occurrence.

I was also troubled knowing that rather than spending the night in that oversized comfortable chair, I would be on the road headed south toward San Diego for the Chargers game the next night. Although our day had been one continuous uphill climb, we still needed to make the drive to meet our 49ers fans who were waiting for us to interview them. It took us nearly two hours to get back to Concord and another hour to drive to the house of the family we were interviewing in Ripon. Once again, we were late. The sun had set and that meant greeting new people with an apology for our tardiness.

It turned out that our fans were a young family with a newborn son living in a small, but extremely well-kept, house. The wife greeted us as if we were long-lost friends while the husband was a little more reserved and timid. They were all three dressed in 49ers jerseys, and the infant was playing with a soft 49ers football. The amount of 49ers memorabilia was not overly intrusive yet made it obvious where they stood on which NFL team was theirs.

The wife had been our point of contact and the primary subject of our interview, since she was actually the driving force behind this 49ers family. When the interview began, she recounted stories of her late father, a huge 49ers fan who had involved her in his football obsession early on. She smiled and seemed to float on the couch as she told us about wanting to stay home with him to watch the game instead of going to church with her mother. We asked if they had gone to the game that day and she sheepishly admitted that it was too far away, too much of a hassle, and too expensive. Another reminder that the NFL, as well as other professional sports leagues, have successfully priced their fans out of the stadium experience. As much as the stadiums of my youth are slowly dying, so is the attendance of the families of four that used to actually go to the games.

There were a few teams whose fans I was a little nervous about interviewing. As rivals of the Dallas Cowboys, the 49ers had always been on the receiving end of my football hatred, but the kindness and generosity of this young family helped ease my fears. The heartfelt story told by the wife had touched me as not only a passionate sports fan, but as someone who grew up in a family where football was a normal Sunday activity. Even though we had drastically different teams, I could relate to her on a personal level—teams did not matter, we shared a bond through football, and that was all that really mattered.

After the interview we drove for about three hours to Fresno. We all were ready to find ourselves out of Hail Mary and enjoying the creature comforts of a budget motel, but Fresno did not provide us with a multitude of options when it came to motels in our price range.

Exiting the freeway, we were confronted with three off-brand motels that provided little in the way of shelter or security. I do not mean off-brand as in Super 8 or Motel 6, I mean off-off-brand, as in the Sleep-E Inn where some of the letters were hanging upside down—

not able to handle their lot in life representing a roach motel—and ready to fall to their demise.

The first option looked to be the least expensive as well as the least secure. The lobby was a booth similar to the drive-thru window at a fast-food restaurant, only the glass looked to be bullet-proof. We pulled in and found a parking space. Even Hail Mary had an uneasy feeling about staying the night at this particular motel. I did not turn off the engine, fearing that if I did and things did not work out, we would be stranded at the motel if she decided not to start. Grayson approached the window while Eric and I became more fearful with every passing moment. Either Grayson went unnoticed by the front desk staff or somehow we had missed the countless clues leading up to the motel takeout window that it was abandoned.

Undaunted, we moved on to the next budget motel on the strip and determined the lack of five-star service at our first stop was probably for the best. The next one was better than the first, but not by much. Once again we found a parking spot and waited while Grayson went to find us a room. Success came in the way of a two-bedroom suite or, at least, it was a suite to us with three beds, which meant everyone got their own.

I must have been weary from the long day of traveling from Concord to Candlestick Park to our interview and finally to Fresno, because I did not gain a full appreciation of just how bad our motel was until the next morning. My uneasiness about our accommodations and leaving Hail Mary to fend for herself in the darkness of Fresno had provided another sleepless night, knowing the morning light would bring with it the ability to leave the red-light district of Fresno and the realization that I would be visiting another stadium I had longed to see since childhood: Jack Murphy Stadium in San Diego.

The stadium has a new name, now. A corporation decided to desecrate another of the long-standing treasures of the NFL in visions of selling more widgets. I hoped for its sake that it was not counting on me to purchase its widget to make up for the cost of commercializing one of the things I hold sacred. At least it has not torn the stadium down in favor of a new one with no history or character, but with plenty of overpriced suites and concessions. I fear that men in fancy suits and a silver shovel will break ground on a new stadium soon, and maybe even in a different part of California. With their hard hats perched atop their heads, their smiles somehow meaning to make us feel okay about losing another pillar of our fandom.

It seems nothing stops the gears of profit—not history, not morals, not fans, not anything—because as fans we have been conditioned to accept the selling out of our sports souls so others may profit. I will only refer to the stadium as Jack Murphy Stadium or simply, "The Murph" because that, and the home of the San Diego "Super" Chargers, is all it will ever be to me.

Every NFL stadium features a field that is 100 yards long with ten-yard end zones on the north and south sides of the field. But not all stadiums are created equal. What separates the great stadiums from just a 100-yard field surrounded by seats is the history and memories of that rectangular parcel of land we call a football field.

For me, Jack Murphy Stadium was Merlin Olson and Dick Enberg on NBC calling the late afternoon game between Dan Fouts and the Chargers playing an AFC West rival like the Raiders or Broncos.

The picturesque sunsets over The Murph were beautiful and bittersweet at the same time, since sunset meant the weekend was ending and another long week of school was about to commence before there would be more football. There was, of course, *Monday Night Football* with Howard Cosell, Frank Gifford, and Don Meredith, but I was only allowed to stay up for the first half of the Monday night games. I missed Tony Dorsett's ninety-nine-yard run against Minnesota and countless other pivotal moments in NFL history that transpired during the second half of *Monday Night Football* games, all in the name of education. I have an undergraduate, graduate, and almost a doctoral degree, but none of my inspiration for higher education came from missing the last half of *Monday Night Football.*

The game in San Diego was the first *Monday Night Football* game of the year and, unlike all those games in childhood, I would be able to watch the entire thing from beginning to end.

We had managed to contact a fan known simply as the "Charger King." Every time we had called to schedule an interview, a female would answer the phone, "Charger King's phone." Charger King never answered the phone and we never spoke to him directly.

Other than confirmation that we would be able to interview him, the specific section of the parking lot, and the instructions to look for a camper with a Chargers flag above it, we had little to go on in our search for the mythical Charger King. We entered the parking lot feeling a little like we were looking for some sort of San Diego godfather or a tailgating Sasquatch, because at this point Charger King was little more than an urban legend.

You would think finding a trailer with a Chargers flag flying above it would not be that difficult, but campers with Chargers flags were not exactly in short supply in the parking lot. Grayson became frustrated with us aimlessly walking a vast parking lot looking for someone who may or may not even exist. He decided to ask someone outside a random camper where we might find the Charger King.

"How do you know about the Charger King?" the Chargers fan asked with a puzzled look on his face.

We might as well have been outside the gates of Area 51 and asked about an alien. His question was at least confirmation that there actually was a Charger King. The fan whom Grayson had spoken with instructed us to remain where we were standing and that he would be back shortly.

"This guy has no clue where Charger King is," Grayson said with a look of disgust. He wanted to move on, but I did not see any harm in waiting a few minutes for the alleged Charger King if our go-between could actually furnish the man himself.

The go-between came back with news that his highness would see us, but the "King's Coach" had to be cleared of peons before we were allowed an audience. The waiting period gave Grayson long enough to interview the go-between, who we learned had been a Chargers fan for 28 years.

"My grandfather took me to my first game here at Jack Murphy Stadium," he said. And with all of the resiliency of a confederate soldier still referring to the South as Dixie, he stated, "I still call it 'The Murph.' I do not know and do not care what the real name is now." The tone of his voice evoked a passion bordering on hatred for the naming rights of the stadium having been sold to the highest bidder.

From the outside, the camper of the Charger King looked as if it could only fit about six people. It did not seem fit for a king, but one thing I was learning on this trip was to accept things for what they were and to never judge a book by its cover.

One by one, Charger fans began filing out of the camper and down the flimsy stairs leading to the parking lot. Like clowns coming out of a small car, the line of Charger fans exiting the camper seemed to never end—if there was one fan that exited there were fifteen.

After the last person made their way outside we were summoned inside to find what we can only assume was a man dressed in a Chargers jersey over full-size shoulder pads, football pants with pads, football cleats, and a robe draped over the back of his uniform. His face was covered with the Burger King mask. To his right was a female dressed in Chargers gear with what looked to be custom-made Chargers sunglasses that intentionally, or unintentionally, obstructed the view of her face. There were other people in the camper who made the earlier mass exodus out of the camper that much more impressive.

Once inside the King's Coach we were welcomed by a few members of the inner circle and the king himself. Our first interview question was to inquire how the elaborate Charger King persona got started, which was met with a deafening and awkward silence.

"Charger King, let's start with you." Grayson said, quickly recovering from the fear that we may soon be thrown out of the King's Coach.

The Charger King told how he was summoned by his father, Zeus from Mount Olympus, to be a super fan of the San Diego Chargers in order to guarantee a Super Bowl victory for the franchise.

"The Charger Kingdom looks to the Charger King for inspiration, and the king always has a smile on his face," the Charger King said, ending the interview by looking at the camera with his permanent, eerie smile.

Being in the camper with the Charger King was one of the more surreal experiences of the trip, making us question if what our eyes were seeing was actually reality. I was mesmerized by the Charger King with his muffled speech and creepy smile.

Charger King was asked to sign a waiver for the documentary, and asked if it was okay if he signed it as "Charger King." We told him that, unfortunately, we would need his real name. After leaving the camper, we purposely shuffled the waivers in our camera bag so we would never know the true identity of Charger King. To this day, his identity is somewhere among the nearly 100 waivers we collected during the trip and I intend to keep it that way. The greatness of that day and being in the camper of the Charger King would somehow be tarnished if I knew the name of the man who was behind such an elaborate pretense.

We made it into the stadium and the game had not even started yet when a woman one section over managed to spill beer on two ladies sitting in front of her. Whether it was accidental or not was left for the police to decide when they arrived to halt the barrage of haymakers the women were throwing, and sometimes landing. These pre-game festivities were as disturbing as the pre-game in Denver was exciting. We considered it a waste of beer and tickets. While two ladies were escorted out of their section in handcuffs, one was allowed to return even though her level of sobriety probably prevented her from seeing a single play.

Even the unexpected and unwanted excitement in the stands could not tarnish my image of Jack Murphy Stadium. My eyes panned across the top of the stadium where flags from each NFL team waved in the Pacific Ocean breeze. I was contently soaking everything in, thinking to myself that I had finally made it to The Murph!

The Chargers, for all intents and purposes, had the Texans beat by taking a 28-7 lead. The lead, like our time in San Diego, would not last however. With less than ten minutes to go, Houston Texans linebacker Brian Cushing made one of the best interceptions I have ever seen and returned it for a Texans touchdown. The game was suddenly tied and the Texans got the ball back. With time expiring, Randy Bullock kicked the game-winning field goal: Texans 31, Chargers 28.

CHAPTER 2

Saving Birdman

Houston, Philadelphia, and Pittsburgh
(Six games and 6,007 miles)

Some people think football is a matter of life and death. I assure you, it's much more serious than that.

– Bill Shankly

There were no real issues with Hail Mary from Denver to San Francisco to San Diego, and it was time for our first attempt at adjusting the valves and changing the oil.

Grayson and I soon learned that we had forgotten nearly everything John had "taught" us. In our defense, since our maintenance tutorial with John, we had met a leprechaun in Denver and a guy wearing the Burger King mask in San Diego, not to mention interviewing Al Roker of the *Today* show—a lot to take in for our first week on the road. But I was eager to prove to the others, and especially myself, that I could actually perform the maintenance and keep Hail Mary purring down the road. I excitedly put on the cheap, paper coveralls I purchased in Austin for just this occasion, and reached into our storage container to pull out all of the tools and parts I would need to adjust the valves and change the oil.

I felt like Bob Ross the PBS painter, about to turn a blank canvas into beautiful clouds, trees, and maybe even some water. It is not an overly complex process to adjust the valves on an air-cooled VW engine: Just rotate the belt until the appropriate gear is lined up, go underneath the engine where the valves are located and adjust them for that particular gear, then rotate the engine belt to the next gear and so on until you have adjusted all four sets of valves. The maintenance, including the oil change, should only take about thirty minutes.

For me, reality landed in the parking lot of a shopping center in El Centro, California when I could not turn the engine belt. I laid on the ground outside of the Starbucks for at least an hour contemplating where I had gone wrong. Not just in the maintenance of Hail Mary but in life.

It is difficult to stop the slide of self-pity once it begins. El Centro was the first time, but not the last, that I seriously questioned the sanity of the trip. Being on the road for four months would give me plenty of time to contemplate the meaning of life, and in particular my own. But where had I gone so wrong that I would find myself lying in a parking lot, thousands of miles from home, with the sun going down and a vehicle that may or may not make it another 100 miles? I wondered if I would ever see home again merely because I could not rotate the belt. In my head I had been over the steps we learned from John, and to the best of my recollection we were following them exactly.

I was a broken man at this point. My father may have been correct in his first assessment of Hail Mary and his recommendation to sell her. I started to think about the absurdity of inspirational quotes like "I have never met a strong person with an easy past" and "Stars can't shine without darkness." I decided that the people behind inspirational quotes have obviously never driven a VW Bus. A VW Bus owner has quotes like "It's not an adventure until something goes wrong." If an adventure requires something to go wrong, this was not our biggest adventure but nonetheless an adventure.

The road had won during our travels west and, despite my best efforts, the road was going to take round two as well. I may have been broken, but was not too proud to call John and ask for help. "Did you take the bus out of gear?" was his first question.

The silence from my end told him all he needed to know. The students he had faithfully tutored in the skill of VW maintenance just a couple of weeks earlier had failed him miserably. We were off the phone thirty seconds later, staying on just long enough for me to apologize to our teacher and become re-energized with the feeling that we were about to be on our way back to Austin, or at least that is what I thought. The valves were no longer an issue and if I did remember one maintenance tip for the rest of the trip, it would be to make sure Hail Mary was in neutral before I tried to adjust the valves.

During our travels to the West Coast, I would periodically look out the back window to see if there was smoke coming from the engine. The VW Bug thirty years ago that I watched catch fire on the side of the road and John's advice of getting everything out of the bus if it catches fire because we were not going to put it out gave me a heightened level of paranoia. I had also Googled "VW Bus Fire" before leaving on the trip, which was about as smart as Googling "parachute not opening" just before you go skydiving.

Changing the fuel filter was not an issue, but changing the oil led to our next bit of unnecessary drama. I accidentally spilled oil on the engine, and to someone who has been around engines, specifically VW engines, this would not be an issue. To someone who forgets to put the VW Bus in neutral when adjusting the valves and someone who made the fateful error of watching Hail Mary's brothers and sisters meet an untimely death due to an engine fire, this tragedy was close to reaching Defcon 5.

Looking back on that episode of my life I was probably overly cautious about driving with spilled oil on the engine but, erring on the side of caution, we wiped down the engine and went to a local Wal-Mart to get engine degreaser. Embarrassing as it is in retrospect, we also called AAA to see if they had any ideas. Like I said, we were erring on the side of caution and the last thing I was going to do was go up in flames in this God-forsaken place they call El Centro.

Our next game was in Houston and we had a little less than a week to get there. If we got back to

Texas early, the plan was that we could actually spend a little time with our families before heading to the Northeast. The El Centro episode was on a Tuesday evening and I was determined to be in Austin on Wednesday. Even if it meant driving at night, we were going to make it.

That night I became aware of how desolate a place the highway can be. Miles and miles of New Mexico without so much as a dead animal in the middle of the road or another vehicle. The thought of being stranded on the side of the road in New Mexico made the El Centro experience seem like Disneyworld, so I began looking upward. Maybe searching for divine intervention or maybe I was just tired of staring out into a black abyss.

For those who have never driven a split-window bus, you basically sit on top of the road with nothing in front of you but possibilities. Consequently, there is not much above you but sky. The deep darkness of the road was endless; the landscape free of the buildings and lights that burden the geography of urban areas, stripping away its true beauty. The panoramic view provided by Hail Mary made it seem like we were driving in the sky, which itself was struggling to contain the abundance of bright stars. It was one of the most unforgettable moments of the entire trip. I knew I could live a lifetime and never see a sky like that again. "The darkest nights produce the brightest stars" is another motivational quote and our dark night had definitely produced the brightest stars. Not only was the sky breathtaking, but my confidence was continuing to recover from that dark time in El Centro. The sense of freedom settled on me along with the feeling that this was not just a trip, but my life.

We arrived at NRG Stadium early Sunday morning excited that we had an interview scheduled with the leader of the Houston Texans band. Our thinking was that the documentary we were filming would be great public relations for all of the teams, so we had a cavalier attitude that every team would be willing to work with us, especially because NFL Films was producing its own feature about our tour. The Texans organization and the band leader did not see it quite the same way we did, however. The front office of the Texans was contacted about our request for an interview and decided they needed to make their presence known. We were happy to speak with anyone we needed to and make whatever concessions necessary to make the interview and the documentary the best it could be.

Anyone who has ever taken a ride in a VW Bus knows how devastatingly hot it can get on the inside during the summer because there is no air conditioning. The only air blowing through the vents is the hot stuff from outside, and 100-plus-degree air is never refreshing. We had been in stop and go traffic, typical of a game day, for the better part of thirty minutes in the same unforgiving Texas heat we had left just a week before. By the time we finally emerged from Hail Mary we were not exactly picture perfect with beads of sweat dripping down our faces. Just another one of those perks when you are particular about the vehicle you drive to every NFL stadium. Our distinguishing taste in transportation meant we were hot, and there was not much we could do about it except grab our camera bag and head to the rendezvous point for the interview.

We were greeted by the bandleader, who was obviously apprehensive about being interviewed for fear of what the Texans organization might think; maybe even consider removing him and his band from the sidelines. It was also readily apparent that the bandleader really was not going to provide an interesting interview so we offered him a way out. Instead, he called a woman from the Texans front office to meet us.

The conversation was pleasant enough to begin with, when she asked us a question to which she thought she already knew the answer. "Have you guys been drinking? I smell alcohol on your breath."

Her question really surprised us, since Grayson had not had a drink in over ten years. It was not even ten o'clock on a Sunday morning, which in Texas means you cannot even buy alcohol yet. The only items in our hands were our camera bag and the talent release waiver for the bandleader to sign. Our look of disbelief and forceful denial of her accusations seemed to convince her that we were indeed completely sober.

Having struck out in our first interview of the day—the interview with the bandleader was predictably unemotional, uneventful, and unusable—as well as our first meeting with anyone affiliated with an NFL team, we decided to peruse the fans in the Yellow Lot on the other side of the street in our search for more fertile ground for interviews.

Houston Texans fans have long been known for having some of the best tailgating in the NFL. A quick scan of the Yellow Lot made it obvious that, if anything, the tailgating at Texans games was understated. The smell of smoked meats hung heavy in the air and despite it being two hours before you could legally purchase alcohol, there was no shortage of people consuming it. Just not us.

I managed to talk my way into playing quarterback in a pickup game of three-on-three football in the lot. Figuring the camera would love to see my throwing prowess I immediately took command of the huddle and marched my team down the field, a few feet short of the end zone—without throwing a touchdown. I felt an overwhelming sense that I had let everyone down; my new teammates, my travel companions, the people who were going to watch the documentary, and maybe even Hail Mary herself had all seen me fall short of the greatness I knew I had within me.

My role on the team changed to rushing the opposing team's quarterback. Not exactly the glamorous, take control of the huddle, white-shoe wearing Reno Hightower leading the troops to victory I thought I was destined to become when I asked to play in the game.

The quarterback for the other team was about five and a half feet tall, in his mid-forties, with a visor holding back his silver highlighted hair. His sweat-soaked hands grabbed the oblong ball, which was actually more round than football shaped. He gave me a quick glance, checked his receivers at the line of scrimmage then quickly called out, "Set ... hut." I fell back into coverage about fifteen feet from him. He cocked his arm ready to fire a strike to one of his receivers down the field, but as soon as his arm started to come forward, the oblong ball slipped out of his hand and flew—uncontrollably and inexplicably—toward my waiting arms.

My first thought was that my eyes were somehow deceiving me, but my next thought was if there was someone close enough behind me who could tackle me just yards away from the previously elusive end zone. After grabbing the ball out of the air, my last thought was just run like hell and do not get caught. I raced to the end zone untouched and was about to receive the adulation that I had rightfully deserved and expected while playing quarterback from one of my teammates, when the other teammate, with me in mid-flight, looked like he was about to tackle me. In the history of touchdown celebrations, that may have been the most awkward. Nevertheless, victory was ours!

My personal display of athletic prowess was short-lived. We were here to film a documentary, after all, and needed to interview Texans fans. Grayson and Eric began to interview a diehard Texans fan who, along with his wife, had remodeled an old school bus into a tailgate party on wheels. It was an impressive engineering marvel with an equally impressive tailgate surrounding it.

Within the same parking lot, we found two fans from Canada who would make any American football fan cringe. "There is nothing like this in Canada," they said. "We don't get to drink at our tailgates. They stopped that a long time ago."

That comment got me scanning the crowd for another possible interview. There was one person who caught my eye, but not because he had the most face paint or the most elaborate costume, but because he was wearing a Buffalo Bills jersey. I could not remember who the Bills were playing that day, but it was not the Texans. His presence in the parking lot begged the question of why anyone would wear a Bills jersey to a Titans vs. Texans football game. He looked as if he had a pleasant disposition with a smirk that was not quite a grin, but gave the impression that he was enjoying everyone else enjoying themselves regardless of the teams playing.

I do not recall how I started our conversation, but the story of him being a Buffalo Bills fan came up—another example of why I took this trip—stories from complete strangers who bonded with me through being a football fan.

I explained to him what we were doing, and he started telling me the intricacies of Buffalo and, specifically, Ralph Wilson Stadium. I had not been excited to go to Buffalo at this point. It was more of a let us get this over with so we can cross it off our list kind of destination. Not that my new friend's description made me think we should get in Hail Mary after the game and go directly to Buffalo, but he did make it seem tolerable.

Grayson, who grew up an Oilers fan, came over after the Canadian interviews concluded and started talking about the Houston Oilers epic collapse in what is commonly referred to in football circles as "The Comeback" game. To this day it remains the biggest comeback in NFL history: The Oilers somehow relinquished a 32-point lead to a backup quarterback named Frank Reich and the Buffalo Bills. Who does that? Houston does that, and Grayson was all too aware of the stigma surrounding the Oilers and Houston sports.

The fan dressed in a Buffalo Bills jersey had actually been at that game with his family. He told us that as soon as the Bills fans started to file out of the stadium thinking it was hopeless, he continued to upgrade his seats until he had one of the best seats in the house for one of the most memorable games ever played. Grayson, to his credit, took it all in stride when our friend declared it to be one of the greatest games of all time.

"It has kind of been downhill ever since," the fan quickly admitted, an understatement as Buffalo is the only team to lose four consecutive Super Bowls during those glory years of the franchise.

As a young sports fan, I had traveled many times to the Astrodome. It was a majestic place and I could not imagine a bigger stadium. I remember touring the Louisiana Superdome as part of a family vacation, and the tour guide said you could fit the entire Astrodome into the Superdome. To a young but proud Texan that could not possibly be true. The Astrodome was huge, it was the "8th Wonder of the World" and everything is bigger in Texas. Although I guess they would not say it if it were not true, I have held a grudge against the Superdome since that tour. Now it is thirty years later and the Astrodome is in the shadow of NRG Stadium. There is no better example of what the NFL and sports used to be and what it has become than the visual of seeing the lifeless Astrodome next to NRG Stadium.

Suddenly the quote at NFL Films, "Life is Good. Football is Better." came rushing back to my mind. Is it or was it? A question I would contemplate before, during, and after the trip. The fate of the Astrodome is undecided; the Houston Oilers moved to Nashville and became the Tennessee Titans, the Houston Astros moved to Minute Maid Park in downtown Houston, and the Houston Livestock Show and Rodeo is no longer held in "The Dome." My idea was always to renovate it and have the Texans and Astros play throwback games a few times a year in the Astrodome. My idea may be more for me than actually makes business sense, but without a tenant the Astrodome faces an uncertain future. If they tear it down, a significant part of me will die with it.

The game between what became of the Houston Oilers and the current football franchise in Houston turned out to be a really good one. A week after recording the largest comeback in franchise history, the Texans erased an eight-point, fourth-quarter deficit, and DeAndre Hopkins scored a three-yard touchdown in overtime that gave the Texans the win. It would be the last win of their season. They finished with a 2-14 record. Their head coach was fired, and their starting quarterback was traded to Oakland for a sixth-round draft pick.

From Houston we headed north to Philadelphia. We were becoming accustomed to being on the road with Hail Mary, and she with us. In Tennessee we started seeing signs for Volkswagen Drive and once again grandiose visions began to cloud my mind. I suggested we make an appearance at the Volkswagen plant in Chattanooga. We all seemed to share in the lofty expectations of how we would be treated once we reached the gates of the mother ship, so without hesitation we detoured from our route.

Our expectations were met by a security guard who was no more interested in Hail Mary than he was in cutting off one of his extremities. The tepid welcome we received from the fine folks at Volkswagen was just another example of how my imagination was outpacing my reality for this trip. With not so much as a free T-shirt we were back on our way to Philadelphia, but before we left we decided to play catch in front of the Volkswagen sign.

People look at you kind of funny when you play catch in random places like in front of a Volkswagen plant. Some may be envious, contemplating the possibility of stopping their own lives to be part of the game, but others may just see it as foolishness undertaken by those who refuse to succumb to the serious business of adulthood, of accumulating things in an earnest yet misguided attempt at finding true happiness.

There is a saying that people do not have souls. We are souls that merely have a body. The acquiring of things in our quest for gratification only serves to hide our souls behind a layer of brand-name possessions. I am convinced the world needs to play catch a little more and take itself a little less serious.

Our trip to Philadelphia included working with NFL Films to get some external shots of Hail Mary going past the iconic landmarks of the city and taking a tour of the NFL Films facility in Mount Laurel, New Jersey. To a fan of the NFL, that tour is worth the physical and mental anguish of going on the road for four months in a '67 VW Bus.

If our resources for the documentary were the epitome of a no-budget film, then the facilities at NFL Films were the polar opposite. As impressive as it was from a production standpoint, the artwork on the walls was equally so. Every few steps were marked by another classic image of NFL football. Players, games, and moments that had been so much of my childhood were being relived; even those that had been dormant for years in the deep recesses of my mind came back to life in an instant. These images and teams had provided the color of my youth. The original scores of NFL Films were the soundtrack of my childhood.

Steve Sabol's artwork lined a few of the walls. He had educated us on his "pop art" in 2011 when we interviewed him at the Super Bowl in North Texas. Items he had collected over the years like buttons, ribbons, tickets, and advertisements—predominantly pin-up girls—were married to images of football players and coaches, then given a title that was often a double entendre.

I actually own one of his pieces titled "The Cowboys Quarterback." I bought it the same year we interviewed him. I had to decide between buying the artwork and buying a ticket to the Super Bowl—not that they cost the same amount of money, but if I bought one I could not justify spending the money on the other. But while there is a Super Bowl every year, there will only be one Steve Sabol.

His parking space at NFL Films is still reserved and adorned with film cells along each side, so it stands out from the rest of the lot. A flag that reads "SDS" for his self-appointed nickname "Sudden Death Sabol," flies next to that of the NFL and a flag of the defending Super Bowl champion. His office is filled with notecards on every player and coach who collected an NFL paycheck, still carefully organized underneath a big window, waiting patiently for their author to return.

The collectibles outside his office were still perfectly placed as if there were an impending photo shoot for an interior design magazine. There is even a seat reserved for him in the theater where all of the programs are reviewed by staff and scrutinized to maintain the quality of the NFL Films brand. One day very soon they would see Hail Mary on that screen for the feature NFL Films was producing on us, and I stopped to think that somehow he would be sitting in that chair watching it with a contentious smile as if to say "These are my kind of guys."

The producer for our feature on NFL Films met us outside of Geno's Steaks. Cheesesteak in Philadelphia is much like barbecue in Texas. You have your place of choice and you do not visit the others. Geno's is one of those places, with Pat's King of Steaks being the other. After a few laps around the block so NFL Films could get various angles of Hail Mary passing by the landmark that is Geno's, the producer hopped into the backseat to give us directions to our next stop.

His first impression of the accommodations afforded by our beloved Hail Mary left me with a lasting memory and a reminder of how different she is from what people expect and what we have become accustomed to with modern transportation. His first reaction was not terrible, but it was not "This is awesome! Can I come with you?"

"Wow," he said as if he needed to buy time to process his surroundings. His face expressed considerable doubt with a fleeting hint of admiration. Then in the next breath it was "This is cool."

It was not an overwhelmingly positive endorsement for Hail Mary, it came across as more like when someone asks if another person is attractive and they are not. They pause, trying to think of some encouraging words while not telling an outright lie. Without lying, our producer was saying she had a really good personality.

The VW lifestyle is not for everyone, and I did not see our producer investing in a Volkswagen Bus in the near future. Most people who learned about Hail Mary and our travels openly volunteered to be a passenger, as if somehow she has the power to free them from the bondage of adulthood. They all open the door and sit down with a sense of optimism or certainty, which eventually fades after spending an extended period of time with Hail Mary.

In reality, very few people would actually take this trip without the creature comforts of a modern vehicle. The luxuries of today's automobiles make us forget about the necessity of a vehicle to get from Point A to Point B—a necessity that was never a guarantee in Hail Mary, which made this trip a true adventure. Nevertheless, our producer was honest, so we did not hold it against him.

We arrived at Lincoln Financial Field extremely early on game day, especially given the fact that the game was on a Thursday night. The stadium parking lot was not open yet, but our interviewee warned us that he enters the parking lot as soon as the gates open, so if we wanted his interview, we needed to be there early.

We parked Hail Mary outside the front gate of the stadium alongside the other diehard Eagles fans, and found our guy.

I do not know if our interview was with the most devoted Eagles fan of all time, but after hearing his story I cannot imagine him not being in consideration. In addition to wearing an authentic jersey, pads in his pants, and actual football cleats, his face was covered with green paint on one side and silver on the other. He had a basic wrap on his head with the Eagles logo prominently displayed on his forehead. And his devotion to his team was on permanent display, thanks to the large Eagles logo tattooed on his right arm. If being a fan was like playing poker this guy was all in.

During the interview he started rocking back and forth with nervous excitement—not about being interviewed, but in anticipation of the gates opening. After about five minutes a horn blew, his signal that the gates were about to open and his football spirit would be set free again after a long offseason. Eagles football was his heaven, and he was about to be on cloud nine.

He apologized for having to leave, put an Eagles sticker on the back of Hail Mary and quickly headed for his football euphoria. We pulled into the parking lot after the long line of Eagles fans had made their way through the gate and joined in the tailgate festivities. With more than ten hours to go before kickoff, we decided to walk around and take in as much of our environment as we could. Somehow we managed to make our way into the stadium without being noticed by security.

It was a beautiful sunny September day and an equally spectacular stadium. The Eagles had played at Veteran's Stadium until 2003. "The Vet," as it was affectionately called by Eagles fans, was by all accounts home to one of the worst playing surfaces in the NFL, and the conduct of fans at the games made the jail in the basement of the stadium a necessity. In

1999, Eagles fans cheered when legendary Cowboys receiver Michael Irvin lay motionless on the field. It was the last game Irvin would ever play in the NFL and left this Cowboys fan with a lasting bad impression of Eagles fans.

The Phillies also played at Veteran's Stadium, and I was a Pete Rose fan. Some of my most vivid baseball memories growing up were watching Rose, playing for the Phillies, rounding second base with his batting helmet struggling to keep up with him and finally giving up the good fight, falling to the ground as he made his way to third base with his trademark headfirst slide. Youthful indiscretion and Pete Rose led me to slide headfirst when I played little league. I was always reprimanded for it, the umpires claimed it was not safe and threatened that if I did it again I would be thrown out of the game. I did not care. I played the way Rose played the game.

In addition to the Eagles and Phillies, the stadium hosted many Army-Navy football games. The Army-Navy game was always played at the end of the regular season of college football and before bowl games. On occasion, the game featured a player who had an opportunity to play in the NFL, but that was a rarity. The first player I remember featured in the game with a real chance to make it in the NFL was Napoleon McCallum. To me, his name had the same ring to it as the BYU quarterback, Robbie Bosco. He played for Navy, which, if I had to pick sides in the game I would have gone with, simply because legendary Cowboys quarterback Roger Staubach went to Navy. McCallum ended up drafted by the Raiders and played a few seasons, mostly on special teams. Those memories all made Veteran's Stadium a special place to me.

The Vet had been replaced by Lincoln Financial Field, a modern stadium with solar panels on the outside, and sans a jail on the inside. We had managed to find a way inside the stadium shortly after the gates to the parking lot were opened. The green grass, the newly painted field, and the empty stadium were all primed for the excitement of a Thursday-night game and the return of former Eagles coach Andy Reid, who was now the coach of the Kansas City Chiefs.

The *Thursday Night Football* television crew for the NFL Network were on the field in their suits, minus the jackets, throwing the ball around. Seeing them pretend to run down the field was further proof of my theory that it is impossible to stand still and play catch with a football. Their smiles and enjoyment for simply playing catch brought a smile to my face as if I was on the field with them.

The jubilant look on the faces of the NFL Network crew playing catch on the field inspired us to return to Hail Mary, get our football and start playing catch ourselves.

The Eagles fan we had interviewed that morning found us again with an energy as equally intense as when we first met. He told us that he would like to tell another story on camera and, sensing that it was important to him, we quickly found our equipment and began filming what would be the most remarkable and unbelievable story we would hear the entire trip.

In the first interview, he had told us how he had morphed into his current persona. How he was encouraged to wear the shoulder pads by a friend and how the metamorphosis continued with the face paint and eventually the full uniform. His appearance was, by most people's standards, enough to put him in the top one percent of all fans, but his second interview revealed a higher level of devotion to his team—more than any of the players have, much less other fans.

His story began when he was lying on his couch one day. The playoffs were going to start that week and for the first time in a long time his Eagles were in them. Suddenly, he was overcome with an intense pain in his side that forced him to the floor. The pain did not subside, yet he refused to go to the doctor for fear he may miss the playoff game. He tried to live a normal life as best he could for that week, even worked out several times at the gym. When game day finally arrived, playing in pain he cheered the Eagles to victory. After the game he immediately went to the hospital and learned his appendix had ruptured while he was lying on the couch. Death was now less than twenty-four hours away for our Eagles fan, who was immediately rushed to emergency surgery.

To say some fans live and die with their teams is usually nothing more than a cliché, but not in this case. We would ultimately talk to fans all around the NFL, but nothing we heard could approach the sacrifice made by this fan on behalf of his team.

My seat for the Eagles game was in the far reaches of the stadium. Jamaal Charles was the running back for both the Chiefs and my fantasy football team, The Rottens. Although I could not cheer aloud for my guy, I expected big things from him in the game.

A few minutes before the game started I made my way to my seat, or at least what I thought was my seat. Of all the stadiums I visited on the trip, the seating for Lincoln Financial Field was the most confusing to navigate. I marched my way toward the top of the stadium and found three empty seats in my row with one of them displaying my seat number. I settled in nicely to my surroundings thinking I would probably be joined by a couple of fans who were coming from work and consequently getting there after the game had started.

I was wrong, and soon confronted with the error of my ways by a "Gym, Tan, Laundry" Guido from New Jersey. He and his two goons hovered over me as if to threaten me before they even knew I was a Cowboys fan. Thankfully, they never asked my favorite team, since I do not know if it is in my being to not say I am a Cowboys fan, regardless of the immediate danger the divulgence of such information may put me in. Our relationship, however, never made it to second base. Guido did not have much to say but did all of the talking. "These are my fuckin' season tickets. Get the fuck outta here," he said. I tried several times to ask him if I was indeed in the wrong section and where my section might be. “These are my fuckin’ season tickets. Get the fuck outta here,” was his only response.

He may have needed things repeated for him three times for him to understand, so that could be the reason we found ourselves in our current predicament. I, however, completely understood the first time Guido told me. All I really wanted was to find my seat. After all, who tries to sit in someone else's seat five rows from the top of the stadium?

While Guido saw me as his adversary, I had no other option but to see him as the stereotypical Eagles fan other fans warn you about when going to games in Philadelphia. The same fans who cheered as Michael Irvin remained on the ground back in 1999 just because he was wearing a Cowboys jersey. The truth is, Guido and I were not so different. We pretend to be based on the team we follow or, in this case, the seat we mistakenly sat in. It is this misconception that leads to rudeness or in the words of Guido, “fuckin’ rudeness.”

Thankfully, other fans around me told me how to find my section, and understood my confusion. Their kindness was proof that not all Eagles fans are like Guido—the vast majority, like the fan we interviewed and those who helped me find my section, are actually quality people.

Looking back, it was probably destiny that made me change seats. My new seat neighbors were welcoming, and I started telling them about my trip.

As I looked down the long flight of stairs, I saw a guy with a full beer in his left hand and a motorcycle helmet painted like an Eagles helmet in his right. From his unorthodox gait while climbing the stairs it was obvious that this was not his first beer of the day. My attention, along with everyone else's in my section, was on this guy navigating his way back to his seat. The now impending carnage was providing the entertainment that a Chiefs blowout over the Eagles could not.

As he reached the row before mine his mind wrote a check his body could not cash and he began to plummet toward the stairs. That is not entirely accurate—his face began to plummet toward the concrete steps. Since I was in the aisle seat I extended my arms to catch him. To his credit, and my dismay, he never let go of the beer or the helmet. I found myself holding up the Eagles fan, his face inches from the ground. His beer and helmet firmly in his grasp, it was apparent he would rather sacrifice his looks than relinquish either item in his hands.

With the help of others, we sent the Eagles weeble wobble back on his way. There was a resounding cheer that may have been for me saving the Eagles fan from certain bodily harm, or it may have been that he had found a way to get back on his feet without spilling a drop of beer or scratching his helmet. Either way, that was a bigger highlight than the Eagles provided all night, losing to the Chiefs 26-16.

I could imagine Guido's critique of his team's performance as, "Fuckin' Eagles," and somehow I considered that a personal victory.

Philadelphia has the best pregame in all of football. Capitalizing on the city's *Rocky* fame, the team even has Adrian from the franchise's second film urging the team on. "There's one thing I want you to do for me...Win...Win!" she cries from the big screen.

I was ready to suit up and cover the opening kick after seeing the pregame in the stadium and feeling the electricity of the crowd.

After the game we found ourselves sitting in Hail Mary while Eagles fans tried to make sense of their team's dismal performance and escape the parking lot. Just like the song from the *Rocky IV* soundtrack: "There's no easy way out. There's no shortcut home." The parking lot was gridlock, so we sat watching cars trying to outmaneuver one another only to move up three feet.

One of those vehicles jockeying for position was a minivan with a family of four. Parents with their two young boys who, at first, reminded me of my family back home. Grayson, who was in the passenger seat of Hail Mary, interrupted the Hallmark moment in my head by starting to yell at the minivan. Apparently one of the boys had noticed our Texas license plate, so he rolled down the window, and clearly, within earshot of his parents, began taunting us, telling us to go back to "fucking Texas." That sentiment did not sit well with Grayson, who had now begun to trade barbs directed toward how the parents were not doing anything about their unruly children. I was amazed but, thanks to having met Guido, not completely surprised. Maybe the

Eagles should reconsider that jail in the basement of the stadium.

At this point, we had spent three weeks on the road and navigated our way across the United States, which means one thing to VW owners: time for maintenance. The nightmare that was El Centro had become just another echo in the journey, replaced by a perceived slight of our greatness at the Volkswagen manufacturing plant in Chattanooga and a misunderstanding at the Knights Inn somewhere in Virginia.

Needing to adjust the valves and change the oil again brought a heightened level of anxiety that would gradually fade as we became more experienced in VW maintenance and our work became road tested. This time, the maintenance also brought to our attention that we had two bald tires in the back and a belt that was deteriorating with every passing mile.

Tires for a '67 VW Bus are not easy to find and, not knowing New Jersey that well, we decided to press on to Pittsburgh and hope for the best with our tires and our belt.

I probably should mention that we did not have windshield wipers, either. They gave out on us in El Paso on our way from El Centro to Austin. Since they stopped working in the middle of the windshield, I made the executive decision just to take them off completely and rely on RainX. While that decision may sound a little short-sighted, so far it had not been an issue—mostly because we had not seen a cloud in the sky, much less rain.

While I am fully disclosing issues with Hail Mary, I probably should also admit that I had never taken her out in the rain before this trip. To judge if she was road ready, my father and I drove her back to Austin from Las Vegas. We drove through mountains and nearly froze to death because the heater was not working, but we made it without issue and without seeing any rain.

Just about halfway between Philadelphia and Pittsburgh we came face to face with a driving thunderstorm. The kind of storm that stranded Gilligan on an island for three years and, looking back on it, Gilligan was probably better equipped than we were to handle the storm. Drops of water were coming from the vents above my head as I steered Hail Mary the best I could with two bald tires. Then the floor began to take on water. The skies were angry that day my friends, and rather than try to push on in a windshield wiper-less Hail Mary we decided our time would be better spent assessing the water damage inside the bus and waiting out the storm at a gas station.

We eventually made it to Pittsburgh late that night, or it might have been early Sunday morning. It being a Steelers football weekend in Pittsburgh meant the probability of finding a motel anywhere near the city was not in our favor.

"Sold out, Steelers are playing!" was the response from the best budget motels in East Pittsburgh—as if we were in town for a jigsaw puzzle convention and totally oblivious to the fact that there was a football game to be played. Had they not heard of the legend of Hail Mary?!

We stopped at the Hampton Inn, which would have been the nicest hotel we stayed at all trip, but they were out of rooms as well. What it lacked in rooms it made up for in parking, though. It had a big, spacious, well-lit parking lot with plenty of spots available, so I backed Hail Mary into the most inconspicuous spot we could find. Grayson took the back, Eric the middle seat and I slept across the front seat. I always tell people we stayed at the Hampton Inn, we just did not stay inside the Hampton Inn.

The thing I began to realize the more I drove Hail Mary is that people are fascinated with VW Buses and want to take a look at her. We always took the time to listen to anyone's VW story, whether it was three in the morning at a gas station or driving to a game. I would catch some people trying to take a picture of her, doing their best to not let anyone know what they were doing. If I saw them, I always asked if they got what they needed or if they wanted to be in the picture, too. The only time the magnetism of Hail Mary was an issue was when we were sleeping in the parking lot of a motel or fast-food restaurant. People would approach the vehicle, not knowing there were three guys sleeping in it. They did not mean any harm; they just could not help themselves. To be woken by strangers early in the morning was not only a shock to us, but to them as well. For this reason, when we slept in Hail Mary we always tried to wake up before someone took notice of her. We did, however, get confused looks when they did not see anyone walk to the VW Bus and get in, yet it drove off.

The Steelers game was at night, but we had managed to schedule an interview for much earlier in the day with a life-long fan, requiring us to arrive at the stadium before noon. PNC Park where Pittsburgh's baseball team, the Pirates, play, and the home field of the Steelers, Heinz Field, are very close in proximity, so much of the public parking is shared. That day the Pirates had an afternoon game against the Reds, so parking was at a premium and the lot attendants were attempting to charge Pirates and Steelers fans for both games. The inflated parking prices did not sit well with three guys who had survived a tsunami and slept in a waterlogged VW Bus, so I volunteered to find a parking spot and wait in Hail Mary while Grayson and Eric went to get the interview.

If I had to do it over again, I would have gone to the Pirates game. PNC Park, with its picturesque view of downtown Pittsburgh visible just beyond the outfield bleachers, is supposed to be one of the best baseball stadiums in Major League Baseball. Although growing up I had a strong dislike for the Steelers, the Pirates were always tolerable if not "rootable." I know that is not really a word, but in this instance rootable means you are not a fan of a team, but if your team is not playing you can actually hope a different team wins. A lot of fans watch the Super Bowl and cheer for the team that to them is rootable, because unfortunately their team is not playing.

Sometimes big games are more like presidential elections where your vote is seen as the lesser of two evils. Really hoping both teams lose—which is not possible—you go for the team you dislike the least. I happened to find something appealing, or rootable, about Dave Parker, Willie Stargell, Bill Madlock, Mike Easler, Kent Tekulve and the rest of the Pirates team of 1979.

My dislike for certain teams has been largely tempered by my appreciation for the love and devotion their fans have for those same teams.

Terry Bradshaw, the Pittsburgh Steelers quarterback from its four Super Bowl wins in the '70s, is now on the FOX NFL pregame show. Despite two of his Super Bowl wins being at the expense of my Dallas Cowboys, I have grown to like him and look forward to his weekly, mindless banter with his colleagues. Bradshaw is now like an uncle whose antics call his sanity into question, leading your parents to warn you about ending up like Uncle Terry, but at the same time make him contagiously fun to be around.

An hour or so later, Grayson and Eric returned to Hail Mary with a renewed energy and excitement for the trip. They went on and on about the heartfelt story the Steelers fan had recounted to them. I had not been at the interview, but they even had me excited. Watching the interview, it was impossible not to build up empathy for this fan and, consequently, I suddenly found the Steelers to be that much more rootable.

For the interview she had worn a Steelers jersey with the number thirty-nine. To a non-Steelers fan, and perhaps many members of Steelers Nation, that number is largely insignificant. But she indicated that the jersey "had a lot of stories behind it," so it was apparent the number and that specific jersey were meaningful to her.

First it was the number of Bobby Walden, who punted for the Steelers in the late '60s and most of the '70s. The number later belonged to her favorite Steelers player, Darren Perry, an eighth-round draft pick in 1992. Not expected to make the team, much less a contribution, Darren Perry had captured our fan's attention. She admitted that her father may have been the biggest Perry skeptic, but despite the long odds and her father's assurance that the Steelers had wasted a draft pick, our fan was unrelenting in her devotion to the new number thirty-nine. Perry, to his credit and that of our fan, led the team in interceptions his rookie season.

Our fan also enjoyed a history of being affiliated with the team. She talked about how she started working as a vendor because that was the only way she could get into the stadium to watch the games, and how her sections liked her because she stopped selling during the actual plays. Later in life, she became a sideline photographer for the Steelers, which to any sports fan, is like Rocky the Colorado Leprechaun leading you to the pot of gold at the end of the rainbow. Short of scoring the Super Bowl winning touchdown and being carried off on the shoulders of your teammates with confetti flowing uncontrollably from the roof of the stadium, it could not get any better.

Her last story was how she felt the Steelers Super Bowl in 2011 was a gift from her father who had passed away shortly before the game. The Steelers lost that game so "gift" may be a strong word or maybe she was not his favorite child. Regardless, it was obvious the Steelers were an important part of the people of Pittsburgh.

There was another fan we interviewed as we walked toward the stadium shortly before kickoff. He had short-cropped hair that stood straight up, due in large part to an abundance of gel. His mustache and two-day stubble could not hide his jovial disposition that showed in his smile and gleeful eyes. There was something about his energy that drew us to interview him. He immediately offered his hand as he introduced himself as, "The Gooch." When asked what the Steelers meant to him, the strength to contain his excitement and happiness suddenly left his body. "It just makes me happy. It's my life, my wife, kids, family, all my friends," he told us.

Although the stadium had changed, the Steelers fans have not, and Myron Cope should be in the hall of fame. Although I am a die-hard Cowboys fan, I believe, without question, that Myron Cope needs to be in the hall of fame. Go to any Steelers game—home or away—and you will see why.

In 1975, Cope was the radio broadcaster for the Steelers and was ordered to come up with a gimmick for the playoffs that year. What he created is as universal a symbol for Steelers fans as the stereotypical foam finger is to other fan bases. The

Terrible Towel and its creator, Myron Cope, are two of the most beloved characters in not only the history of the Steelers, but the city of Pittsburgh.

The Terrible Towels were out in full force for the game against the Bears. Even as a Cowboys fan, I can appreciate looking out across the stadium at an endless ocean of yellow towels being waived by their owners, summoning the stadium to a fever pitch. It would not have been a Steelers game had there not been Terrible Towels.

The Bears took control of the game early, and the ocean of Terrible Towels evaporated into a few puddles spread throughout the disgruntled stadium. The Bears won the game 40-23, and with the loss the Steelers started the season 0-3 for the first time since 1986, but the personal investment the fans make in their team and the pride they have for the Steelers is something I will never forget. I will never be a fan of the Steelers, but after being in Pittsburgh for a game I understand it. And more importantly, I appreciate it.

I also appreciated the old Steelers home, Three Rivers Stadium. All that remains of the old stadiums like Pittsburgh's Three Rivers is the grainy NFL Films footage that provided countless hours of entertainment for me when I was growing up.

Sort of like how I feel about Hail Mary. While she is not the main character in our story, she adds an element to our journey that a new car could not possibly provide. Much the same way the current generation of stadiums—such as Heinz Field—although much nicer and newer, are void of any character or history. The hallowed grounds where so many of the iconic images captured by NFL Films have all but been extinguished.

CHAPTER 3

Road to Mexico

St. Louis and Kansas City
(Eight teams and 6,857 miles)

It's not what you look at that matters, it's what you see.

– Henry David Thoreau

After the game there still were not any motel rooms available near Pittsburgh, but it was more or less irrelevant at this point because we only had a few days to make it to St. Louis for the Rams game on Thursday night. Normally three days would be sufficient for the 604-mile trip from Pittsburgh to St. Louis, but truth be told anything can happen when driving Hail Mary. If we missed one game, our quest for every NFL stadium in one season would be lost. Consequently, if our temperamental choice of transportation was willing to go, we needed to get moving to the next stadium before she changed her mind.

The Steelers game was on a Sunday night, so we headed west immediately after it was over. Knowing we could only drive a couple of hours toward St. Louis that night meant we needed to either find a budget motel or, at the very least, a safe parking lot of a motel for the night.

We had spent the previous night in Hail Mary and, while Grayson and I were willing to do it again—mostly because we were running low on money—I also got the sense that we both enjoyed the sometimes suffering that life on the road inherently brings. Eric, on the other hand, was approaching his breaking point and it was only September. Grayson and I relented and decided to get a room at a motel in a remote part of West Virginia. Our accommodations that night were closer to the Bates Motel than the Ritz Carlton, but somehow better than Hail Mary if only marginally.

The next morning checkout was at eleven, but we never made it that far into the day. The construction crew renovating the motel had begun their day's work at nine. They may have started before that, but I refused to think about regaining consciousness until at least nine. They also spotted Hail Mary, and it was not long before everyone on our team—except me—had made their way to the parking lot.

When I was pitching a television show to the Travel Channel, a friend of mine sent me an email that read, "Keep climbing ... your peak will be very high." Another friend, who has known me over thirty years, told me before I left on the trip that if he were going to climb a mountain and could only take one person with him, it would be me. His reasoning was that no matter how bad I felt or what the circumstances were, if I said I was going to the top of the mountain then I would make it to the top of the mountain.

As I lay on the motel room floor in my sleeping bag, awake, but with my eyes not yet introduced to the day, I heard my two friends in my head, urging me to keep climbing to the top of the mountain. I also could hear Grayson talking football to the construction crew. There was a pause, and one of the workers proclaimed his allegiance to the Miami Dolphins. "Fuck the Dolphins! This is Steelers country!!!" another worker quickly sniped.

I could imagine that worker pulling out his Terrible Towel and waving it as he claimed the motel parking lot in the name of the Steelers. Suddenly I remembered the mountain I was climbing and the reason I was climbing it. It was not only that I wanted to see every NFL stadium, but because people like the construction workers wanted to see every stadium. They would have traded places with me without much consideration, so how is it that I could find myself still in a sleeping bag with St. Louis on the horizon?

From this point on, Hail Mary seemed to want to hold a grudge against us and became an unwilling participant in our travels. Sometimes she was less than that and did not participate at all. Every morning after Pittsburgh I prayed to the VW gods that she would just start. Praying to get us to where we needed to be that day could wait until we got on the road. Just to be able to hear that distinct voice of a VW engine was no small victory and not one the team ever took for granted.

Hail Mary's gas tank is a little over ten gallons, small compared to modern vehicles. To further complicate things and force us to have to stop more frequently, her gas gauge is as accurate as a third-string quarterback. This meant having to stop every

150 miles or so. It was not terrible because it afforded everyone the ability to stretch their legs, get something to eat, and generally broke up the monotony of driving across the country. But when your vehicle is Hail Mary, every stop is another opportunity for her to show how fragile the relationship between owner and VW Bus can be, and calls into question who actually owns whom. We had unwillingly relinquished the control of our travels to Hail Mary, deepening our dependence on others to help us make it from stadium to stadium.

We drove throughout the day and deep into the night. The days of not wanting to drive at night were trumped by the necessity of getting to the next stadium. Worries of what might happen if we do drive at night were replaced with the thought that as long as she is running we will keep driving. But after filling up with gas and buying enough rations to get us to the next stop, Hail Mary refused to start. Repeated attempts were made to resuscitate her, but no amount of praying or swearing could breathe life back into our weary road companion, so we pushed her away from the pump and into a parking space on the far right side of the convenience store.

Every time we had issues with Hail Mary we would convene like referees after a pass interference call to talk about what each of us saw as the issue. These meetings were about as fruitful as those referee huddles since we were not mechanics and had the video to prove it. How would we ever figure out what was wrong with her?

We quickly called the cavalry that is known by most people as AAA. We were not overly optimistic that whoever AAA sent out could truly help us. It may have been more that we just did not want to go through this experience alone and felt more comfortable having a total stranger look her over to verify we were indeed in trouble.

It was generally the same reaction everywhere we looked for help—with a shrug of their shoulders and a hand running through their poorly groomed goatee, they would explain how they had never seen one of these buses much less worked on one. And with that pearl of wisdom, like Santa Claus wiggling his nose, they were never to be seen again.

We were easy to spot, and the AAA guys were easily recognized as well—the look of bewilderment as soon as they turned into the parking lot gave them away. After thirty minutes of waiting, the cavalry arrived, this time in the form of a husky blond kid in his late 20s. I had always swore to myself that I would never refer to someone younger than me, but clearly an adult, as a kid, but since it seemed to fit him I made an exception. He listened to our issue for about five minutes and by all indications was about to shrug his shoulders and place his hand over his surprisingly goatee-less chin.

"You know what your problem is?" he knowingly asked in the same tone that a cop uses when he pulls you over and asks if you know why he pulled you over. "It's your starter," he said. "It means it's going out. All you have to do is tap on it while you turn the key and it should start."

I quickly grabbed a dormant piece of camera equipment and gave Grayson the key to turn on my command. I slid under the VW Bus, began tapping the well-concealed starter and gave the command to turn the key, not knowing if the engine would start or if I was going to make it out alive. The purr of the engine never sounded so good, and I quickly made it back to my feet with a sense of relief and an even bigger sense of accomplishment.

To this day I have no idea why tapping on the starter would get Hail Mary going. Sometimes in life the important thing is not understanding how something works, just that it works. It would work for us on countless occasions until we had enough money for a new starter or Hail Mary forced us to buy one.

The entire trip—if we went directly to each city—was a little over 26,000 miles, but rarely, if ever, did we take the shortest route to our destination. Maybe that was the reason for Hail Mary's grumpy disposition. It was not that we wanted to see the country or that we were only four short hours away from the second-largest ball of twine on Earth; it was out of the necessity to find a place to stay for the night.

St. Louis was one of those places where we traveled off the beaten path to find room and board. Centralia, Missouri, is a town of a little over 4,000 people north of Columbia and between St. Louis and Kansas City, meaning we had to drive past St. Louis to get there.

We arrived the day before the Rams game and would be back after the game to wait to drive to the Chiefs game on Sunday, making this home our base of operations for the next few days.

I could tell you how Eric was related to this family but I would probably be lying, so it is not important. What is important is how welcoming and nice they were to all of us. We had everything we needed, including a home-cooked country breakfast. After four weeks on the road, you start to appreciate food that is not a bag of Doritos and a blue Gatorade.

I took the basement the first night and slept on the couch. The basement was a dark, peaceful sanctuary, and with no checkout time I was able to get some much-needed rest.

The dog from across the road seemed to like us and spent more time in our yard than his own. That was fine with us and, truth be told, if he had not belonged to someone we would have found room for him in Hail Mary.

We were scheduled to meet NFL Films the morning of the St. Louis game. Anytime NFL Films wanted to meet us I would get a call or email from the producer asking if we had time to meet with their camera crew. I always thought it to be a polite but strange question. Do we have time to meet with NFL Films? As if three guys going to every NFL stadium in seventeen weeks would want to do anything other than meet a camera crew with NFL Films.

We never worked with the same crew twice, but it was always the same modus operandi: Two or three guys wearing NFL Films shirts in an unmarked minivan. For St. Louis they gave us an address of a parking lot of an abandoned building in East St. Louis.

If you have never been to East St. Louis I recommend avoiding it at all cost. The city is actually in Illinois, and as the name states east of St. Louis, and boasts a violent crime rate almost six times that of the national average. We had rolled through the city in Hail Mary like an ice-cream truck at an elementary school, and everyone had taken notice.

When we found the meeting location, I was ready to contact our point person for the day to let him know we were moments away from being robbed at gunpoint. While that may or may not be true, there were safer places for Hail Mary. But before I could make the call, a white minivan pulled up next to us and we quickly learned what they wanted us to do.

To be honest, NFL Films could have told us to drive Hail Mary backward, down the wrong way of a one-way street, yelling "we're drunk" and we would have done it. Knowing that at the end of the trip we would be featured on *NFL Films Presents* was a pretty big carrot for us. In the short term, getting out of East St. Louis was a more immediate carrot, so we were eager to please.

We had managed to line up an interview with "Ram Man" before the game, so after a few shots of Hail Mary driving past various landmarks we graciously bid farewell to our friends at NFL Films and made our way to the parking lot next to the Edward Jones Dome. It was mostly vacant as you might expect for a

Thursday night home game of a mediocre team. That did not, however, prevent us from finding a jovial pair of fans to pass the time with until Ram Man made his way across the parking lot. They had a red Dodge truck that contained everything they needed for a tailgate, including beer that they quickly offered us and I even more quickly accepted.

It is a common misconception that because we went to thirty-two NFL games alcohol figured prominently into our game-day experiences. Truth be told, we were always working: to film a documentary; to get Hail Mary from one stadium to the next; trying to set up interviews; and surviving from one day to the next. Alcohol rarely played a part of our trip, so to actually have time to enjoy a cold beer and the company of football fans was a welcome diversion from the logistics of our journey.

We figured someone who goes by the name Ram Man has to be a visually remarkable individual, and he did not disappoint. It was a few hours before the game and I doubt that any of the players had their shoulder pads or pants on, but Ram Man did. It may have been midday on a Thursday, but to him it was game day.

As a fan of an NFL team, you are only guaranteed eight home games. Knowing this, and being realistic that his team was only going to reach the minimum number of games and not make the playoffs, Ram Man was embracing every moment.

Grayson walked across the parking lot to retrieve our latest interview subject. When he arrived at

Hail Mary, it was clear he was over six feet tall, but with his ornate, custom-made Rams hat perched on top of his head he looked closer to seven feet.

Maybe hat is the wrong word to describe what he was wearing. It looked as if he had gone out and killed an actual ram and was wearing its head on top of his, much like a king wears his crown. His full regalia included Rams sunglasses, wristbands, shoulder pads covered by a custom Rams jersey with "Ram Man" stitched on the back, authentic Rams football pants, a sweat towel—yes, a sweat towel—and Rams socks and shoes. He told us that someone had once offered him $5,000 for his Rams hat but he turned them down.

During the interview, Ram Man sternly professed his love for the Rams, ceremoniously putting the former owner of the Rams, and "St. Louis' own," Georgia Frontiere on a pedestal because she moved the Rams from Los Angeles to St. Louis in 1995.

This interview was the first time I had ever heard kind words spoken about the former owner of the Rams who inherited the team after her sixth husband mysteriously drowned. She promptly fired the president of the team—who happened to be her former stepson—and moved Los Angeles's first professional sports franchise east to St. Louis.

In the world of sports, players change teams and teams change cities. I found it interesting how fans could easily justify taking a team from a different city when it worked to their benefit, but when it did not it became "shady dealings." Ram Man's story was not the only one we would hear about how the relocation of a team positively or negatively impacted the psyche of a city. Los Angeles has never forgiven Georgia Frontiere, and has never stopped loving the Rams.

Since football teams are measured by wins and losses, Grayson would often ask the fans how important winning is.

"True football fans don't care. Look at the Cleveland Browns," Ram Man declared. "As long as you are playing football in your city, wins and losses don't matter. At least they're going to be here next year."

His statements, which seemed to be of a fan deeply afraid of losing his team, turned out to be prophetic. The St. Louis Rams moved back to Los Angeles in 2016.

Ram Man had been generous with his time and provided the type of insight into the hearts and minds of football fans we needed for the documentary. Still hours before kickoff, we moved Hail Mary to the parking garage that would be her home for the night and walked to the St. Louis Arch.

With our football in hand, the field that the Arch stands on was calling us to run around and play catch. It was one of those rare moments for us on the trip where we had free time to actually see a little of the city. Grayson and Eric wanted to go to the top of the Arch and soon found themselves crammed into the pods that jettison visitors to the top. Having already been in the Arch years earlier I decided to remain outside with the football.

Walking around the base of the Arch I heard "Psst. Here!" My gaze was still focused on the football I was tossing around in my hands. "Psst. Here!" I heard again.

I finally looked up and saw someone in a 49ers jersey giving me the international "I'm open" sign by raising his hand above his head while pretending to run a pass pattern. Some people can deny a man his God-given right to play catch, but not me. I quickly jumped into my best throwing position, looked the defense off, and fired a strike twenty yards down the field.

There are universal truths in this world, and one of them, as I have said, is that it is impossible for people to remain in one spot when playing catch with a football. We have to either run patterns, jog to the other side of the field or do some imitation of a wide receiver running, pretending that a sidewalk or the edge of the road is out of bounds. It is not our fault we do this. It is innate, part of our DNA as football fans.

Here is another universal truth about playing catch: Despite only pretending to run patterns or tiptoe the sideline, it somehow wears you out. After about five minutes of playing catch, we introduced ourselves and, on the benches outside the Arch, began to talk football.

He was a die-hard 49ers fan from Chicago, and his wife had bought him tickets to the game—his first 49ers game ever!

The way old people talk about how a candy bar was a nickel when they were growing up is how sports fans talk about great players and games when they were growing up. We reminisced for almost twenty minutes, knowing the NFL would never be better than it was when we were growing up, recounting fond memories of seasons long gone. Grayson and Eric returned to find my new friend and me talking football and they soon joined in. We had nowhere else to be at the moment and honestly did not want to be anywhere else.

The Edward Jones Dome in St. Louis has always had a corporate label tattooed to its existence. As you might expect of a facility with a corporate name birthed in the mid-'90s, it has very little character. The overly concrete exterior is neither warm nor intimidating, so it is difficult to imagine the "Greatest Show on Turf," as the Rams offense was called from 1999-2001, calling this stale, unimaginative building home. Not to be overly critical, but this stadium simply was not blessed with the good fortune of possessing NFL history to provide some much-needed charm.

If the stadium had little charm, the game had even less. When you sit in different stadiums with different fan bases, you inherently root for the home team, feeding off the excitement of those around you, and I soon found myself a Rams fan for the night. Unfortunately, it was a miserable night to be a Rams fan.

The Rams had given away T-shirts touting the team's middle linebacker, James Laurinaitis, before the game. At the start of the game, fans were proudly wearing their shirts or waving them like improvised Terrible Towels.

After Rams quarterback Sam Bradford missed a wide-open receiver for a touchdown, the free shirts quickly became cotton projectiles. It happened almost in unison; as if the entire stadium was throwing in the towel to surrender to the 49ers. The Rams ended up losing in a fashion as unremarkable as the stadium they played in, 35-11.

On the way back to Hail Mary I walked past someone who was as out of place as I would be winning Olympic gold in figure skating. A young, attractive female, maybe in her twenties, whose looks were fading at an unnatural pace thanks to the hardened life of being homeless, was sitting outside the stadium where thousands of people passed by after the latest Rams loss.

I glanced at her, and our eyes met for what seemed to be an eternity but was actually less than a second. She was holding a sign that was a typical account of her current situation that I did not take the time to read. I have never given money or food to a homeless person based on what they scribbled on the blank canvas of an equally homeless piece of cardboard. Since eyes are said to be the window to the soul, most of the time my decision to help out is dependent on what I see in a person's eyes. Looking at her eyes, I saw someone who did not want to be there but life had given her no other options.

If I had one regret of the entire trip, it would be that I did not offer to help her. I am not sure if it was the shock of someone so out of place or selfishly not wanting to risk getting trampled by the stampede of

Rams fans, but for whatever reason I passed on helping someone in need.

It is not the money or a meal that I could offer that would have made a difference, but merely the fact that someone stopped and cared. She made me think of the John Steinbeck quote, "I wonder how many people I have looked at all my life and never seen." It was obvious that nobody had taken the time to care about her, and I shamefully had not made the effort to see her either. My life will never know the hardships she has faced, because even in my darkest hour, I knew I would always have Hail Mary to call a friend and home.

Kansas City, the next stop on our trip, is about 250 miles away from St. Louis. Their proximity to each other meant we could remain stationary for a couple of days and take advantage of the free room and board graciously provided by our hosts. The break also gave us the opportunity to explore our surroundings, so we decided to interview a couple of Cowboys fans about twenty miles from our current headquarters.

Mexico, Missouri, got its name from early settlers who either lacked the material to build a new sign or the gumption to make one. The story goes that settlers found a wooden sign pointing to the southwest that read "Mexico." Instead of thinking of a different name and going through the painstaking process of sending out the appropriate mailer, not to mention the sign issue, they just decided to go with it as the name of the city.

While its town square left a lot to be desired on a Friday night, Mexico did offer us the possibility of home-cooked food. We eased Hail Mary into a parking spot in front of the Liberty Diner, which judging from the number of people visible through the large windows surrounding the building, we had either stumbled upon *The* place to be or the only place open. If the rolling billboard that is Hail Mary was not sign enough to alert the locals that we were from out of town, our deer in the headlights look once we walked through the front door and approached the hostess probably did the trick.

The décor, furniture and even the uniforms of the workers were from around the time of those early non-sign-building settlers. That may be a slight exaggeration, but it is quite possible the seats in Hail Mary were newer than the seats in the diner.

Segregated into two distinct halves, Liberty Diner's smoking and non-smoking sections were separated by a doorway. In the middle of the diner was the hostess stand/souvenir cabinet.

As we approached the hostess we were visible to everyone in the diner, regardless of their allegiance to smoking. When the natives became aware of us they seemed to stop eating, placed their forks in the middle of their plates and paused mid-conversation.

Slowly their attention began to focus on us. There was a long awkward pause, and running out the front door we had just entered and praying Hail Mary would start found its way into my consciousness. In the moment of truth, one of the locals broke the silence and, in a painfully begrudging tone, exclaimed "Howdy!"

As if the king had spoken and given his approval, everyone went back to their conversations and largely ignored us for the rest of the evening. The food was forgettable, but the hospitality at the Liberty Diner will be with me for the rest of my life. Maybe they still talk about the night three strangers arrived riding in a 1967 VW Bus. Given that the diners that night are the descendants of the founding fathers of the town, who considered that coming up with a new name and sign was too much work, I seriously doubt it. But I still think about Mexico, Missouri.

The Kansas City Chiefs, and even the Royals, were always teams that I found to be rootable. The first image that comes to mind when I think about the Chiefs and what brought them into my football conscience was the NFL Films footage of their legendary coach, Hank Stram.

On the sideline at Super Bowl IV, Stram was encouraging his offense—led by Len Dawson—to continue to "matriculate" the ball down the field. His jolly persona was captured on camera, and I became aware of not only the Chiefs, but got the word matriculate introduced to my lexicon. I have read the definition of matriculate several times, and am not sure Coach Stram was using the word correctly, or for that matter if the countless times while growing up I urged my team in the neighborhood to matriculate the ball down the street. But ask any football fan and they will give you the football definition of matriculate thanks to Coach Stram.

The Chiefs relevance resurfaced in my football world with players like Derrick Thomas, "The Nigerian Nightmare" Christian Okoye and, both playing out the winter of their careers, Joe Montana, and Marcus Allen. The Chiefs have not won much since the days of Coach Stram, but those players made Arrowhead Stadium a magical place to me. Always known as one of the loudest stadiums in professional football, as a football fan I was excited and almost obligated to submerge myself into the mystique of Arrowhead.

If it was not game day, just looking at the stadium provides nothing that really separates it from the Edward Jones Dome in St. Louis. While it is not a dome, there are ample concrete facades on the outside that give it a lifeless character.

Kansas City was the only city in which we did not have interviews scheduled before the game, so we were left to aimlessly walk the parking lot in search of interesting subjects.

Intrigued by two heavily bearded fans about to crack open their first beer of the day, we asked why they were Chiefs fans.

"Because that is the greatest stadium in all the land," one of the fans responded in a deep voice as he pointed toward Arrowhead, almost as if we were on top of a mountain with clouds lying at our feet and below the clouds a stadium made of gold.

I am not ready to anoint any stadium as being the greatest in the land, but what separates Arrowhead from a lot of stadiums—including the Edward Jones Dome—is the character of the atmosphere both outside and inside the stadium. Not the concrete façade of the stadium itself, but everything that makes up game day at Arrowhead Stadium. From the plumes of smoke rising from the countless barbecue pits generating a tantalizing smell that permeates the air surrounding the stadium, to the sun-baked field engulfed by a sea of Chiefs fans all in red make for an incredible sports experience.

We found a much older Chiefs fan and asked him for an interview in hopes that he may be able to provide a different perspective.

"Why is Kansas City the best tailgate?" Grayson asked, feeding off the previous fan's comment about Arrowhead being the greatest stadium.

"Because of the fans, of course," our middle-aged Chiefs fan replied. "We've been doing this forever. Since the '70s, the red, it's just awesome."

He told us his parents had been season ticket holders since the franchise moved from Texas in 1963. He then began to roll off the names of historic Chiefs players as if he was watching them play in his mind.

"Mike Garrett, Otis Taylor, Nolan Smith, Super Gnat," his tone gave the impression that he longed for those days of being in the stadium with his parents watching those great Chiefs teams. I know from personal experience that just a brief mention of former players of your team can be a cathartic experience for a football fan.

I had seen the stadium and the field countless times on television while growing up. And although the Chiefs were not perennial Super Bowl contenders, they were always on the cusp of being a playoff team. Occasionally we build something up so much that it cannot possibly live up to the vision in our minds, and other times we find ourselves content, or even excited, that the vision actually came to fruition.

To me, Arrowhead Stadium was one of those times on the trip where I was completely content with enjoying the game, the atmosphere, and the loudness of the Chiefs fans. I did not get to try the barbecue, though, which is reason enough to go back to Arrowhead, but honestly, as a football fan I do not need another reason to go back. The stadium and its atmosphere stand on their own merit. If you do not like Arrowhead Stadium and the fans in Kansas City, you are not really a football fan.

The Chiefs were playing Eric's New York Giants and the quarterback he held in such high regard—yet I had little use for—Eli Manning. As the game wore on I could imagine Eric sliding lower and lower in his seat in a feeble attempt to hide his public allegiance for the Giants that was sitting on top of his head in the form of a bright blue cap with "NY" monogrammed in white letters.

The Eli Manning I said was finished before the season even started did not disappoint. He finished the game completing less than half of his passes, throwing an interception and fumbling twice. The Chiefs beat the

Giants 31-7 and, for one day at least, Arrowhead Stadium was the greatest stadium in all the land.

CHAPTER 4

In Need of a Hail Mary

Cleveland and Cincinnati
(10 teams and 7,903 miles)

Football fans share a universal language that cuts across many cultures and many personality types. A serious football fan is never alone. We are legion, and football is often the only thing we have in common.

– Hunter S. Thompson

The Monday after the Chiefs game we began our journey to Cleveland for the Browns game the following Thursday, and I was lucky enough to have a friend who lives in the area.

Patrick Hazelwood and I had gone to grad school together at Georgia Tech. He is the type of sports fan after my own heart, planning vacations and business trips around sporting events. We had been to Lambeau Field together, saw the second to last Phillies game at Veterans Stadium in Philadelphia and drove from Atlanta to San Antonio for a Final Four. Needless to say, we saw eye to eye when it came to being a sports fan.

After graduating, Patrick moved to Cincinnati, so he offered up his house as a temporary refuge from the road. We gladly accepted as we were always low on cash and Cleveland was less than a day's drive from Cincinnati.

Patrick had bought a house in a nice area of Cincinnati, but it was the worst house on the block. In much the same way I had planned this trip with visions of grandeur and a spark in my eye, I think my friend had torn away the walls and in some cases the floors of the house. To say it was not the Ritz Carlton would be an understatement, but it did not come with the price tag of the Ritz Carlton. On the bright side, it had running water, a place to sleep, free internet and an Xbox. Another amenity is that it was within walking distance to a coffee shop and a sports bar.

The first night in Cincinnati, Eric and I walked to Millions Café for a beer. The place looked to be a typical sports bar from the outside, and did not disappoint with its surplus of fried food, cold beer, televisions, pool tables, and shuffleboard. We were the only two in the bar and found a petite brunette whose personality was anything but small. She smiled and offered us menus and, most importantly, a cold beer. Not to sound like I am an alcoholic, but it tasted so good and was our just reward for keeping Hail Mary on the road.

Cincinnati brought us some much-needed rest, and while it was not home there was something comfortable about staying at my friend's house. I liked Cincinnati, and its proximity to other NFL cities meant we would get to spend a lot more time there. Staying at the house instead of the Ritz Carlton also gave us the opportunity to once again try our hand at VW maintenance. We decided it would be a good idea to film Grayson and me doing the maintenance. By this time we were not cocky about our ability to adjust the valves and change the oil, but it was not a huge point of contention either.

It still took us longer than someone who knows what they are doing, and we most likely became more soiled than the average VW mechanic. Nonetheless, part of the pride of ownership for me is being able to work on Hail Mary myself, and someday I would like to be able to talk intelligently to other air-cooled owners about vintage Volkswagens. Despite traveling the country in a VW Bus, however, that day remains a long way off.

Grayson and I had completed the maintenance and made ourselves presentable for another night at Millions Café. Our big personality bartender was aware of our journey and offered to introduce us to a Bengals fan who had grown his beard out and decorated it for game days.

It is possible that Hail Mary could have sounded worse as we drove the short distance to the bar, but I do not see how. I have never heard any engine, much less a VW engine, sound that bad. It pained my heart to hear my beloved Hail Mary struggle for her life.

Mechanical problems rarely correct themselves, and this was no exception. The more we drove, the sicker she sounded. I did not rest easy that night knowing that something was drastically wrong with Hail Mary. Only vintage VW owners may understand this, but you form a bond with your VW much like and, in some cases, more so than, your significant other. Like most significant others, when you make a mistake they yell at you, and Hail Mary had been yelling at us since we finished our latest attempt at maintenance.

There is one part of this debacle that I have not mentioned because I would like to forget it. While we were changing the oil, fuel filter, and making a poor attempt at adjusting the valves, we noticed Hail Mary's belt was being chewed up rapidly and needed replacement. Changing the belt was never part of our lesson from our mechanic back in Austin. In spite of that, our maintenance bravado had manifested itself into attempting to replace the belt ourselves.

I have found there to be a few universal truths anytime I am performing maintenance, whether on Hail Mary or simple home-improvement projects. The first is that I can always take things apart; the second is that I will not be able to put things back together, but on the off chance I can, the third universal truth comes into play; I will always have parts left over.

Grayson and I could not have been digging a deeper hole for ourselves had Hail Mary been a backhoe instead of a VW Bus. We managed to unscrew the top nut that appears to the untrained eye to hold the belt in place. As expected, the belt loosened and slid off, but with it came all these extra parts called shims. With the shims came the uneasy feeling that we were now officially in trouble.

To me, the major utility of YouTube is to either show you how fools are out there doing things they should not, or proving how big of a fool you are by showing you in about three minutes how to do something you could not figure out in three hours. To date there were no videos of our journey on YouTube so the world could not see how big of fools we were. Instead, we were the fools who took the belt off by unscrewing the top nut, which introduced us to shims. There was a person on YouTube who had taken the belt off and on in about five seconds using a screwdriver while the engine was still running. As soon as we saw the video, silence blanketed the back room of the dilapidated house that would now definitely be our home for the next few days.

The silence was broken by one of us verbalizing the realization that we were indeed in trouble. Collectively, we were like Wile E. Coyote when he finds himself over the cliff. For a fleeting second, he remains in the air then suddenly drops to his demise in the canyon below. Wile E., despite his intentions, never catches the Road Runner and we, despite our best intentions, were not going to be able to put the new belt on.

The video propelled us into action, and by action I mean we called every member of the VW clubs in the Cincinnati area hoping someone could tell us how to put the new belt on and what to do with the shims.

We managed to contact a guy named Bob, who by his admission was the default president of a local VW club. As was the case most times we spoke with someone from a VW club, their tone of voice carried a certain amount of disbelief and they would eventually volunteer to meet us where we were. I guess they figured the roads were safer without us on them, and they could not bear to think of what further damage we could inflict on our beloved VW if left to our own devices.

Bob managed to get our new belt on using a screwdriver while the engine was running, a first for him. He also brought with him a light-heartedness that at the time was somehow comforting. As fleeting as the feeling of comfort was, it had been nice to share this experience with a complete stranger who was only brought into our lives through our inadequacies as mechanics and my love for a vehicle.

We had begun our maintenance odyssey on Tuesday that included going to the bar with a VW Bus that sounded like she was in an iron lung, and meeting Bob. The next morning I woke up and went through the maintenance again—I just needed to make sure that the valves were indeed adjusted properly. Not far into the process I discovered that not only were the valves not spaced properly, but that I could no longer adjust them at all. The nut on the exterior of the valve was at its end and could not be adjusted back down. John, our mechanic back in Austin, never went over this situation and no matter how thoroughly we had videotaped our lesson we would not be able to nurse Hail Mary back to health.

I looked through the most trusted book on VW maintenance, *How to Keep Your VW Alive* by John Muir, but to no avail. He did not cover this issue, either. We had managed to create a situation so foreign to the

VW community that it was not represented in the bible of VW maintenance and had never come up after sixty years.

It was Wednesday, and we needed to be in Cleveland the next day for interviews and the Browns game. We had lined up a personal tour of the Cleveland Browns headquarters with the director of the Browns fan club and a tailgate with Pumpkin Nation. All of that was now in jeopardy with Hail Mary suffering from a previously unknown ailment. We had dodged a major bullet yesterday thanks to Bob and his magic screwdriver, but now we were in real jeopardy of missing a game with Hail Mary facing possible season-ending surgery.

The great thing about VW people is that they truly care about those who share their appreciation for vintage VWs. Bob called us the next day to make sure we were still doing okay and that we had not attempted to pull the engine or anything. We assured him that the engine was still there, but we had managed to find ourselves in another less-than-ideal situation. Either Bob understood the gravity of the dire straits we found ourselves in or he had become suddenly aware that the name of our VW Bus was more than a name—it accurately described our situation and the odds of us making it to every NFL stadium. Either way, he put us in contact with one of the few places that had a chance of resuscitating Hail Mary and keeping our journey on schedule, Drew's Off-Road in Hamilton, Ohio.

I would estimate that Drew's Off-Road was, at least, a sixty-dollar cab ride from where we were in

Cincinnati. That is just an estimate of course because we always rode in the wrecker that was towing Hail Mary. Let us just say the all-too-frequent experience of riding with either the tow truck drivers or in Hail Mary on the back of the tow truck could be a book within itself.

Tow truck drivers seem to be opinionated people in that they do not mind sharing their opinions. Maybe they feel obligated to do so in an attempt to escape the awkward silence that always seems to fill the cab of a tow truck. That day I learned a lot about the family that owned the Bengals, race, and other nuggets of information I had forgotten by the time we reached our destination.

Drew's Off-Road is a modest place, not far from the main road in Hamilton. A dirt road led us behind the building to the garages. There to greet us was Brian with his toddler daughter in his arms. "What is that?" he asked her as he pointed to Hail Mary. "A split-window VW Bus," she replied without missing a beat.

It was almost like she could have told us the year it was built, the size of the original engine, and where it was produced, as well as the original paint scheme, but stopped short so as not to flaunt her knowledge of VWs in front of hack mechanics like ourselves. If she had been around yesterday with a screwdriver, chances are we would not have needed to call Bob.

Brian proved to be the entire trip's biggest asset in keeping Hail Mary on the road. After a brief introduction, he told one of the stories that I am always interested in knowing: How and why people become fans of air-cooled Volkswagens.

As most good stories start, he had met a girl who liked VWs, so he bought a Beetle and started working on it. The girl did not last, but he was hooked on VWs and at this time in my life I was grateful that girl had come into Brian's life. He also said something in passing that was interesting.

We had called him earlier that day and he said he did not have much going on. Typically, he said, he would have been too busy to look at Hail Mary. While Brian and the others at Drew's Off-Road were great at working on VWs, they were even better at being good people.

That is one of those things about owning Hail Mary and spending a lot of time with mechanics—or on the side of the road—you get introduced to a lot of interesting people you would not normally have a chance to meet. The issues we perceived as unprecedented in the VW community were less like when scientists discover a new species of fish in the Indian Ocean and more like a simple issue of having an automobile that is nearly fifty years old. Parts are going to wear out, and sure enough, our valves needed to be replaced. Although a simple procedure, it was something that we, the Three Stooges of VW maintenance, could not have done on our own. Even if we could have, I would have most likely ended up with leftover parts after reassembly.

"We had heard you guys were in town and were wondering if you were going to stop by," said the cashier as we were paying our bill. Do what? Had we become famous, were people finding out about the documentary before we were even done filming? The cashier said they had a couple of calls telling them about us. I quickly asked if Bob, our savior from the day before, had called and the cashier responded that it was not him.

So Drew's Off-Road knew about us being in town, wondered if we were going to make it in, and Brian, who would normally be too busy, was not on the day we needed his help. Some people would say that was mere coincidence, but I like to attribute it to the mojo of Hail Mary. She is a special girl and once again we were on schedule for Cleveland.

The Chicago Cubs have been the lovable losers of Major League Baseball. They have not won a World Series since 1908 because, allegedly, they are the victim of a curse involving a goat. Despite this supposed curse there remains a large contingent of baseball fans who bleed "Cubbie Blue."

If professional football had a version of the Chicago Cubs, it would have to be the Cleveland Browns. Although the Browns have won professional football championships—the last being in 1964—they have never played in a Super Bowl.

I was not sure what to expect from Cleveland. I had only driven through the city once and, from what most people said, the nickname "The Mistake by the Lake" seemed to fit. Growing up, I did not mind the

Browns. I remember having a football card of the Browns quarterback, Brian Sipe, and thinking he looked pretty cool. For some reason the logoless, tanish-orangish-brownish, helmet offset by the brown jersey of the Cleveland Browns had always appealed to me, as did the team's fan section in the old Cleveland Municipal Stadium, the infamous "Dawg Pound," which was notorious for being one of the rowdiest collections of fans anywhere in the NFL.

In the late '80s, Browns fans were presented with consecutive years of complete heartbreak. The AFC Championship Game, played on January 11, 1987, in Cleveland, will be forever known for "The Drive." With five minutes and two seconds left in the fourth quarter, John Elway, the Denver quarterback, orchestrated a ninety-eight-yard touchdown drive to tie the game with seconds left: Denver won the game in overtime and advanced to the Super Bowl.

A year later in the AFC Championship Game played in Denver, the Browns were driving for a game-tying touchdown when Ernest Byner fumbled the ball on the two-yard line with just over a minute left. The fumble essentially ended the game and allowed the Broncos to go to the Super Bowl for the second straight year at the expense of the Browns. Since "The Fumble" game in 1988 the Browns have rarely made it to the playoffs much less the Super Bowl.

We were fortunate enough to make contact with the person working for the Cleveland Browns organization who was in charge of its fan clubs around the world. She was gracious enough to invite us to the corporate office in Berea, just outside of Cleveland. As a franchise that had never played in a Super Bowl and had not won a championship of any kind since before Hail Mary was born, I was expecting modest accommodations at best.

Once parked, we crossed the street to the team headquarters, which from the exterior, looked like any suburban office building—reminiscent of my opinion of the Edward Jones Dome in St. Louis—functional, but with little character. Honestly, the only way I knew we were in the right place was the Browns flags hoisted on flagpoles as if they were claiming land for a country.

If the outside was ordinary and lacked character, the inside was anything but. Once we were through security and walking around the offices, I was completely enamored with the Browns. The walls were filled with pictures of great players in Browns history followed by inspirational quotes. In what appeared to be a conference room was a large panoramic shot of the stadium on game day. Judging from their facilities and the atmosphere around the team, if the Browns were considered the lovable losers of the NFL they did not like that moniker and were doing something to drastically change that image.

There is just something about a football or baseball field. It is an indescribable energy, a heightened awareness that I rarely experience outside of the sports world. The practice area, with its perfectly painted yard lines and Browns logo in the middle of the field, beckoned me for a game of catch. While the practice field had without question seen faster athletes and quarterbacks with better arms, it would never see someone who enjoyed playing catch more than me.

Our interview with the head of the Browns Backers was conducted on a couch in the main corridor of the offices. Some people were working feverishly in their cubicles while others had more segregated offices. It felt like we were in the eye of the storm.

It was impossible for me not to be excited about going to the game after seeing the panoramic picture in the conference room and listening to our interviewee describe Browns fans. "This town has fun with football!" she exclaimed.

Cleveland and fun are usually not synonymous for people who have never been there, but I was beginning to get a vastly different impression of the city and the Browns. Browns Backers may be the most impressive collection of fans anywhere in the NFL, and the way Cleveland embraces its team is truly special. The Cleveland Browns have 370 fan clubs around the world, with one on every continent including Antarctica.

By the time our tour was over, I was ready to put on a helmet and pads to join the resurrection of Cleveland. At the very least, the quotes on the walls had prepared me to give the pregame speech. It may not have been the caliber of "Win one for the Gipper," but without question it would have gotten the job done. Maybe those two AFC title games would have turned out differently had I been in the locker room before kickoff.

Our time at the Cleveland Browns headquarters was brief, but that was simply the way things had to be on a trip like this. Our ambitious goal of every NFL stadium in seventeen weeks kept us from staying in one place for very long.

We returned to Hail Mary who evidently had taken the tour of the facilities as well and was not quite prepared to leave. She would not start and, if our time with the Browns had been football euphoria, we were quickly reminded that we were dealing with an aging and sometimes unwilling VW Bus. In the world of sports, Hail Mary would be considered a veteran past her prime. I guess in that regard Hail Mary could be considered a metaphor of the Cleveland Browns: She looks great but does not go anywhere. We found two guys willing to give us a jump and hoped that was the only issue we would have with her that day.

We also had made contact with Browns tailgaters known as Pumpkin Nation. They were expecting us for the game and we arrived at the parking lot well before the party started. Their RV was in place next to the Barley House, and a few people were starting to mill around even though it was still a full eight hours before game time.

We were greeted by "Pumpkinhead" himself and instructed to pull Hail Mary through to the back parking lot. It was difficult to tell who was more excited about the game, us or Pumpkin Nation. The atmosphere in Cleveland was as if they were playing the Super Bowl, when in reality it was a Thursday-night game against the Buffalo Bills. The opponent did not matter. Cleveland is a football town and celebrates its Browns.

The original Cleveland Browns moved to Baltimore and became the Ravens in 1996. The city was without a team until 1999, when the Browns returned to the NFL as an expansion team. What makes Cleveland's situation unique is that they were allowed to keep their nickname. The Baltimore Colts, St. Louis Cardinals, Los Angeles Rams, Oakland Raiders and Houston Oilers all either took their nicknames with them or the franchise that replaced them decided a new one was needed. Cleveland kept the Browns and, after talking to the people in Cleveland, we discovered that meant everything to them. Taking the Browns out of Cleveland would be like taking pilgrims and turkey out of Thanksgiving.

We were progressively getting closer to game time, and by mid-afternoon Pumpkin Nation was alive and well. An invitation to climb atop the RV was an opportunity we could not pass up—I have never been atop a tailgate vehicle—and from that vantage point we were able to get some good footage for the documentary. The roof of the RV was tenuous, though, so it was important to not get lost in the atmosphere and to especially be cognizant of where you stepped. I am not good with heights, and the last thing I wanted to do was instigate a riot by stepping through the ceiling of the Pumpkin Nation RV. The view from the top of the RV combined with the energy we experienced from the crowd when they found out who we were and what we were doing was intoxicating. My world had never looked or felt more perfect.

The female fan who had led us to Pumpkinhead was a striking brunette, in her 40s with perfect teeth and hazel eyes that did a poor job of concealing her love for the Browns. I was never prepared for what the female fans we interviewed would say. It was difficult to overcome the stereotype that a female is a fan because it is the thing to do on a Sunday afternoon in the fall. For some, their knowledge and appreciation of their team and football is limited to the team colors.

The female fans we had interviewed on the trip so far were anything but stereotypical, and Cleveland was no exception. "Lyle Alzado stole my heart in elementary school," she said. "He was on the news and showed a Super Bowl ring. He promised Cleveland a ring. One of the many disappointments of being a Browns fan."

Transitioning to defend what she had just said about disappointment, she continued, "We have championships. Just not Super Bowls. Very important."

Her closing statements may be my favorite of any of the interviews we did the entire trip. She compared the book, *The 1980 Kardiac Kids: Our Untold Stories* by Don Cockroft, which focuses on the Cleveland Browns during the 1980 season, to "dating your first love all over again. The boyfriend you never give up on." I had never personified my love for the Dallas Cowboys in such simple yet eloquent terms. "I love the sound of football," she offered without further encouragement. We were immersed in that sound with her and could not imagine a better place to be for football than Cleveland.

You would think a Thursday-night game between two teams that had not won a Super Bowl, and that included the starting quarterbacks for each team leaving the game due to injuries would not be that great, but it was awesome. The Browns and Bills went back and forth most of the game, but Cleveland—behind its second-string quarterback, Brandon Weeden—won the game 37-24. It was the first week in October, the Browns, with their win, were in first place in their division and Cleveland celebrated like it was the first week in February and the team was finally bringing home the championship.

Late Thursday night we were driving back to Patrick's house so we could avoid the expense and potentially traumatic experience of another seedy motel room. We had just begun the 250-mile trek back to our humble abode in Cincinnati when we needed gas. It was early Friday morning, and while I found it somehow acceptable to be stuck on the side of the road for mechanical issues, it was not acceptable to be forced to hang out on the side of the road because I did not give Hail Mary what she needed most, gas.

There was a highway sign indicating a gas station at the next exit—a remote part of Ohio just outside of Cleveland. There were no hotels, fast-food places, or even other gas stations on this particular sign. The gas station was nowhere in sight as we pulled up to a stop sign at the end of a T intersection. We looked as far as we could to our left and our right, but the thick black night had effectively concealed any hint of the gas station rumored to be at our chosen exit. I do not know why we opted to go right, but we did, and it was evident almost as soon as we turned that this was not the direction of the gas station. I remembered seeing a sign that clearly stated that U-turns were not allowed, but at the blessing of the others in Hail Mary, and since there was no one else on the road, I figured it was safe to turn around while hoping the gas station materialized on the other side of I-71.

A little bit of information about Hail Mary and other split-window VW Buses: They all have standard, four-speed transmissions, do not have power steering, and if not dramatically modified can barely break the speed limit in a school zone much less on an interstate highway. Point being, a VW Bus was not the official vehicle of bank robbers or anyone who may find themselves in a police chase. I began to make the illegal U-turn, which is more difficult without power steering and on an unfamiliar road. A simple U-turn was magically transformed into a spectacular four-point turnaround. As soon as the U-turn was completed I looked in my rearview mirror to see what looked like the beginning of an alien abduction with a myriad of bright, blinding lights signaling that they had indeed arrived and we would be unwillingly boarding their spaceship soon.

I quickly came to the realization that, despite the convincing endorsement I received from my cohorts in Hail Mary for making the U-turn, local law enforcement did not share in that endorsement. I looked for a place to safely pull over to serve whatever sentence making an illegal U-turn carries in the state of Ohio. The road we were on had one lane in each direction with no shoulder and no street lights to illuminate our path, much less the side of the road. Not wanting to risk the safety of the aliens behind us, Hail Mary and I continued to drive in hopes that the sign for the gas station had not been a mirage, and that we would soon be able to get some much-needed gas along with a ticket for the illegal maneuver I had orchestrated moments earlier.

At no time did we exceed thirty miles an hour or drive in a serpentine in hopes of losing the sheriff and his posse. It should have been readily apparent that we could not run and hide in a 1967 VW Bus with huge "Foam Finger Nation" signs on each side and in the back. Our license plate is "TAILG8" which should also make us easy to find and less likely to run.

Evidently, these cops had missed the obvious signs that we were not in any real danger of becoming fugitives before their very eyes. As soon as we brought Hail Mary to rest at the gas station I looked in my side mirror to find the lead officer out of his patrol car with his right hand hovering near his gun. I quickly glanced up to see his face drawn with anger.

With a snarl he yelled for me to get out of the vehicle. At this point it became apparent that this would not be a drive-thru transaction but would require some explanation and possibly negotiation.

I tried putting him at ease by telling him what we were doing, proudly showing him the stickers on the back of Hail Mary indicating where we had been, and told him where we were going. Evidently the officer was not much of a football fan, or possibly a disgruntled Browns fan still living with those conference championship losses from the '80s. What he heard me say and what I inadvertently told him was that I was driving a vehicle after being at a place where large amounts of alcohol was consumed. "You been at the Browns game?" he asked.

Not wanting to get our friendship off to a bad start, I told him that we had indeed been at the game. He then asked if I had any alcohol to drink. Since lasting relationships are built on trust and telling the truth, I informed him that I did have a beer at about three in the afternoon, but had not had any alcohol since.

I was pretty confident that over the twelve hours since consuming that light beer it had probably burned through my system or, at least, that is what my high school health class led me to believe to be true. The officer was not that convinced, so he raised a pen to eye level and instructed me to follow it without moving my head. By this time I could see his partner in the background had a grin on his face because he believed all of my answers and knew his superior was headed down a dead-end street. Maybe he was the football fan of the duo and was smiling because he imagined himself in the VW Bus.

The lead officer continued to press on and interrogate me about my alcohol consumption. Interestingly enough, he never really mentioned the illegal U-turn, and I never received as much as a warning. We filled Hail Mary with gas, and talked to the attendant who had witnessed everything. "That guy is a dick," he consoled us. "He does that all the time." We put the Browns sticker on the back of the bus and were soon on our way back to Cincinnati.

The house on Herschel Avenue in Cincinnati was beginning to feel like home, or at least as close to home as we could feel on the trip. Being at the house brought with it a routine: Go to Lookout Joe's on Linwood for some morning coffee; work on getting interviews; play a little Madden on the Xbox; then Million's in the evening.

Patrick was not always home during our stays, but when he was we often branched out from the normal routine. He introduced us to Terry's Turf Club that, once you got inside, had a phenomenal hamburger. Outside it was like a horror film where you walk the plank of light-up signs of people who waved and looked at you as you made your way past them to your untimely death.

Graeter's Ice Cream was often the dessert of choice. I cannot remember much about the flavor of ice cream I got because the pretzel cone was just that good.

On one occasion Patrick decided he wanted to take us out for Chinese food. Based on his recommendation and the fact that we had built up an immunity to the fried food at Million's we were more than happy to go with our tour guide.

I do not know Cincinnati that well, but I have been to enough places to know when you are not in the safest of neighborhoods. The Chinese food place was not very well lit and, other than the Asian couple working behind the counter, showed very little signs of life. From the looks of the place and the looks of them, I could easily imagine them trying to warn me about buying a Mogwai, and not to get it wet or feed it after dark for fear it would turn into a Gremlin.

The gentleman was watching a small, square television with rabbit ears that provided the highest-quality picture standard-definition sets from the early '80s could provide. The woman acted as if she knew Patrick, but judging from the vacant restaurant, it could have been either excitement or shock that someone came to eat, actually having very little to do with my friend. The walls featured pictures of a thriving restaurant where people came to celebrate special occasions or simply enjoy the company they chose to keep. The pictures were as old as the television set. I began to contemplate what had happened to the restaurant and how it came to be in its current state. By the time I could gain enough courage to explore my surroundings further, our to-go order was ready, and we were on our way.

After eating while overlooking the skyline of the Cincinnati night, we moved on to the University of Cincinnati football stadium. It was open to the public, and we were more than ready to throw the football around and attempt a few field goals on a real field with real goalposts. We drew an audience of students who passed by on their way to other parts of campus, but as quickly as they came to see what was going on, they left in disgust over the ineptitude they had just witnessed. In my defense, I never claimed to be a field goal kicker and have attempted fewer than ten in my lifetime. After all, what kid dreams of being a kicker? I was always Roger Staubach or Danny White, never Rafael Septien. For me to be able to kick a thirty-yard field goal after eating Chinese is asking a little much. Regardless, it was still a welcomed relief to living life on the road and working to film a documentary.

One of the best things we experienced on our trip was getting to meet different people from various parts of the country who brought with them their life experiences as either fans of football or VWs, but most importantly as a person. Despite being an avid sports fan since birth, I had never contemplated the people behind the face paint at games. Why do some fans choose to outwardly and overtly display their fandom on their face or wear a full uniform while others like myself are content with a cap or T-shirt? It is a fascinating question, and I would love to be able to answer it for you, but despite interviewing fans of every NFL team I still do not have a clue. I have lived and died with my Dallas Cowboys every year I can remember being on Earth. I cried when we lost three straight NFC Championship games in the early '80s. I have forgotten more plays and players in the history of the Dallas Cowboys than most people know, yet I would never wear shoulder pads or face paint to a game.

Our favorite Million's bartender followed up on her offer to introduce us to one of the most interesting fans we would encounter the entire trip. The Friday night before the Bengals game we came front and center with "Misled Cincinnati" himself.

When the bartender mentioned him to us that first night at Million's, I could not tell if she was drunk or if it was me who was feeling the effects of finding a beer oasis in the middle of our trip. Her description of Misled painted a very unusual picture of a football fan: He had a long beard that he painted and sometimes used to hold his beer, and his bald head and face were a blank canvas, painted orange with black stripes like the Bengals helmets. She had not told us his name and we did not know what he looked like for sure and simply went on the word of our Cincinnati bartender that such a person existed.

Misled walked in with a black hat, a VW shirt, his trademark beard, and his attractive, blonde fiancée, and it was obvious he spends considerable time in the gym. He greeted us with a smile as if we had been friends for years. Misled is what I consider to be an obvious free spirit. I do not know if he viewed us in the same lens because of our VW Bus or the fact that we were temporary vagabonds traveling around the NFL. Whatever it was, I knew without even really talking to him that Misled was one of the good guys, and that behind the façade of his three-year-old beard was someone who, for the most part, shared my views on life.

I thought about how amazing it is how some people come to power. I do not mean in the sense of power as the President of the United States or a CEO of a Fortune 500 company. I mean power as in leading by example, making the world a better place and having others look up to them.

Misled uses his "epic" beard to better his community and the lives of others. He is a mainstay for not only the Bengals, but also Cincinnati's baseball team, the Reds. His propensity for growing facial hair has garnered him face-time on local and national media and won fourth place at the Beard Nationals in 2011. Yes, there is such a thing as the Beard Nationals and, believe it or not, Misled has beard sponsors.

The beard actually led him to NFL headquarters to meet with Commissioner Roger Goodell. "Being there and seeing every Super Bowl ring but not seeing one for your team is not a good feeling," Misled told us about the trip.

According to Ram Man in St. Louis, real football fans did not care about winning as long as the team is playing in your city. But since the Cincinnati Bengals have never been the subject of relocation rumors, Bengals fans like Misled place a higher priority on winning. In some ways, the team staying in Cincinnati is taken for granted, so getting a Super Bowl ring is the priority.

On game day, we shadowed Misled as he prepared at a restaurant close to the stadium. His fiancée, the engineer and architect behind the beard, is responsible for taking his latest idea and making it a reality. She started by easily coating his head and face with orange paint, then gently, but with purpose, applied the black stripes. The beard took a little more attention but soon his look for the Bengals game was complete.

Following Misled around we began to realize how difficult it is for him to actually get anywhere. Every few steps another fan wanted to take a picture or have him pause so they could gawk at the craftsmanship and fine detail that went into his game-day preparation. He told us his notoriety stemmed from a beard he originally grew on a bet with a co-worker, and I kept thinking to myself that it was just a beard, but knew it was really much more—it is someone daring to be different and refreshing while at the same time himself.

As I write this, I begin to think again about it being just a beard, but again, it is more than just an unwillingness to shave. It is a reflection of what most people would like to be, but do not dare step out of what they know in order to become who they know they are. Beards may not be it for everyone; it may be a different hairstyle, a different way to express ourselves or even traveling the country in a '67 VW Bus. Whatever it is, most people are afraid to be themselves, which is what makes Misled Cincinnati such a social phenomenon around Bengals games.

After the game we met at a restaurant, El Coyote, where Misled, conveniently for us, had a monthly tab in exchange for personal appearances. The restaurant has a mechanical bull, and you would expect someone from Texas to have one of these in their living room growing up or, at the very least, is an expert on riding the real thing.

Until that night, my life was void of any interaction with the top of a bull, mechanical or otherwise. I was convinced after seeing my traveling companions try somewhat successfully to maintain a seat for eight seconds that I could tame the beast. After all, Eric is from New Jersey and he could ride it—by ride I mean not fall off immediately—so how difficult could it be? I had seen Grayson and Patrick tame the bull without any real problems, Again, I mean they did not fall off immediately, so how difficult could it really be to ride a mechanical bull?

The young, attractive female hostess who evidently drew mechanical bull duty that night asked me who my favorite team was. "Dallas Cowboys," I replied. She had a flirtatious smirk on her face as I straddled the mechanical beast, ready to show the world how we do things in Texas. Slowly I raised my left arm above my head signifying I was ready for "go time."

Now, when you get on a mechanical bull you are at the mercy of the person in control. No matter how innocent and sweet that person looks, they hold your life in their hands. It is kind of like getting a haircut—they can make you look as good or bad as they want.

"Dallas Cowboys, huh," she said softly, then immediately jerked the control, throwing the bull, which I now know as Widow Maker, into a spin that this cowboy could not control. In less time than it took me to tell the little darlin' my favorite team, I was on my backside staring at the ceiling of El Coyote. I was upset with her for blatantly discriminating against my team, but even more upset that I was from Texas and could not tame Widow Maker.

Riding Widow Maker would be the perfect opportunity to use falling off the mechanical bull as a metaphor for life and how when life throws you off you grab the bull by the horns and show him who is boss. Widow Maker did not have horns and if it was not evident by now that we would get back on the bull that was this trip and Hail Mary no matter how bad she threw us, it soon would be. For now, it was time to saddle up and head to Chicago for a Bears Thursday-night game. I was excited to be going to Chicago and seeing Soldier Field again.

CHAPTER 5

The Long Way to New York

Chicago, Buffalo, and New York
(14 games and 9,121 miles)

When Brian told me he grew up in New Mexico, I told him I thought it is cool that people from other countries play football.

– Terry Bradshaw

For me, Chicago had always been a magical place, due in large part to sports. I did not know anyone who did not watch the Cubs on WGN, and while it was not my favorite team, midday baseball during the summer was better than no baseball at all.

Chicago has two baseball teams. No city has two baseball teams unless it is New York. Chicago is not New York which led this kid in Texas to begin to wonder who is this Chicago? I knew a little about Chicago's other baseball team, the White Sox: Ron Kittle hit home runs; Harold Baines had a great name and even better afro; the White Sox played at Comiskey Park; and the players wore jerseys that reminded me of beer-league softball. The Cubs were special with Harry Caray, the ivy on the outfield wall, Ryne Sandberg at second base, and Andre Dawson in right field. Lee Smith was a big presence on the mound and, over at first was Leon "Bull" Durham, who to me always looked like he had better things to do than play first base for the Cubs, but his nickname made his outwardly lackadaisical demeanor cool. The Chicago Bulls were gaining prominence with Michael Jordan, and I will never forget being in a sports bar in Chicago in 1997 when Steve Kerr hit the shot that gave the Bulls yet another title.

But before the Bulls, and even before the Cubs and White Sox, there was Soldier Field and the Chicago Bears. For a young sports fan this team and this place helped create the legendary place they call Chicago. The mystique had long been forged with players like Butkus and Sayers, but the Bears came into my football lore in its 1985 championship season. Payton, McMahon, Gault, Singletary, William "The Refrigerator" Perry, and others had made household names of themselves, not only for their talent on the field, but for their music video and song, "The Super Bowl Shuffle."

The Bears had characters, and Soldier Field seemed to have an ambiance oozing of football past and present. The stadium, with its columns and concrete façade that read "Soldier Field," was the closest thing we had to the ancient Roman Coliseum east of the Mississippi.

I say had because the Soldier Field we saw the Bears play in on the trip was not my Soldier Field.

"I would never say that Soldier Field is an architectural landmark," said a representative of the prestigious architectural firm that renovated the stadium. "Nobody has copied it; nobody has learned from it. People like it for nostalgic reasons. They remember the games and parades and tractor pulls and veterans' affairs they have seen there over the years. I wouldn't do this if it were the Parthenon. But this isn't the Parthenon."

That statement is proof that architects do not play football, do not understand it, and should not be in charge of renovating the Parthenon of professional football.

A Chicago architectural critic dubbed the renovated Soldier Field as the "Eyesore on Lake Shore," and others view it more like a spaceship landed on Soldier Field. As a football fan, it is difficult to think taxpayers knowingly funded $475 million for the "improvements," and the architects heartlessly cast aside the reason people like Soldier Field so much—for nostalgic reasons—to create a spaceship nobody in their right mind would copy. Nice job architects!

Soldier Field is not a bad stadium, but gone is the football ambiance it once had. As a football fan I feel cheated out of the Soldier Field experience that had given Chicago its mythical status. Strangely, I do not look at the city in the same way since the renovation.

Wrigley Field has lights, but no Harry Caray; the beer-league softball team on the south side has respectable jerseys and won a World Series; the Bulls are mediocre; and Soldier Field is a spaceship.

Anything the city lost because of recent sports developments was not lost on the Bears fans we met. We were contacted by Da Superfan Nation through Twitter, and after hearing their introductory voicemail I realized we needed these guys for our documentary.

The guy on the voicemail spoke with a very thick Chicago accent, the kind that gives outsiders a false impression of arrogance and entitlement. That is not meant as an insult, because, to a person, everyone I met was friendly, outgoing, and most of the time smiling. Their accents give them character, and the two guys of Da Superfan Nation were definitely characters. Their picture on Twitter had a strong resemblance to George Wendt as a Bears fan on *Saturday Night Live*.

Every time we spoke on the phone they never broke character or spoke without an accent, and by the third conversation I was beginning to believe that this was no act. These guys were legitimate, real-life George Wendts.

Hail Mary, along with the fact that the world headquarters for Da Superfan Nation is located outside of Chicago, made us late for our interview. When we pulled up, there were a couple of guys there to greet us with warm smiles and friendly handshakes. What they did not have were mustaches and aviator sunglasses. These fans, by my standards, were young kids, probably in their early 20s. What happened to George Wendt, the accents, the glasses, the false arrogance? Where is Da Superfan Nation?

From our brief conversation before turning the camera on, it was apparent that this was going to be a good interview whether Da Superfan Nation made an appearance or not. These guys loved Chicago sports—specifically the Bears—and it was more than a game for them, it was a family affair. They were cousins and had been going to or watching games together practically since birth. After a brief conversation outside they welcomed us into their house and led us down to the basement where the history of Chicago sports was readily on display.

Other than the obscure and strangely out-of-place picture of Joe Namath on the wall, the space was inundated with Chicago sports teams, dominated by the Bears. Maybe Soldier Field should have had these guys redesign the stadium, because these two obviously got it. They understand what sports and, in particular, the Bears, are all about and their importance in the world. No self-respecting sports fan would have desecrated a temple like Soldier Field with such callous disregard for the cultural significance of the stadium, especially these two.

Our conversation was casual, and even while filming it seemed more like talking to old friends than an interview.

Food is a big part of tailgates as well as part of what makes Chicago famous, so it should come as no surprise that food plays an integral part of Da Superfan Nation.

"The food tradition, laid down by our forefathers is divided into groups," they told us. "There is sausage, beef, and other meats, and vegetables like

French fries. If you are on a diet, fried chicken is the way to go."

They also talked about how the city of Chicago changes from being divisive based on its loyalty to their baseball team, to being unified in the name of the Bears. I have always thought one of the great attributes of sports is how it brings people together, and there may be no better example of that than Chicago. "Every single regular season (Bears) loss is equivalent to a post-season Cubs loss," they told us.

The Cubs teeter between absolutely terrible and playoff contenders where they eventually collapse, leaving their fans completely heartbroken, but not surprised.

To hear how important the Bears are in comparison to the Cubs speaks to how much Chicago is truly a football city. The Bulls, Cubs, White Sox and Blackhawks could win their respective championships every year and it still would not have the impact of a Super Bowl on the psyche of Chicago.

The interview was winding down, so I asked about Da Superfan Nation. It was like I had given a toddler permission to play in the mud—these were toddlers and the Chicago Bears were their mud.

The accents started, the aviator glasses and mustaches were taken out of their storage boxes, and it was show time. Here were the guys we came to interview! Even their dog, Ditka, was let into the basement. And one of the guys grabbed a guitar and started to improvise a song about Walter "Sweetness" Payton and, of course, Coach Mike Ditka.

Da Superfan Nation had made the statement that Chicago would not exist without the Bears, and after spending the morning with them I had to agree. I would have been content just sitting in their basement and watching the game with them, but we were scheduled to meet with NFL Films in Chicago so we made our exit knowing that this would not be the end of our friendship.

To almost anyone else, the nondescript, unmarked minivans used by NFL Films are just part of the street scene, but to us they stuck out like a 1967 VW Bus. The rendezvous point to meet our latest crew was outside the famous Chicago Theatre. As we pulled up behind the white minivan, an older gentleman with glasses and a goatee leaped out of the van with a sense of purpose. His energy and excitement for his job were readily apparent. While I would like to think that was because he was excited about our project, I had a feeling this guy loved his job and life in general. He handed us a parking pass that was like gold to us—not because we could not walk from a parking lot around the stadium, but because we did not have to pay for parking. That meant the money could be used for the infrequent hot meal or the all-too-frequent shady motel. We instantly bonded with our NFL Films contact and were soon on our way, slowly cruising in front of the theater marquee then to Lake Shore Drive, Navy Pier and finally Soldier Field.

NFL Films always had a camera guy and a driver for the minivan. The camera guy would instruct us to either speed up or slow down, and the driver, on his command, would frantically position the minivan around Hail Mary to get the best shot possible. In this particular instance, the camera guy was in the back of the minivan with the door open to get footage of us from the front. He told me to get as close to him as possible, but what he did not understand was that Hail Mary did not have disc brakes, which makes the required stopping distance a lot farther than his minivan. I had also recently started to feel a change in the brakes, and not for the better. The brakes seemed different, and it took us longer than normal, even for a VW Bus, to stop.

I managed to keep a safe distance from the cameraman and felt a sense of relief when it was over. We finished early in the day and had a chance to spend some time in Chicago before the game that night. When you are in Chicago you have to eat pizza, and with the parking pass from NFL Films we could now afford to get some without worrying about how to pay for gas or having to lower our motel standards any more than we already had. On the recommendation of our friends at NFL Films, we went to Lou Malnati's, and it did not disappoint. If hanging out with Da Superfan Nation is not reason enough to go back to Chicago, the pizza alone makes the trip worth it.

My seat for the Chicago game was the most expensive ticket of the entire thirty-two games. Face value was a little over $100, which, considering my budget for the trip, represented the high-rent district. I guess I can thank those wonderful architects for the inflated ticket prices. Even if they are not directly responsible, they should shoulder some of the blame. On the bright side, the inflated ticket prices gave me a lower-level end-zone seat. I had the obligatory drunk guy and girlfriend sitting next to me, and in front of me were three brothers who obviously enjoyed the company of each other. They may have been just friends, but bonding over the Chicago Bears made them, for all intents and purposes, brothers.

The game once again featured Eric's New York Giants and Eli Manning. We were almost halfway through October and the Giants still had not won a game. Manning led the league in interceptions and was clearly determined to prove me right when I proclaimed before the season that his career was over.

The brothers in front of me seemed to be in one continuous high-five as they watched the Bears beat the Giants 27-21. Eli Manning did his part by throwing three more interceptions—including one for a touchdown. With the loss, the Giants were 0-6 on the year.

At this point in the trip, my Dallas Cowboys still had a little life left in their season, but not much. What I thought was going to be a continuous barrage of friendly football banter between Eric and I during the trip had turned into more like the relationship alcoholics have with their AA sponsors. Each of us ended up sponsoring the other at various times of the season.

While I remember almost everything about our trip—the places we went, the people we met, the motel in Fresno's red light district—I have an extremely vivid recollection of Buffalo. I was not looking forward to

Buffalo. Next to Cleveland, people rarely say nice things about the city, but treasures are sometimes hidden in the most unassuming places. Although I was not a big fan of the Bills, always considered the other team in New York, that mindset changed when we pulled into Hammer's Lot the night before the game.

An open grassy field, the lot was across the street and down a long block from Ralph Wilson Stadium. Since it was the night before the game, a few people were already there and it was obvious everyone knew each other. These people were more than friends; they had become family because of the Buffalo Bills.

We had spoken to Hammer, the gentleman who owns the grassy field—both of which are practically institutions at Buffalo Bills games—and as we entered the lot a bearded man wearing a Bills jersey and cap approached Hail Mary as if we were expected.

Our new friend introduced himself as both Pinto Ron and Ketchup Kenny. He showed us where to park, told us to make ourselves at home, and let us know that Hammer would be there shortly. Behind him was an old red Ford Pinto station wagon, which, judging from the way it looked, I had no confidence in it making it around Ralph Wilson Stadium much less outside of Buffalo. The more I examined the Ford Pinto, the more I began to feel confident in our chosen mode of transportation. While a VW Bus could catch fire, Ford Pintos were legendary for blowing up, which would have given us very little opportunity to get our stuff out, much less survive. My confidence in Hail Mary, however, would soon be proven to be completely without merit. For now, though, I could say that we were fortunate to not be driving the red Ford Pinto.

Pinto Ron began his story with the Pinto, of course, but also told us how he had not missed a Bills game, home or away, for the last 25 years. I started to call up the limited knowledge I had of the Bills history and imagined how awesome it was that he was there for it all. The upside was that he had been to four Super Bowls. The downside was that he had witnessed four straight Super Bowl losses.

Pinto Ron described what a Bills tailgate looks like at Hammer's Lot, a majestic tale of devotion to a football team and tailgate glory. He talked about the Pinto, showed us the jug of milk from the first Bills Super Bowl and told us how he cooks on top of the vehicle.

I wanted to ask how, over the 25 years since the Bills first Super Bowl, he had managed to keep the milk from curdling and the rationale behind keeping it. Clearly, I was better off not knowing certain things, so I did not ask.

He said he cooks bacon on top of a saw, uses an Army helmet for stir-fry and takes shots out of a bowling ball.

Just let that sanitation nightmare sink in for a minute: A saw that has been through countless pieces of wood and probably has some accumulation of rust; an Army helmet that had probably seen its fair share of sweat; and quite possibly the most unsanitary piece of his tailgating equipment—a bowling ball for shots. How many people had put their fingers in that bowling ball during its playing days and how many had put their mouths on it to drink a shot are questions best left unanswered for me.

He then confirmed the legend of Ketchup Kenny: During a memorable tailgate with friends, he had a hamburger with nothing on it and asked them if they had any ketchup. His friends began to douse him with ketchup, getting some on his barren hamburger, but the majority of the bottle ended up on Pinto Ron himself. This has become a ritual or right of passage for Bills fans as Pinto Ron transforms into Ketchup Kenny at every Bills home game.

While his stories were bizarre and would leave a normal person in complete disbelief, on a trip like this it is better to accept things for what they are and not ask too many questions or think about things for very long. Hammer later told us that at any given tailgate it could be a manager of a local strip club cooking on one side of Ron/Kenny's hood, while the person cooking on the other side could be a professor at the local university. Somehow this all made sense to us and everyone in Hammer's Lot. These people were not managers of strip clubs or professors; they were Bills fans.

There were a couple of people who stuck out from the rest of the fans at Hammer's Lot because they were wearing the colors of the Cincinnati Bengals. Although the Bills and Bengals were playing the next day, I could not imagine that many Bengals fans were making the trip to Buffalo for the game. We approached them and, from their mannerisms when we introduced ourselves, it was evident that these were not ordinary Bengals fans.

In their best broken-English they told us their story of being not only Bengals fans but fans of all American football. They were from Russia and traveling around the United States for the entire month to watch American Football. The Cold War was trumped by football. These were definitely my kind of guys.

Their overt devotion to the Bengals begged the question: Why the Bengals? Apparently one of the guys had put every team name into a hat and drew out the one that would become their team, and that team happened to be the Bengals.

In the same tone as Ivan Drago confessing that he must break Rocky, one of the fans said, "Only Bengals fan in Russia, only sport for me, only football, and only Bengals," as he proudly displayed the orange and black tattoo of the Bengals logo that occupied most of the real estate on his right arm.

Grayson quickly turned to the Russian's friend and asked why he liked football. His response made me proud to be an American and validated my early indoctrination into the sport. "I think it's the best game in the world," he said. "Very sportish for me and real men to play in it. It's beautiful, spirit of America to me."

Football and sports being a universal language, our interaction with the Russians was proof that we all want the same thing, a win on Sunday and just one Super Bowl before we die.

Hammer's Lot was truly a football melting pot. We met two other guys who were obvious Bills fans. One was from England and had moved his family to Buffalo to be closer to the Bills—every football fan needs a wife like that. He said he became a fan after accompanying his father to an NFL game in London between the Eagles and the Bills. His father picked the Eagles and he, being the defiant youth he was, went with the Bills. He said he also met a couple of students from Buffalo University who explained the game of American Football to him and warned him there would be consequences for his manhood if he did not cheer for the Bills.

The other guy was from Australia and proclaimed his fondness for Hammer's Lot and Bills fans with a smile that slowly moved across his face, eyes shifting to the big open field that would soon be home to "his family." It was evident to the Australian that football was more than what happened on the field. Hammer's Lot and the Bills fans held a special place in his heart and, for that reason alone, my image of Buffalo would be forever changed. Buffalo had become more than a place to visit on my way to see every NFL stadium, it became a place I wanted to make part of me.

All of that aside, Hammer is one of the nicest people I have ever met and greeted us excitedly with open arms. He is a hard-working blue-collar man, typical of the type of people found in Buffalo. By just talking to him you can feel his pride in owning the lot where so many congregate before Bills games. "I may've overpaid for the property," he admitted, "but they only make so much."

The land is valuable and I am sure the Bills would love to buy it for themselves, but the real value to Hammer cannot be measured in dollars and cents. He lives in the house across the street, and when we met he told us he had to mow the yard because his wife would not be happy if he did not do it before the game. He then offered to take us to Duff's for wings when he was done. While that sounded great, the daylight was fleeting and I had never seen anyone mow a yard at night. A few moments later we peered across the lot and saw Hammer in the distance mowing the yard by moonlight. I immediately thought that this guy is special.

The wings at Duff's that night were as good as I have ever eaten and Hammer picked up the tab, which made them taste even better. Since good wings are known for their inspirational qualities, as we sat at Duff's talking about life, Hammer floored us with this profound statement: "Sometimes you just have to put your oar in the water to see how far you can go."

While it was not directed at us, it easily could have been—we had figuratively stuck our oar in the water and would soon be paddling upstream.

Hammer told us there was a motel on the other side of the stadium that we could walk to, but we opted to pitch a tent and stay in Hammer's Lot instead. Despite my earlier misgivings about the city, Buffalo marked another point on the trip that I was completely content, believing this is actually happening and that we are going to make it to all thirty-one NFL stadiums.

Although I was content in Kansas City experiencing Arrowhead Stadium, it was nothing like the contentment I felt in Buffalo. I was truly living in the moment at Hammer's Lot. That would soon change, but, for now, it was good to discover that places like Hammer's Lot and people who shared a passion for football existed.

I audibled out of sleeping in the tent and instead slept under the stars. I was awakened by the sound of tailgaters getting ready for the game, kids playing football, and a dog's wet nose checking to see if I was dead or alive. I was alive, more than I had ever been in my forty years on Earth, and it was all because of ... Buffalo?

People kept telling us about Texas red hots and how we had to try one when we were in Buffalo. They are not an institution and do not receive the notoriety the wings get, but they are close, at least in the conscience of the people in Buffalo.

Being from Texas, I feel obligated to try anything with the name of my state on it as if I can verify the authenticity or legitimacy of the Texas name, although the authority to judge all things Texas probably ended when I put my bull-riding prowess on display in Cincinnati

Nevertheless, we had game-day-morning interviews lined up with Bills fans known as the Bell Ringer, Dapper Don, and Wagonmaster. They suggested meeting at Louie's Texas Red Hots, which is within walking distance of Hammer's Lot as you go toward Ralph Wilson Stadium.

The Bell Ringer is the jester of Buffalo Bills fans. His custom-made costume is ornate with bright splashes of blue and red accompanied by bells that jingle at the slightest movement. He is an older gentleman, as are Dapper Don and Wagonmaster, Bell Ringer stands about five feet tall, and his eyes light with passion when he talks about Buffalo—specifically the Bills. What the Bell Ringer does not have in stature he makes up for in passion for the Bills and kindness toward others. He thanked us repeatedly for the interview, not knowing how much spending time at Louie's with him and his friends meant to us. "Buffalo is a blue-collar town, and without football we would have nothing in the fall," he told us, almost defiantly.

His wife soon reluctantly joined us and shyly talked about her role in Bills games. She, with the Bell Ringer at her side, recounted the checklist for preparing the tailgate meals. You could almost see her envisioning her list as she went through the week of preparations for Bills home games. We could tell right away that the Bell Ringer's devotion to his Bills was only surpassed by his affection for his wife. Loyal not only to his wife and the Bills, he proved his loyalty to his friends as well, making sure to leave enough time so we could interview Wagonmaster and Dapper Don.

If the Bell Ringer is the jester of Bills fans, then Dapper Don and the Wagonmaster were the Bills fan equivalent to the two older men in the balcony of *The Muppets Show*, only not as bitter or angry or self-appointed know-it-alls. Each wore a western-style Cowboy hat, and the Wagonmaster had a western vest while Dapper Don wore a suit with a Bills tie.

"Fans of other teams just took the wrong exit on the freeway, that's just their team," Dapper Don said and urged us not to hold someone's team against them.

If there is one lesson I learned from this trip, it is not to hold someone's team against them. I enjoyed the countless conversations with everyone we met during our four months on the road, despite only one being a Cowboys fan. I do not know if anyone put it better than Dapper Don did by crediting these apparent shortcomings in selecting a football team to simply taking the wrong exit on the interstate.

Ralph Wilson Stadium is probably not as nice as some major college football stadiums, and there is nothing from the outside that would signify it as being a significant landmark in the Buffalo area. Rich Stadium, as it was originally named, was opened in 1973 and is what you would expect from a stadium over forty years old. Other teams and other cities tear down their old stadiums for a new, more glamorous home with luxury suites and large replay screens. Somehow, Ralph Wilson Stadium fits the people of Buffalo and the Bills perfectly.

Despite all the flash that has permeated professional sports, Buffalo has managed to repel all of the temptations of the modern football world, leaving a refreshing football oasis that is Ralph Wilson Stadium, the Buffalo Bills and Hammer's Lot.

People have asked me what I considered the best stadiums we visited on our trip, and I reply the same way every time. If it were just the building, then it would be the Dallas Cowboys and Jerry Jones's magnificent stadium. A stadium that is, even by modern NFL standards, untouchable. Having said that, if I had one place to visit for a football game or if I could relive one experience from the trip it would be Hammer's Lot and Buffalo.

The actual game was as good as the tailgate in Hammer's Lot. The Bills fell behind 24-10 heading into the fourth quarter but, reminiscent of that playoff game against the Oilers twenty years ago, they were mounting an improbable comeback with a backup quarterback. With just over a minute left in the game, Thaddeus Lewis connected for a forty-yard touchdown with Bills wide receiver Marquise Goodwin to tie the game. Although the Bengals eventually won the game with a field goal in overtime, the Bills and Buffalo had put on a football experience that I would remember for the rest of my life.

Our next two games were a week away in New Jersey, first the Jets and then the following night the Giants. The schedule gave us a chance to fly home for the week after Buffalo, and then fly back in time for the games in New Jersey. The Bills experience was great, but we had not been home in over a month and, excited to see family again, we began driving through rural western New York.

I did not know what I was expecting, but western New York has rolling hills and farms, which I was enjoying because it reminded me of Texas. We were, however, a long way from home both literally and figuratively.

My contentment with the Buffalo experience and reminiscing about Texas would quickly change when, on the two-lane road with cars in front of us and passing us going the other direction, our brakes went completely out.

I pushed on the brake pedal, and it stuck to the floor. Racing down the hill, I told Grayson to pick the pedal up off the floor. He quickly did and I pressed it once again, hoping that Hail Mary would respond this time. She did not and the pedal was once again stuck on the floor. My first thought was: Is this how it is going to end?

In times of distress, all the things that go through your mind is amazing. In high school I would have been voted the least likely to be killed in a VW Bus, because at that time I wanted nothing to do with old cars. If it was not a fast car, it was not the car for me. My friends would never believe it. Then I thought about my kids and what they would think if they knew the peril of the current situation and how far away from home I was.

I quickly glanced to the side of the road and looked for a place to land Hail Mary to make it the safest crash possible. If I were on the outside looking in I would imagine we looked like something between an Indiana Jones movie and *Scooby Doo*.

Then I thought of my father, who seems to have a knack for both finding himself in these situations and getting out of them. Knowing him, if he were here he would probably downshift. Downshift! Slow her down and land her on the side of the road as best we could. Miraculously, it worked. Downshifting to slow Hail Mary down was not the miracle—the miraculous part was that I had thought of it. We were now stranded on the side of the road eight hours away from our flights home, which were going to take off with or without us in twelve hours.

We spent the first futile moments after we got out of Hail Mary searching for a repair shop. Clearly we were not thinking, because what mechanic would be open on a Sunday evening in rural, western New York? None, and we did not have time to wait around for someone to maybe answer our prayers and return our call.

There was a house across the road and I thought about asking if we could leave her there for the week and try to find someone to fix her. From the looks of the house, though, we were just as likely to be greeted with a man wearing a hockey mask, revving a chainsaw, as we were to be greeted by a helpful person. Thankfully I never had to knock on the door, because we found the clo sest VW dealership to the crash site and had Hail Mary towed using Patrick's AAA account. By the time we reached the dealership back in Buffalo, the rain we had experienced on our way to Pittsburgh had tracked us to New York, or at least that is what it seemed.

Hastily, I grabbed an envelope and wrote down the issue we were having with Hail Mary, then slipped the instructions with the keys into the night deposit box. A cab hurried us away into the night to the airport where we rented a car and drove to Newark in time to catch our flights home.

For the first time on the trip we were missing part of our team, and as we drove off with Hail Mary standing in the drizzle of a Buffalo night I had to tell her that everything was going to be okay and we would see each other again. I honestly did not know if she needed the reassurance or it was more to comfort me, since I was not even sure I believed everything would be okay or that I would ever see her again.

When I landed in Houston I started calling air-cooled VW people in Buffalo to see if they could help Hail Mary in her time of need. It was a weird feeling talking to someone over the phone you have never met and immediately asking for a favor. Our latest issue with Hail Mary was not the first time, or the last, that she had blessed me with the opportunity to begin a new friendship by requesting a favor. I never got used to it, but it became a necessity throughout our four-month trip.

Back when we had our tutorial on VW maintenance with John, we met another mechanic who was working with him. He wore camouflage shorts and a gray ribbed tank top, and had long flowing white hair that extend from his chin by three or four inches. He is the stereotypical Vietnam vet who has had issues since coming back from the war except I do not know if he had ever been in a war.

Throughout the maintenance lesson, he looked out across the lot of vintage VWs in various conditions. Like Moses ready to part the Red Sea, he told us that all of these older cars have a mojo about them that he feels when he works on them. Normal people would think this guy is crazy and maybe I did too, at first, so I offered him an out. "Oh yeah?" I asked, giving him the ability to retract his statement.

He did not retract his statement but reinforced his belief in mojo and specifically the mojo of Hail Mary. That day I did not have the same conviction of my new friend to profess the mojo of Hail Mary publicly, but his statements reinforced what I already knew on the inside: She has mojo. We might use it all up during this trip, but thanks to her and her mojo we were going to make it.

Mojo can take on many forms and, in this instance, it took on the form of selecting the right VW dealership at which to leave Hail Mary. I say selecting, but what I mean is to be forced to leave her at the closest VW dealership. That dealership, as I learned from various members of the air-cooled VW community in Buffalo, was the only one in the area with an experienced vintage VW mechanic, who also was a prominent member of the VW fan club in Buffalo.

After talking to the dealership while waiting for my connecting flight to Austin, I felt confident that Hail Mary was getting the care she needed and we would be reunited soon. What I was not sure of was the best way to get Hail Mary from Buffalo to where we were staying in Newark. That ended up involving a different kind of bus and a different kind of uncomfortable.

In professional sports, specifically football and baseball, fans are mostly defined by their favorite teams but also form an allegiance to a specific conference or league. As a fan of baseball, you identify yourself as a National League fan or an American League fan—depending on if you like the designated hitter or prefer pitchers to hit for themselves. Some believe that this difference forces a different style of play. I always thought of the National League teams as being more inclined to steal bases and bunt to manufacture runs one or two at a time, while the American League teams were more likely to create runs by getting people on base and hitting the ball out of the park to get three or four runs in an inning.

Incidentally, my team growing up was the Houston Astros, a National League team at the time, but now belong to the American League. Imagine the emotional trauma this causes a baseball fan; my allegiance to a certain style of play was called into question.

I do not know if there is anything to my theory, but the same could be said for the NFL but to a lesser extent—you are either a fan of the American Football Conference (AFC) or the National Football Conference (NFC). I do not think there is a difference in strategy between conferences, like in baseball, so the rationale for being for one conference or the other is completely unfounded. But I, being a Dallas Cowboys fan, always found myself an NFC guy.

I also liked CBS, which broadcast NFC games and its pre-game show, *The NFL Today* with Brent Musburger, Irv Cross, Jimmy "The Greek," and Phyllis George better than whatever pregame show was on the network—NBC at the time—for AFC games. I liked the announcers John Madden and Pat Summerall (CBS) slightly better than Dick Enberg and Merlin Olsen (NBC). Even if the broadcast teams were even, Phyllis George, a former Miss America turned sports reporter before the days of the female sideline reporter, swayed my vote for CBS. She would definitely make an NFC fan out of most young, male football fans. Maybe working with her set the wheels in motion years later for something Brent Musburger said during the broadcast of a Florida State University (FSU) football game when the cameras panned to a very attractive female FSU student.

"Fifteen hundred red-blooded Americans just decided to apply to Florida State," he commented. He was right in my case. After seeing what the crowd looked like at an FSU game, I considered going back for a Ph.D.

Musburger is now almost as famous for his in-game zingers inspired by female college football fans as he is for his actual play-by-play ability. And to this day I am not sure what Phyllis George did other than tip the scales for *The NFL Today*, but I am glad she was there.

Growing up an NFC fan I paid little attention to the next team on our schedule. They were rarely on television in Texas since they were never really in Super Bowl contention.

The team itself was filled with colorful characters like Mark Gastineau and Mark Klecko of the "New York Sack Exchange." I thought Freeman McNeil and Richard Todd were good players and looked cool in their jerseys, but other than an AFC title game in 1983 there was not much reason for a Texan to know too much more about the Jets. Although more recently the team had experienced two AFC title games, it lost both of them and was mired in the middle of the Mark Sanchez drama that included the infamous play known as "The Butt Fumble."

Needless to say, the Jets futility had once again provided little reason for the football world to pay attention. The occasional entertainment provided by the sideshow of head coach Rex Ryan and the New York media left me to contemplate why we cared, why there was all this national attention for the Jets, who were, after all, still just the Jets.

One of those recent AFC title games provided the background on the Jets fans we were scheduled to interview. All five of them had met on Craigslist for a road trip to Indianapolis to see the 2010 AFC Championship game between the Colts and Jets. These guys understand what life and football are all about, and their spirit of adventure along with their willingness to accept what life as a football fan brings are all things I find admirable. They also have an understanding that most people in the world are great—something we were finding out the more places we visited.

We met four of the five fans in the basement/Jets fan cave of one of the organizers of the trip. When we entered the house there was a binder full of football cards in plastic sleeves. Nothing takes me back to childhood—specifically 1980—like Topps football or baseball cards. That was the first year I remember collecting the entire set of cards, not just Dallas Cowboys, and spent countless hours thumbing through them, learning names and putting them in sequential order according to the number on the back. I quickly glanced at the cards in the binder and everything I ever knew or thought or learned about the Jets from Topps football cards came rushing back to me.

I considered that this might be the only evidence of Jets fandom in the house, but the short trip down the stairs to the basement quickly shot down any fear that these Jets fans would not be good interviews. I imagined a glowing green light seeping out of the basement at night if a Jets game was on television—the walls were an inferior opponent in containing the shelves of Jets memorabilia that surely emit a glowing green light that is unmistakably the J-E-T-S, Jets! Jets! Jets!

With a Joe Namath autographed football here and a Jets pint glass there, the room was as complete as a sports fan of any team would ever dream. There was one non-Jets-related item in the room, however—a ticket to the main event at the World Series of Poker.

If there is one event that I would like to attend more than a Super Bowl, it is the World Series of Poker. I inquired about the ticket and one of the Jets fans, with a grin as if replaying the entire tournament in his mind, proudly said that he had won entry into the WSOP and had the time of his life. A lot came out of our time with these Jets fans, including confirmation that I had to start training for the World Series of Poker when this trip was over.

All four of the Jets fans were perched on bar stools facing the camera with various Jets memorabilia surrounding them. The positive energy and emotion radiating from their posture and voices was somewhat surprising to someone familiar with the Jets inept history. They recounted how everyone got together and told us all about the trip to the AFC Championship itself. The game, in typical Jets fashion, started out promising but ended in disappointment. After being up 17-6, the Jets relinquished twenty-four unanswered points and lost 30-17, extinguishing the Super Bowl hopes of Jets fans in an otherwise successful season.

The pain of the loss had been diluted with time to these Jets fans, but left lasting memories and friendships to be enjoyed for seasons to come. "What do you remember most about the trip?" Grayson asked the group. "I remember laughing my ass off!" the Jets fan on the end chimed in after a moment of silence.

The other fans were in agreement and, as soon as the silence was broken, each shared something about the trip that they still held in their hearts. It was apparent the trip had been about so much more than a football game.

Grayson had long been a proponent of the belief that unless a team wins a Super Bowl it is a failure, and I had long subscribed to that same theory, since as a Dallas Cowboys fan anything other than a Super Bowl win is unacceptable.

After meeting these Jets fans and listening to their story, though, I started to think maybe it is not about that elusive Super Bowl victory. What if it is more about sharing the experiences of being a fan with others than it is about winning and losing? What if it is more about connecting with people and sharing emotions with others than it is about touchdowns? What if sports teams, like VWs, were simply a conduit to unite us in victory and defeat? If that is the case, the Browns fans we met in Cleveland have it right, and those fans living in anguish after seeing their teams fall short of the Super Bowl year after year have it wrong. Maybe fan clubs on all seven continents is better than a team with seven championships. Maybe, but I bet there are a lot Cleveland Browns fans who would like to find out.

We were still without Hail Mary, and I was the only one with a ticket to the Jets game, so I took the rental car and went to MetLife Stadium. Going to the games in anything other than Hail Mary was uneventful and more of an experience to be endured rather than enjoyed. The games themselves and the stadiums were different of course, but getting to the stadium was merely mundane without her, and this particular game came with a certain level of anxiety for me personally. Not necessarily because the Jets were playing their rivals, the Patriots, but for what I had to do after the game.

To get Hail Mary back where she belonged—with us—I needed to take the rental car back to the Newark airport, catch a city bus to the Greyhound station and get on another bus, which would take me to my transfer station in New York City that would eventually take me to the Buffalo station and hopefully reunite me with Hail Mary. Then I would drive her back to New Jersey for the Giants game the following night. It sounded easy enough: A rental car, a few buses, and a taxi, and ten hours later I would once again be behind the wheel of Hail Mary driving her directly back to the stadium I had just left.

The rental car return and finding the city bus to take me to the Greyhound station in Newark was simple enough. After that things got complicated. I walked into the station in Newark and saw the Broncos vs. Colts game on the small television hanging from the ceiling. I had been looking forward to that game for a long time and even considered including it on our schedule, since Peyton Manning's return to Indianapolis would have been nice to see in person. Although I had been looking forward to this game, the rest of the bus station was disinterested in it if not completely unaware that the sport of football existed at all. At this point I realized things are what they are and to make the best of the situation I would just focus on the game itself, largely ignoring my surroundings or the difficult road back to Hail Mary.

I remember nothing about the game; the same game I had been looking forward to just a week earlier. My fear of missing my bus to New York City began to consume me and the lack of organization and announcements at the bus station only fueled my fear. I walked outside to separate myself from the non-football fans loitering in the station and to hopefully ease my fear with some fresh air. The Hail Mary mojo must have been working, because I found the correct bus and soon made the short trip to New York City. If my situation in Newark was frustrating, not to mention unsanitary, then I can only describe my circumstances in New York City as apocalyptic.

The lack of signs, workers, and any desire to help from the few workers I could find made navigating the Greyhound station in New York City excruciatingly painful and mentally exhausting. The fact that most of the terminals were closed added to the distinct possibility that this was an abandoned bus station. My sense of accomplishment getting there was quickly replaced with the fear of missing the bus to Buffalo or something even worse. Maybe there was no escape. Maybe my destiny was not for my life to end on a rural road outside of Buffalo. Maybe I was destined to live like Teenage Mutant Ninja Turtles in the bowels of a city, existing only in the shadows.

While that may be extreme, I found the correct terminal for the bus to Buffalo and sat on an empty plastic seat looking around, wondering where all these people were going. I started contemplating where I was going and if this was truly how my life had turned out. I do not know if it was acceptance of my situation, a sense of defeat, or an undeterred sense of determination, but in that moment of my greatest despair I realized this trip had changed me.

"Doesn't matter how bad he is hurt or how difficult it looks, Rhett will keep climbing and get to the top of the mountain," I heard the voice of my friend say. So for now, to keep climbing meant getting up and getting on that bus to Buffalo.

To my surprise the bus was completely packed, so I was forced to take the last seat in the back—next to the restroom. I was exhausted and slept as best I could through the countless people passing me on their way to relieve themselves, as well as the countless stops along the way.

Hearing the driver call out the different stops and knowing that I was getting closer to my destination, yet realizing I needed more sleep if I was going to make the drive back to New Jersey, I began to hope the trip would take longer.

I do not know how much sleep I actually got that night and probably owe the passenger sitting next to me an apology. I am sure being next to me the entire night was not the most pleasurable experience for him, because I discovered that if sleeping in Hail Mary was uncomfortable, sleeping on a Greyhound bus filled to capacity is excruciating.

As the day was breaking I came to terms with the realization that I would be driving back to Newark on next to no sleep. We finally pulled into the station and I was soon free of the shackles of the Greyhound bus, but my trip was far from over.

My cab driver, much like the tow truck drivers I encountered during my journey, refused to sit in silence. Silence leaves people alone with their thoughts, which inherently makes some people uncomfortable.

He said he was having issues with women and kindly shared his views on the fairer sex while driving me to the VW dealership. Normally his issues would not interest me, but they provided reassurance of how fortunate I was to even be on this trip. Despite facing a day-long drive back to New Jersey, I was lucky. I hoped my cab driver would soon be able to resolve his woman issues and wished him well as I left the cab. As for my problems with the fairer sex, I was optimistic and naive thinking that these were the last issues I would have with Hail Mary.

I arrived just as the service department was opening. Surrounded by computers and the latest automotive equipment—none of which could help Hail Mary—I talked to an adviser who was able to retrieve my keys. He muddily detailed what work had been done on her in much the same way people do when they are singing a song but do not know all of the words.

I was soon on my way to Newark, wondering if I would be able to stop and if so for how long. That is the thing about having your brakes go out. The feeling of being almost helpless and thinking that the end could be near never leaves you completely and raises your anxiety level, even on the good days.

At this point in the trip, it was a frequent occurrence at a gas station to see me under Hail Mary tapping the starter while Grayson turned the key. On my way back from Buffalo I decided to stop for gas outside of Freehold, New Jersey, on my way to MetLife Stadium, but stopping for gas was a risky proposition. I knew I would probably have to tap the starter to get her running again, but would not be able to do it on my own. It was equally as risky to keep going and potentially run out of gas. I knew without gas Hail Mary stood no chance of running, but there was a sliver of hope that she would fire up after stopping at the gas station. That sliver of light that was hope soon turned to complete darkness. After giving her some gas, I waited with bated breath as I turned the key in the ignition—the silence was deafening. I had effectively stranded myself at a gas station just hours before the start of the Giants game.

In New Jersey you cannot pump your own gas, it is a state law that an attendant has to pump the gas for you; to this day I have not learned the rationale of that asinine law. Nevertheless, it opened the door for me to strike up a conversation with the attendant and explain to him the process of tapping the starter to get Hail Mary running.

From the looks of him, he had been in homeroom at a local high school that morning, and his apprehensive demeanor left a lot to be desired as a potential partner in starting Hail Mary. I unwillingly recruited him, and as he walked in front of Hail Mary he peered inside. With his eyes opened wide and his mouth even wider, he began to talk himself out of his ability to perform the simple task of turning the key. I guess he thought I was asking him to board a spaceship and fly me to Mars.

Fearing that I may lose my co-pilot on this mission, I quickly reassured him that it was easy and walked him through the process again. I slid under the bus and started tapping while simultaneously yelling at the attendant to turn the key. Nothing. I tried again and still nothing. Could it be that the starter was finally dead? Could it be that my quest for thirty-two games and thirty-one stadiums in seventeen weeks was over because of an attendant who has algebra homework when his shift ends?

Mojo was about to reenter my life in the form of a former hippie. I would say reformed instead of former, but truth be told neither word is appropriate when describing a hippie. Once you are a hippie, you are always a hippie. The outside may change, but the person on the inside rarely does; especially if they have had a meaningful experience with a VW.

He recognized Hail Mary and felt obligated to tell me his VW Bus experience. It involved weed and may have involved a woman. To be honest, I was more interested in my starter and making a football game than retaining all of the facts of his story, but soon realized that I had nothing better to do than enjoy the company of a guy who was willing to approach a complete stranger for no other reason than a VW Bus.

I was going nowhere fast, but I was confident something was going to work out for me one way or another. What I was not confident of was the attendant's ability to turn a key. Maybe it was fear of it blowing up or maybe he did not know how to drive and his parents had to drop him off at work. Whatever the reason, I was not completely convinced that tapping the starter was not going to work. So I asked my hippie, mojo friend if he would not mind turning the key as I tapped on the starter. It was almost as if that was the real reason he approached me and was just talking to me in the eventual hope that I would invite him to get behind the wheel. Well, his ploy worked and he soon found himself at the reins of Hail Mary.

The sound of an air-cooled VW engine is unmistakable, especially if you are lying under said engine. When she started up, the sound of her engine was the sound of my dreams starting up again. I thanked my cohort in getting Hail Mary started, wished him well and quickly found myself back on the road to MetLife Stadium with my dream still alive!

The Giants game was uneventful, or as eventful as you might expect from a game between two teams with only one win between them in late October. Having seen MetLife Stadium the day before, which with all of my traveling seemed like a lifetime ago, took away the rush I feel when seeing a stadium for the first time. The adventure that was traveling from the stadium to Buffalo and back just a day before made me excited to see it nonetheless. Much like I had spent the entire day working to reunite myself with Hail Mary, the crew at MetLife Stadium had spent all night and day transforming the stadium from where the Jets play home games to the home of the Giants.

We interviewed a Giants fan who wears vanity license plates around his neck during the games. He had about fifteen license plates that had been sent to him by Giants fans from around the country. Most were pro-Giants and some were anti-Cowboys, which I found to be humorous and witty. Funny is funny and to me it did not matter if it was at the expense of my team or not.

The best way I can describe this fan is a Mr. T wearing license plates instead of gold around his neck. He also did not have the anger issues of Mr. T, because, despite being the fan of a winless team he was positive, upbeat and gave the impression that nothing could stop him from being a Giants fan. "If you are born into a Giants family you have no choice," he said. "You are a Giants fan. Trust me."

Our next interviews were living proof of that theory: A group of four fans who were season ticket holders since the days of Yankee Stadium—to give you some idea of how long these guys had been season ticket holders, the last time the Giants played in Yankee Stadium was 1973.

The Giants tailgate was home to about 200 or more fans each game. Their RV was decorated with pictures of family and friends through the years at various Giants tailgates, and the names of the five friends—one is deceased—responsible for the tailgate are inscribed across the side of the vehicle like a Ring of Honor for tailgating Giants fans. They welcomed us into the tailgate and offered us food or anything else their tailgate could provide, but most importantly they offered us conversation and a glimpse inside their world as Giants fans.

"We keep this up for our kids because they don't know what it's like not to come. They will be the next generation," I remember one of them saying.

Sports, unlike anything else, connects generations. It is a family bond that cannot be broken and there was no better evidence of that than these Giants fans.

The game, as I said, was uneventful. Despite having one of the most dynamic players in NFL history, Adrian Peterson, the Vikings offense was truly offensive, managing a lone touchdown on a punt return and losing to the Giants 23-7. The Giants themselves were not much better that night, but at least License Plate Guy and our favorite tailgating Giants fans had something to cheer about.

CHAPTER 6

Home is a VW Bus

Tampa Bay and New Orleans
(16 teams and 10,925 miles)

Whether it's the best of times or the worst of times, it's the only time we've got.

– Art Buchwald

If the Giants game was uneventful, the drive to Tampa more than made up for it. We left on Tuesday morning, needing to be in Tampa for the Buccaneers Thursday-night game against the Carolina Panthers. That meant covering about 500 miles a day in Hail Mary, and consequently having to push her to her limits for about nine or ten hours each day, if not more. This part of our schedule would be a difficult stretch in a regular vehicle much less a 1967 Volkswagen Bus.

We decided it was best to keep driving through the night to make it as far as we could, but Hail Mary started to have issues shortly after the stroke of midnight. Like in Cinderella's tale, our coach was quickly turning into a pumpkin. When we stopped for gas, I checked the engine to find our new belt starting to fray and grooves wearing into the metal where we had worked on it in Cincinnati. At this point we were on

I-95 in rural North Carolina, and I thought the best we could do was drive until we reached civilization and hopefully find a mechanic who worked on VWs. Hail Mary, as she often did, had other ideas.

We packed ourselves back in Hail Mary and headed south on I-95 toward Tampa. At two o'clock in the morning, despite being on a major interstate, rural North Carolina provided a considerable amount of solitude. Not having to worry about other cars, or even the large trucks that made driving Hail Mary a challenge, I became mesmerized by our headlights, which were going in and out, flickering and periodically losing their brightness. I asked if it was just me and received the blindly optimistic, "we are fine" from the other two in the VW Bus.

Later, after my questioning of the headlights persisted, my travel companions relented that the lights were indeed losing power. By this time I had driven in the rain without windshield wipers, stopped without brakes, and in this instance may have used the lack of any sign of life as motivation to drive without lights, knowing that Hail Mary needed help. Help we could not provide on our own and could not find at 2:30 am in rural North Carolina.

After seriously contemplating if we could drive her without headlights, I relented and came to the conclusion that pushing her so hard was only delaying the inevitable. We were not going to make it, and by continuing to drive we risked further, maybe permanent, damage to the girl who was going to get us to every NFL stadium in seventeen weeks.

Hail Mary began losing power, so I exited I-95 and pulled to the side of the road. I gave one last look at the engine by using the flashlight on my phone, realized that it was not wise for us to take the engine apart in the daylight much less in the thick blanket of darkness that surrounded us, and closed the hatch. We did the only thing we could; pushed her off the road as far as we could and called her our home for the night. Maybe in the morning we could work our magic once again to see if we could find help and get her back on the road. We were in desperate need of some more of that VW mojo.

The mojo, this time, came in the way of a mechanic that was just a mile or so down the road. The injuries sustained by Hail Mary, the bends in the road, and the cover provided by countless pine trees had prevented us from seeing the shop the previous night.

Attempting to avoid another tow I tried to start her. As if to take one last gasp of life she miraculously started and made it to the mechanic. The shop was modest with one stall and very little in the way of a waiting room. A man emerged from the shadows of the stall bearing a resemblance to wrestler "Hacksaw" Jim Duggan. His hair was a little shorter, but his beard was shaggy like Hacksaw's. He maintained an intense yet bewildered look and could be confused as crossed-eyes at times. But then, it could have been us and the state of disrepair of Hail Mary that made a man look that way.

In a thick North Carolina mountain accent he informed me that he could not fix her. There was, however, a VW mechanic about ten miles away, he said. Hail Mary was in no mood or condition to drive another inch much less ten miles, so we called a tow truck to make the short journey to what we, once again, hoped to be our last repair. If the tale of our journey with Hail Mary does not prove that hope truly springs eternal, then nothing else will.

The tow truck arrived and, to our dismay, two people got out of the cab of the truck. The lack of room in the tow truck was an issue because, as we explained several times to the operator, we needed enough room for three people in addition to the driver. The dispatcher had assured us that all of us would fit in the tow truck, news that came as a shock to the truck's driver.

Since we were not left with many options and the two tow truck employees were not opposed to bending a few rules or, in this case just downright breaking the law, they told us to ride in Hail Mary, who was strapped to the gurney that was the flatbed of the tow truck. Their last request was for us to stay down if we saw any cops. Somehow I imagined this was not the first time these two had thought about taking evasive action when confronted by the police. What option did we have and how often in life do you get to ride in a vehicle that is being towed?

We soon saw the world from a new perspective, from inside a VW Bus on the back of a tow truck. Normally this would be a surprise, but after the leprechaun in Denver, a fan with a Burger King mask in San Diego, a guy cooking on top of a red Ford

Pinto, and running out of brakes in Buffalo, nothing came as a surprise anymore.

Our time on top of the tow truck was not long, did not involve any police, and we soon found ourselves explaining our situation to the VW mechanic. His lot was much bigger and vintage VWs spotted the field in front of the shop with other older foreign cars. Our latest repair shop was more of what I had come to expect from VW mechanics. And while it was not what I preferred, leaving Hail Mary behind again was the only alternative.

It was now Wednesday morning and we had to be in Tampa the next day for the game. Not knowing how bad Hail Mary's ailment was, if the mechanic would have the right part, and how long it would take to fix her, we opted to rent a car to drive to Tampa. At least we were not leaving her in the rain with a note on some dealership's driveway like in Buffalo. We would only be gone for a day and be back on Friday to pick her up then on our way to New Orleans.

Logic would dictate that this was possibly the last repair we would have to do on Hail Mary because there are only so many parts you can replace. However, owning a 1967 VW Bus as I have learned, defies all logic.

We made it to Tampa in what would be considered record time for a VW Bus, but being in a small rental car we did not exactly get a welcome reception from the *Guinness Book of World Records* when we pulled into Raymond James Stadium.

I discovered that I preferred to travel in Hail Mary for various reasons. Mostly because I had listened to every sound and analyzed every bump or vibration to take every precaution so we did not find ourselves stranded on the side of the road. The constant attention Hail Mary required forced me to be in the moment and enjoy the road more than I did in a modern vehicle. In Hail Mary, it was truly as much about the journey as it was the destination, and driving a rental car simply did not afford that kind of experience, being more about getting from point A to point B.

I knew very few things about the Tampa Bay Buccaneers. They were famous for being the losers of the NFL, historically winning less than forty percent of their games. Their inaugural season they were winless in fourteen games and lost the first twelve games of the following season. Under their head coach, John McKay, the Buccaneers did not play many memorable games.

Coach McKay always had a memorable quip for reporters after the losses, though. "Well, we have determined we can't win at home and we can't win on the road," was his response after one game. "What we need is a neutral site." He was later asked about his team's execution. "I'm all for it," he said.

If the team was famous for its ineptness, it was also infamous for its logo featuring "Bucco Bruce," a swashbuckling pirate with a feather in his cap and knife in his mouth. The pinkish-orangish hue of the logo complimented the players' "Creamsicle" uniforms, but evidently did not strike fear in the hearts of other NFL teams. Ironically, there are probably more of these vintage uniforms in the stands today than there were in 1976.

The Buccaneers may not know how to win football games, but their fans know how to celebrate the sport of football. The vacant lot where we met the fans we interviewed was overflowing with people who did not know, or did not care about, the score of the game or the record of the team. They were there because they loved having a football team in Tampa. They had won a Super Bowl in 2002 but short of that season fans had historically little to celebrate. The fans of the *What the Buc? Podcast* were more interested in claiming their allegiance to a team with a history of struggles than a team with a history of Super Bowls. While the 2002 championship was briefly mentioned, the loss record was a point of emphasis. Grayson asked a female Tampa Bay fan to describe a Buccaneers fan.

"We don't get enough credit. Who goes 0-26 and still flies the colors?" she defiantly responded. Her point validated the extreme lows experienced by Buccaneers fans and their unwavering devotion and perseverance.

Our next interview was with the personality behind What the Buc? The backstory of how someone becomes a fan of a certain team is something I always find interesting.

In 1976, our Bucs fan was four years old when his dad told him: "We have a local team (Buccaneers).

We will root for them and whoever plays the damn Dolphins!"

Since that day, he has been a devoted fan of the Buccaneers and likely rooted against the Dolphins. "We don't have the numbers, but what we have are diehard. We've lived through the worst football possible. We need generations of fans," he told us when Grayson asked about the Buccaneers fan base.

The people of What the Buc? are also interested in helping their community through tailgating efforts. It may sound odd, but the more stadiums we went to and the more fans we interviewed, the more we understood how fans use their affinity for their team to get others involved in their community.

What the Buc? helped fill the local food pantries through donations collected at the tailgates. This act of kindness, in isolation, would be commendable, and knowing that similar things happen at tailgates across the NFL is remarkable, even though they are not official NFL events or supported causes. At the heart of it were ordinary people using their platform of being football fans to help the greater good. I hope the fans in Tampa never stop supporting the Buccaneers and never stop improving the lives of others in their community.

In the game, the Buccaneers quarterback, Mike Glennon, continued the long history of futility the franchise has experienced at that position. His quarterback rating for the game of 23.1—158.3 is perfect—is all you need to know about how it went. The Panthers, behind their young quarterback Cam

Newton with an 86.4 quarterback rating—who was responsible for three touchdowns on his own—beat Tampa Bay 31-13 to keep the hometown Buccaneers winless for the season. Somewhere, Coach McKay is looking down and contemplating his team's execution.

Hail Mary was 600 miles away, give or take a few, but, more importantly, she was in the opposite direction in which we needed to go. With her close to Charlotte and us in Tampa needing to get to New Orleans by Sunday morning, meant we had to drive through the night to pick up Hail Mary then drive her the 700-plus miles to see the Saints play on Sunday. In Hail Mary, this equated to about eighteen hours of driving, and with our frequent stops to get gas it is more like twenty hours. Some days on this trip the road would win, some days Hail Mary would lose, and on a very rare occasion we would win. I was pretty sure the trip to New Orleans was not going to be one of those rare occasions. As long as Hail Mary did not lose it for us we should be okay. Well, okay as much as three guys can be okay after nearly two months living, for the most part, out of a 1967 VW Bus that had the brakes go out and was susceptible to leaving them stranded on the side of the road at three o'clock in the morning in rural North Carolina.

The last time I thought there was a chance we would not make it to every NFL stadium was in Cincinnati when we met Brian at Drew's Off-Road. We had been saved in what I considered at the time our darkest hour. From that point on I expected to have problems, but I still expected to make it. There was a period of adjustment from thinking that this was going to be fun and more like a vacation, to this trip is going to be uncomfortable and sometimes downright painful. Nonetheless, we were going on the offensive against the road and I was more determined than ever that we were going to win!

We returned to our mechanic in North Carolina and found Hail Mary to be in good spirits. To us that means she started and was able to drive on a highway. None of us were qualified to give a stamp of approval, but we were grateful to be back on the road. How long we would be able to stay on the road was, at this point, anyone's guess. The anxiety of not knowing if we would need a tow or be able to make it to our destination when we woke up every morning and after every stop along the way intensified. I began to realize that if we were going to make this trip in Hail Mary, the anxiety was just another piece of luggage or equipment we carried with us everywhere we went.

The road to New Orleans was long, but thankfully without incident. We made good time according to our standards and got to a friend's house Saturday evening with just enough time to get acquainted with our surroundings then meet one of the people we wanted to interview for the documentary.

We met outside a bar near the French Quarter, but safely away from everything the French Quarter and Bourbon Street offer. She was obviously an avid fan of the NFL, especially the Saints. Her soft-spoken demeanor concealed her passion for the city of New Orleans and football.

"You can't be here too long without being swept up in 'Who Dat Nation.' It's just who we are, it's in your blood. Saints football is the backbone of the city," she said. She also mentioned two players in Saints history who had done more for the franchise than any of the others.

Drew Brees, who I had followed since his days in high school in Austin, had successfully done the impossible and made the New Orleans Saints Super Bowl Champions in 2009. The franchise affectionately referred to as "The Aints" had reached the pinnacle of the football world by beating the odds and defeating the Peyton Manning-led Colts in Super Bowl XLIV.

The other player, Steve Gleason, primarily played on special teams—punts and kickoffs. It was difficult to tell from our interview which player had meant more to the city, but, needless to say, each had significantly changed the course of the franchise and the city of New Orleans.

The next morning was game day and we had an interview set up with a couple who told a story that would reverberate through all of our interviews with Saints fans.

Hurricane Katrina had decimated New Orleans in August of 2005, leaving many homeless and hopeless—including the Saints. The devastation wreaked on the Superdome forced the team to play essentially all of its "home" games away from New Orleans until September 25th of the following year. I can remember watching that "domecoming" game between the Saints and the Falcons on ESPN and feeling the energy from the crowd coming through the television. At the time I had no idea that more than five years later I would be interviewing fans about that night.

I now found myself in a small house a short drive from Canal Street, discussing a punt with two people who had lived through the entire event. A punt, of all things! An almost forgotten aspect of football and we were captivated with their story.

Neither of our interview subjects had been football fans until 2006. They said they had spent considerable time in Austin after the hurricane and returned to find there was very little left of the life they once knew. The wife specifically mentioned that the song "When September Ends" by Green Day resonated with her because those were the emotions she felt at the time. Chances are an entire city shared the same sentiment, since Green Day and U2 were playing in the Superdome at halftime the night it reopened. Tickets were sold out and on the secondary market were selling for as much as season tickets. Not going to the game was not an option for the wife and, as any loving husband would do in this situation, he unselfishly offered to buy her season tickets to the Saints.

Four plays in and the game forever changed the Saints and, more importantly, the city of New Orleans. While Steve Gleason will never make the hall of fame, after talking to Saints fans I am convinced he rebuilt an entire city in one play. Ninety seconds into the game, Gleason rushed up the middle of the

Falcons line and blocked a punt that was recovered for a touchdown. The crowd let out a deafening cheer as if they were letting out a year's worth of hostility towards Mother Nature and their seemingly endless battle to bring back normalcy. In fewer than two minutes, the Saints had announced to the world that they, and New Orleans, were back.

The importance of that game, that play, and that team cannot be overstated and is not lost on the people of New Orleans. Outside the Superdome there is a statue of Steve Gleason blocking that punt and convincing a city that it could rebuild.

It is difficult to argue exactly what NFL team is the most important to its city. You could make an argument for all thirty-two teams so I will not pretend to claim I know the answer. What I do know is that there is no other team more valuable to their city than the Saints. If anyone questions that statement they need to spend some time with Saints fans and learn about how a blocked punt changed everything.

Our game was against the Bills and, as I watched it, I thought of Ketchup Kenny, who was actually at the game in New Orleans, and Hammer, presumably watching it on television back in Buffalo. I also thought about our new friends who were Saints fans, and became conflicted as to who I wanted to win. Before our Saints interviews it would have been the Bills without a doubt, but hearing the story of Steve Gleason and how important the Saints were to New Orleans made me want them to win as well.

Drew Brees threw for five touchdowns and the Saints built on an eleven-point halftime lead and won 35-17. The Saints won the game, but the teams, to me, had the faces of the fans we met who had become friends.

Because of this trip, I have been to a lot of places, but I have experienced very few of them. Being in New Orleans, however, I started thinking of all the things I wanted to do and experience like beignets at Cafe Du Monde.

The best-laid plans, however, can be changed by a VW Bus. When we started driving, I heard a rhythmic pinging sound coming from the engine. Bad news, because anytime any sound other than the mellifluous tone of an air-cooled VW engine comes from the back of the vehicle there is something wrong.

We discovered that Hail Mary's air filter had broken off, so we spent the better part of Monday morning trying to fix her. It was the air filter we purchased in Cincinnati, which meant it was virtually brand new. Thankfully, on the advice of John, our mechanic in Austin, I had kept the old air filter. It was dirty and less than ideal, but it was not broken. I quickly reinstalled the old air filter and we were soon listening to the hypnotic purr of the engine as we headed for Miami sans beignets.

CHAPTER 7

A Religious Experience

Miami, Dallas, and Green Bay
(19 teams and 14,313 miles)

After all, is football a game or a religion?

– Howard Cosell

We got as far as Pascagoula, Mississippi, on our way to Miami for the Thursday-night Dolphins game. Despite having replaced the alternator and, to a novice mechanic, every other part on Hail Mary, she still was not running right. The red light on the speedometer kept blinking, and she began to sputter as if she was being choked. Earlier in the trip the sputtering had been an indication that she was overheating, but that was in September during a hot Texas summer. It was now thirty degrees cooler and we were driving at night, so being overheated was not the issue. In some ways it would have been much easier had it been, but once again, Hail Mary was mocking me and my inadequacies as an air-cooled VW mechanic.

The battery was the only other issue that could cause the red light to flicker irritatingly like a child taunting us into believing we were not going to make it to Miami. We managed to convince an Auto Zone to stay open so we could have our battery tested and replaced, if necessary. In a perfect world, the battery would be the issue, we would install a new one, and be back on the road to South Florida, considering the whole ordeal as more like a pit stop at the Daytona 500, only at Hail Mary speed.

Her battery was tested and since it was barely putting out any volts, we enthusiastically purchased a new one with $100 we did not have.

I gave the keys to Grayson before I crawled under Hail Mary to tap the starter, and he quickly jumped into the driver's seat like on *The Price is Right* when they want to give a car away. The contestant picks a key and if it works they drive away in a brand new shiny automobile. If it does not, you hear the stereotypical "we are so sorry—better luck next time" wa, wa, waa music.

I would have rather heard that music instead of the click followed by silence when Grayson turned the key. We could feel the optimism in the air quickly leave the group. We had now passed the tapping the starter phase and would begin the *Little Miss Sunshine* phase of the trip where we had to push Hail Mary to start her.

The next morning was more of the same: Shady motel, Hail Mary not starting and hundreds of miles from our next game with little hope of her issues resolving themselves. The more defiant Hail Mary became, the more defiant and resilient I became. It did not matter if I had to push, pull or drag her around the country to see every NFL stadium, it was going to happen and the sooner she got that through her mind, the better off we would all be.

The sputtering continued until it became incessant, which was right across the Florida border heading to Pensacola—we could not go any farther. At our current rate, we would never make it to Miami, even though we were technically in Florida a day before the game. Grayson began hastily making calls in a venomous tone. He had started to see Hail Mary as a burden that was, at times, more than he could bear. With each call ending in "thanks anyway," our situation became even more dire.

I searched on my phone for the air-cooled VW club in Pensacola and soon found a number for "Wild" Bill. He was truly our last call—it was Wild Bill or nothing. "Wild Bill you are our last hope," was all I said when he answered.

I decided to just lay all of our cards on the table by explaining our situation and giving him our location. It was late afternoon by now and Wild Bill was still at work. You could tell he was moving while we were talking, like he was putting on coveralls in anticipation of working on Hail Mary. He began to talk faster, seemingly from the excitement that we called him and he was our last hope. Wild Bill said he was taking off work early and would meet us at the house of another member of the VW club in Pensacola, Don. He gave us Don's address and an assurance that he would let Don know to be expecting us. Wild Bill said he would get us back on the road. His commanding tone gave us the reassurance we needed and we were quickly on our way to Don's house.

We pushed Hail Mary to get her started and soon found ourselves in the driveway of a house we hoped belonged to Don. There was not an overt sign that a VW person lived there, but we decided to knock on the door anyway. A gentleman with gray hair, glasses, and an Auburn Tigers T-shirt answered the door with a warm greeting.

We started out by apologizing for having to be there at all, but that we desperately needed his help. He hesitantly told us that his plans were to put a new floor in his garage, but that it could wait because VW people are teammates and when one of us is down the others rally and do whatever they can to help their team. Keeping Hail Mary, or any air-cooled VW, on the road is a win not only for the owner but for the entire team.

Don was ready to take our engine out and replace our new, evidently defective, alternator with a new one he had recently purchased. That is the other great thing about VW people: They always have extra parts because you truly never know when you might need a part or three random strangers traveling the country in the name of football knock on your door in need of a new alternator. He tested the alternator and it was low so he checked all of the connections. His examination revealed the real issue; a small wire had not been properly plugged into the alternator, which caused it to under-perform. As soon as the wire was plugged in properly our issue with the alternator was fixed, the red light on the speedometer no longer taunted me, and we were back on the road to Miami and the dream of thirty-two games was still alive. I never got to meet Wild Bill in person, which was a disappointment. I am sure our paths will cross again, maybe when he is driving through Texas and needs some help.

The alternator was fixed and the red light was dormant, either from burning out or we had actually fixed the problem. At this point it did not matter. The torture of the red light was over.

The sputtering, however, was not. We limped along the Florida highways as best we could until we made it to Miami. The issues with Hail Mary were troubling because the next three games would mark our longest drives of the trip in the shortest amount of time.

I said earlier that our initial schedule was for seventeen weeks ending with our triumphant return to Texas from Seattle. The trip from Seattle to Dallas looked good in April when I made the schedule, but after driving through the Rocky Mountains in September and knowing how bad the weather would be in late December we had to find a way to shorten the schedule. There was no way we could make it from Seattle to Dallas in December.

We decided that instead of going from Miami to Green Bay from Friday to Monday, we would make a small detour and go to Dallas for a Sunday afternoon game. Our new schedule meant we would need to drive from Dallas to Green Bay overnight.

"Faith is believing in things when common sense tells you not to," is a quote from George Seaton's film *Miracle on 34th Street.* I am sure he would agree that going from Dallas to Green Bay in one night would take a lot of faith. It would also take a healthy and cooperative Hail Mary.

We went to the Dolphins game and interviewed a traveling therapist from Ohio who had been a Dolphins fan since 1972 when he went to a game with his grandfather. His devotion to the Dolphins was modeled after the band Kiss, with his face painted white, complemented by aqua glitter for eyebrows and an almost Joker-like smile. His Dolphins cycling outfit revealed a Dolphins tattoo on his calf. It was Halloween and his orange hair, along with his makeup, could frighten most trick or treaters. It was apparent this was not the exception, more like the rule, for this Dolphins fan.

"When the schedule comes out in April, I decide where I go for work based on where the Dolphins play," he told us. Accompanying the traveling therapist was a female showered in aqua and orange. "We're Dolphins fans till the coffin slams!" she exclaimed. She said she drives an hour each way to the tailgates—a small price to pay for someone who claims to have a "pavlovian" experience every time she sees something aqua and orange.

The traveling therapist, his friend and the other Dolphins fans in the half-full stadium were treated to a spectacular game. I have watched a lot of football in my life and have never seen a game end like this one.

The Bengals and the Dolphins went into overtime with the Dolphins winning 22-20 on a safety. Unbelievable! All of the NFL games I have watched and none had ended with a safety in overtime. It has only happened three times in NFL history, so chances are not good I will ever see another game end like this one.

Having said that, the ending of the game was anti-climactic. It was unexpected, the fans who were still in the stadium and not celebrating Halloween were on their feet making as much noise as possible when suddenly it was over. The crowd did not get louder, but more or less quietly left the stadium.

Even more unbelievable than how the game ended was how we needed to be in Dallas on Sunday and Green Bay on Monday.

During all of our calls from the side of Florida highways, we did manage to find a place called McNab Foreign Car in Pompano Beach. I scheduled an appointment with Bruce for the Friday after the Dolphins game to get Hail Mary tuned up for the 2,500-mile journey to Green Bay by way of Dallas. I anticipated a long day of getting her back healthy and performing some preventive maintenance to ensure we would not have issues until at least Green Bay.

I met Bruce, a thin, middle-aged man, early that Friday morning. He seemed to have no recollection of me scheduling an appointment the day before. This awkward introduction and his somewhat cranky disposition contributed to us getting along at the beginning like oil and water. He looked at Hail Mary with her stickers and probably saw someone who just considered a VW Bus a marketing tool, discarding the heritage that has made this the iconic road-trip vehicle. At least, that is what I imagined he was thinking since that would have explained his cantankerous temperament toward me.

We walked over to her together and he raised the lid to the engine. The condition of Hail Mary drew immediate ire from Bruce—almost like a chef lifting the lid from a pot of something their understudy was cooking. He scolded parts of the engine as being all wrong and questioned where the seal to the engine compartment had gone. To his point, and my defense, we had a seal when we left Austin and it had mysteriously disappeared somewhere along the way to California to Ohio to Florida. He closed the lid and said he would get to it later that day, but he had some work ahead of Hail Mary.

I decided to just do whatever I could to make it through the day. You do not have to be friends with someone but it does not hurt to be nice, since you catch more flies with honey than with vinegar, and we were focused on getting Hail Mary fixed and seeing some familiar faces in Dallas.

I walked about a half-mile to Dunkin' Donuts to get some coffee and breakfast, but mostly to pass the time. I sat there watching people under the age of sixty-five hurriedly come and go, while those in the November of their lives patiently drank their coffee and read the newspaper. I figured I was probably closer to the Novembers than I was the people quickly grabbing their breakfast and gulping down their coffee, because

I had nowhere to be and, even if I did, I had no way of getting there. Bruce Almighty was holding Hail Mary captive and, while it would be good to be on the road to Dallas, being the calm in the midst of chaos was nice.

My period of reflection led me back to Bruce. I figured we had simply gotten off on the wrong foot; that maybe I had misread him and he had misread me. If indeed this was the case, I could not spend the afternoon just people-watching at Dunkin' Donuts, and he could not spend an afternoon alone with Hail Mary. We both had a story to tell that the other needed to hear.

I walked back to meet Bruce with the urgency and anxiety of a family member outside of an emergency room, because Hail Mary is family. That, and our proximity to the next game after Miami made me feel justified in returning to the repair shop. Bruce had already started working on her and glanced over his shoulder to see me approaching. He was not happy to see me, but did not seem unhappy either, so I took a chance and began to ask questions. He slowly started to open up about the condition of Hail Mary, how an air-cooled VW engine works, his own VWs and his life. I will never forget walking underneath Hail Mary with Bruce. He explained how the heater worked and complimented her overall condition despite not having a seal for the engine. He even gave me the tubes for the heater so we would not freeze to death going to Green Bay. The seal for the engine compartment was back in place and Hail Mary sounded as good as she ever had or at least since I had owned her.

After hearing of our trip, Bruce confessed that he thought he would "find" himself in a VW Bus. He said on a whim when he was much younger, he moved to California in a bus and lived in it for two years. Apparently believing that I had gone on this trip on a similar whim he relented that what we were doing with Hail Mary was "crazy." These buses, according to Bruce, were not meant to be driven like this. Here I stood in Pompano Beach, hundreds of miles from home, and someone finally told me that this was crazy and the Griswold Wagon Queen Family Truckster is not the vehicle you want when taking the tribe across the country.

Some of my fondest memories of the trip are not related to football, but rather in spending time with VW people. Even had I met Bruce before we started this journey I still would have taken it, and at this, the halfway point of the trip, there was no turning back. Nothing could stop us, except maybe Hail Mary catching on fire.

I got the feeling Bruce greeted everybody the same way he initially greeted me in an attempt to qualify them; to see how much they actually care about and love their VW. He is a smart man. The air-cooled VW community is not a prestigious club, but the last thing we want is someone to buy one and not appreciate the vehicle for what it represents—history, memories, families, freedom, dreams, and being able to appreciate having to work on your own vehicle.

Evidently after my return from Dunkin' Donuts, I was granted access to Bruce's club or, at least, qualified for a day pass. A few garage doors down from the stall Hail Mary occupied was Bruce's own VW collection. While Don in Pensacola had a beautifully restored VW Bug, I do not ever recall seeing a VW Bug as nice as Bruce's. It was beautiful and gave me something to aspire to when I restore Hail Mary. More important to me is that Bruce let me into his personal VW sanctuary. I remember that day with Bruce more fondly than most of the entire trip.

The journey to Dallas happened without a sputter, without a red light, without much of anything except for a seemingly endless highway. I was not as excited to see my Cowboys play as I was to be back in Texas, though. I had friends in Dallas who were having a party the Saturday night we were in town. The party was not for me, but seeing familiar faces for the first time in nearly two months made it seem like I was the guest of honor that night.

I drove Hail Mary to the house and, as I walked through the front door, people turned around and greeted me as if they were looking at someone thought to be dead. They all wanted to know about the trip, see Hail Mary in person, and offered their condolences about our alternator that left us stranded in North Carolina. How did they know about the alternator? We had posted something on Facebook, but did people read it? Did people care?

The party, seeing friends in Dallas and knowing that people paid attention to what we were doing could not have come at a better time. Even though we had driven overnight to get to Dallas from Miami and we were going to drive overnight again to get to Green Bay on Monday, these little, seemingly insignificant words energized my mind and spirit if not my body. I was physically road weary, but our glory was still ahead of us.

When the calendar turned to November we were exactly halfway to completion of our journey around the NFL: Sixteen games in with sixteen games to go. Although technically we were at the halfway point, November would without a doubt be our most difficult month.

Having moved the Cowboys game from the end of the schedule to the beginning of November meant we had twelve games scheduled for the month, or roughly three a week for four straight weeks. The good news was that we were getting better about filming our interviews and b-roll of the stadiums, so it took less time per team equaling less time per city. The bad news was that we were going to need to travel over 8,000 miles in one month. We had done fewer than 5,000 the month before, and under 7,000 miles in September. November may prove to be more than either Hail Mary or I could handle.

We arrived at the home of our Dallas Cowboys fan later than expected. She, along with a few other Cowboys fans, greeted us at the door with the customary smile before welcoming us into their world. Originally from Arkansas, Shelby was a fan of Texas history, and that was the driving force behind her obsession with the Cowboys. "I don't know if I knew there were any other football teams," she said during the interview.

And since I did not know there was much history to Texas other than the Dallas Cowboys, we got along well. She told us about her son, who liked the color green and was thinking of converting to become an Eagles fan. "You can be anything in the world but a liar, a thief or an Eagles fan," was her advice to him. During our interview her son was appropriately dressed in a Cowboys uniform, so apparently he heeded her warning.

Shelby's living room was filled with brown boxes stacked on top of each other. It was not until after the interview that I found out the boxes contained the blue foam star hats that Shelby manufactured and sold to Cowboys fans. We walked into another room off of the living room and entered Dallas Cowboys heaven. She had the most complete collection of Cowboys memorabilia I have ever seen, including a piece of the goal post from Texas Stadium.

Texas Stadium was a significant part of Texas history to a young football fan who had grown up idolizing the Cowboys. Like many things in life, it met an unceremonious, if not callous, end after its useful life had been deemed exhausted. I will admit that its successor, AT&T Stadium is an engineering marvel and an architectural spectacle, but it is not the Dallas Cowboys or at least not what they used to be.

Shelby and I discussed the implosion of the old stadium, and she shared her last moments with the stadium with us. "You knew that they had already torn up the field inside but, if you listened really close, there was still that spirit of football inside," she said.

The sense of pain and loss for a stadium is not specific to Cowboys fans. The Redskins, Giants, Eagles—the biggest rivals of the Cowboys—also have suffered the unceremonious demolition of beloved stadiums. That is not entirely true: RFK Stadium has not been imploded, but the Redskins no longer play home games there. To me, bigger and nicer stadiums do not equate to better and, in the case of Texas Stadium, Shelby did not think so either.

AT&T Stadium is definitely the most impressive in the NFL. I do not even know if there is much debate about it, but as far as tailgating and the pregame environment, the Cowboys leave a lot to be desired. Fans will not understand what is missing until visiting tailgates in Cleveland and Buffalo, even Houston. Then it is readily apparent that the Cowboys fan experience has gone the way of Texas Stadium.

I knew someone who worked for the Cowboys, so with the struggling Vikings in town she was able to get us good seats. We had seen the Minnesota Vikings play in New York, so I had a good idea who was going to win the game. But my thoughts were not entirely on the game. Hail Mary needed to have the valves adjusted, and the road to Green Bay was not getting any shorter.

The game provided its share of disappointment and excitement for Cowboys fans and, surprisingly, the Vikings showed signs of life compared to their game against the Giants in New Jersey. The Cowboys must have watched that game as well and expected what I expected, the Cowboys to win big. Tony Romo threw a touchdown pass with less than a minute left in the game to give the Cowboys the much-needed and expected victory, 27-23.

I enjoyed the game and being back in Texas, but it was soon time to leave. The game ended at three o'clock, which meant we had twenty-eight hours to drive nearly 1,200 miles. The maintenance, as it always did, took longer than it should have so we actually left Arlington at close to five o'clock. Now we were down to twenty-six hours to get to Green Bay. With the sun beginning to set we headed north not knowing if we would make it, but understanding that if we did not our goal of getting to every NFL stadium in sixteen or seventeen weeks would be over.

I drove until a little after two o'clock in the morning with no issues. For the first time on the entire trip, Hail Mary outlasted me, and I needed to find a place to rest for a couple of hours.

We turned into a regional fried chicken chain and drove to the back of the parking lot behind the drive-thru speaker. The restaurant was closed for the night, so we thought we had found a place that was secluded enough for some peace and quiet, yet visible enough that we were safe. The peace and quiet was short-lived. The semi-truck that restocks the restaurant pulled to the back door effectively blinding Grayson, who was sleeping in the back.

They were not going anywhere for a while, so it was up to us to move on to a more serene setting.

Motel parking lots are generally a good option for finding a quiet place to get some sleep, so we found one of the shady motels we had grown accustomed to sleeping in and around on this trip. I set an alarm for an hour and a half, planning to wake up and continue driving while the others slept. The hour and a half turned into three hours; I desperately needed the rest, but had put our trip in jeopardy by ignoring my alarm. Hastily, I gathered myself, started Hail Mary and continued to Green Bay.

Green Bay, Wisconsin, and Lambeau Field are special places. There is no other town or professional sports venue like them in the United States, if not the world. To many football fans, Lambeau Field is a holy pilgrimage. The Packers are Green Bay, according to the several people we interviewed who told us that if Green Bay did not have the Packers, nobody would know Green Bay existed, much less go there.

We walked down Lombardi Avenue and found a young couple to interview. The wife had a bubbly personality and was adorned with everything Packers, while the husband was dressed in the dark navy of the Chicago Bears. The wife said there were more people in town just for the Packers game than lived in the city of Green Bay. Whether that is true or not does not really matter. The point is that it could be true, which makes Green Bay and the Packers a truly amazing environment.

The husband's face wore the disdain all Bears fans have of their small-town rival as his wife discussed religion in Green Bay. "Church services are adjusted based on when the Packers play," she said. "Ridiculous!" his rebuttal was similar to what I imagine the Pope's would be.

One priest has actually resorted to spreading the good word and holding mass at Packers tailgates. I am sure that Bears fans have either listened to a game during church or skipped church entirely in favor of watching the game live. Most NFL fan bases live in glass houses when it comes to what they will miss in favor of watching their team play, so nobody should cast the "ridiculous" stone.

Everything about this place is football, and because of that I was in heaven. The Lombardi Trophy is named after the famous Packers coach Vince Lombardi and is given to the winner of the Super Bowl. I had read Vince Lombardi's biography and wanted to go to his old house to put an image with the stories, but we did not have time. We were late everywhere we went, and Green Bay was no exception. Although we were later than I wanted to be, we were still in time for kickoff.

The fiercest rival of the Green Bay Packers is the Chicago Bears, and the two teams met on the Monday night we were in Green Bay. The Bears vs. Packers was a special game for me because these were two old-school NFL teams from the NFC North in the stadium that most NFL fans want to visit at least once in their life.

The game did not live up to the hype because the Packers future Hall of Fame quarterback, Aaron Rodgers, was injured early in the contest. His backup,

Seneca Wallace, did little more than hand the ball off to the running back, which is a stark contrast to Rodgers throwing the ball all over the field. The Bears themselves were depleted at quarterback and were forced to start their first-string clipboard holder, Josh McCown.

The Bears beat the Packers 27-20, and we had beaten the most difficult part of our trip. In five days, we had driven over 2,500 miles and crossed three stadiums off our schedule.

Chapter 8

A Dame Good Time

Minnesota and Baltimore
(21 teams and 15,700 miles)

The reason women don't play football is because 11 of them would never wear the same outfit in public.

– Phyllis Diller

You could count on one hand the stadiums that I was really looking forward to seeing on this trip. Jack Murphy Stadium, Candlestick Park, Lambeau Field, Arrowhead Stadium and the Metrodome in Minneapolis. These are the stadiums that I grew up with as a football fan, the stadiums I spent countless hours watching on television, dreaming about going to, and the few in which I could still see the historic stadiums of the NFL in motion: Jack Murphy was home to those great Chargers teams of the early '80s; Candlestick Park was where "The Catch" happened; Arrowhead Stadium had a reputation for being the loudest in the league; and The Metrodome is where Tony Dorsett, on *Monday Night Football*, ran for the longest run in NFL history. I did not get to see that play live since I never got to watch the last half of the game on Monday nights, but my father was all too excited to tell me about it the next morning before school.

All the same, the Metrodome was one of the places I had to see before it was gone. This was the last season for the stadium and my last chance to reclaim part of me being a football fan as a child. It did not matter if they were playing the Redskins or that the Vikings themselves were not the best team in the NFL. The stadium mattered and I was here to pay my respects.

We had managed to track the Vikings back to Minnesota a week after their game against the Cowboys. While they were fortunate enough to take a chartered jet, we took Hail Mary.

Getting to Minneapolis was not the easiest or most pleasant trip in the VW Bus. A light snow began to fall as we reached the suburbs of the Twin Cities. The heater had not yet been connected in Hail Mary, so the cold wind blowing through her left a lasting impression on all of us, so much so that we quickly stopped at a Target to buy gloves and other cold weather gear we were not expecting to need quite so soon. Most years in Austin we do not see snowfall, especially not the first week in November. Despite Minneapolis and Austin being connected by the same interstate, we were far from the warm comfort of a Texas November.

Do not think I did not consider heading south on I-35 until I saw the Austin skyline. I did, but only fleetingly. It was like being a prisoner in Alcatraz; even if we were able to slip by the guards and start our journey home, there was no guarantee we would make it. More than likely we would meet our demise somewhere along the escape route in our makeshift mode of transportation.

Since an escape from Alcatraz would not be possible, it was for the best if we just bought the gloves and found a hotel for the next three nights, because sleeping in Hail Mary in the cold was not an option.

The Motel 6 was unforgettable, as most of them were during our trip, but as nice as we could afford for three days—the longest amount of time we would stay in one place until December when we had a week between games. Those three days seemed like an eternity.

While walking to the local Starbucks, I saw children playing outside, bundled in their warm winter coats and thought about my children. I truly missed them and hoped they knew it. A large part of why I went on this trip was for them. I wanted to do something that would make them proud of who their father is, and I figured being on the NFL Network was pretty cool. At least when I was growing up, it would have been the coolest thing next to having a dad who played in the games themselves. While I was not sure how my children would feel about seeing me on television, I was pretty sure I knew how they would feel about me coming home and I could not wait.

For now, I had to be content with two full days in Minneapolis primarily filled with the luxury of doing laundry and walking to and from that Starbucks. The people inside drinking coffee would often stare, probably wondering what we did for a living. They would not believe it if we told them, and they truly would not believe we were not making money from the trip, but actually spending it faster than we had anticipated.

I had never been in Minneapolis before, but for whatever reason I had a fondness for the Metrodome from watching Vikings and Twins games on television. The Twins had moved on to Target Field a couple of years before our trip, and had they been playing I would have gone to the game. It had taken me forty years to get to Minnesota, so I really could not say for sure when I would be back and by that time the Twins may have an entirely new stadium.

One of the regrets I have of the trip is not going to the Mall of America. Not because I like shopping or really had money to buy anything, but because the mall itself sits on top of the previous home of the Vikings, Metropolitan Stadium, where Dallas Cowboys wide receiver Drew Pearson famously caught the original "Hail Mary" pass from Roger Staubach. It seems Drew Pearson may have pushed off to catch the ball, a huge point of contention for long-time Vikings fans. For me, a Cowboys fan who named his most valuable possession after that play, I should at the very least have paid my respects and let Hail Mary do the same.

Although I had a certain attachment for the Metrodome, I was not expecting much from it. Kind of like a president at the end of his second term, the Metrodome had little to offer other than simply playing out its final few games. The atmosphere around the stadium was filled with Vikings fans tailgating, apparently oblivious to the frigid temperatures, something that was not, however, lost on me. It was not snowing, but it was cold and windy.

We found two fans who had renovated a delivery truck into the Battle Wagon, what is best described as a mobile living room complete with a fireplace. The mobile, tailgating tribute to the Vikings was almost lost in the sea of people wearing purple, and after a brief conversation from outside the Battle Wagon, we were invited inside to see all of the nuances the owners had installed. I think my favorite piece was the Vikings helmet that had been split in the middle and framed in profile. I remembered they were wall decorations at my Foot Locker when I was growing up in the late '70s and early '80s, but had not seen one since.

Our talk with the Vikings fans quickly turned to the new stadium and how it would impact their ability to do what they do best, tailgate. They told us that the Vikings plan to bus people in for tailgating because the downtown location does not have enough space for onsite tailgating. That made me immediately think of AT&T Stadium in Arlington and how disappointing the pregame environment was for me as a fan. The Vikings had a good thing going with the atmosphere around the Metrodome and I hated to see it go. We offered our condolences to the Vikings fans for their impending loss and made our way to our next interview.

It was a mother and daughter who went to Vikings games together. Vikings football had become a tradition in their family because their father and grandfather, respectively, had been a business leader in Minneapolis and was part of the team that brought the NFL to Minnesota.

The daughter wore big pigtails and a Vikings T-shirt with a purple and yellow scarf that served to accent her devotion to the team. Grayson asked her if she had the opportunity to select her own team. Her response was what we had come to expect from fans all over the country when asked the same question.

"Not really," she said. "I became part of the tradition right away, watching Vikings games from an early age with grandma and grandpa on the couch." Her smile was indicative of someone who did not mind being forced to be part of the family football team.

Even though I was not expecting much from the stadium or the game itself, the game ended up being one of the best we saw our entire trip. The Vikings stopped the Redskins at the four-yard line as time expired to hold on for the victory, 34-27.

The stadium itself was everything I think fans need in a place to watch football. Besides the distinctive white roof, my favorite feature was that it was only two short flights of stairs to the second level. Most stadiums today have a series of long ramps or escalators that make it an athletic accomplishment just to make it to the top. Rarely did I have a lower-level seat, so this feature was particularly relevant to me. Truth be told, other than the unique roof and my personal history with the Metrodome, there was not much difference between it and the Edward Jones Dome in St. Louis.

When I look back and think about the Metrodome, it saddens me to know it no longer stands. When it was imploded, I paused to say goodbye and reflect on the day I had gone to a Vikings game in Minnesota. It is a difficult thing for me to watch a stadium filled with experiences and memories implode; what took generations to build is gone in a few seconds. For me it does not matter if it is Texas Stadium or another stadium like the Metrodome, it still hurts me as a sports fan.

Minneapolis to Baltimore was our longest drive of November, next to the Miami to Dallas to Green Bay experiment. Hail Mary seemed to be in good spirits, so the 1,100 miles in two days was not an issue. It would not be comfortable, but after staying in the same place for seventy-two hours I learned that I preferred being on the road and seeing new things, as opposed to the confinement of a Motel 6 or Starbucks.

We had no issues with Hail Mary the entire way, not even a sputter. An optimist would say this is how it should be, but a VW Bus has a way of turning even the most optimistic people into realists. Be overly optimistic and your bus will leave you stranded on the side of the road with a mechanical issue, or worse, on the side of the road after a fire. Realistically, we knew our bit of good fortune was going to come to an end sooner or later. All we could do was drive her until she had her next issue and hope that we could find our next Wild Bill from Pensacola.

When we got to Baltimore we drove straight to the house of the Ravens fan we were interviewing for the documentary. On the driveway of her ranch-style house is an enormous Ravens logo that had obviously been painted by a professional. I turned to Grayson and Eric and said if the driveway was any indication, we were in for a real treat as far as sports fans go.

We were greeted at the door by a female wearing a Ravens jersey, purple wig, and face paint. The person behind the Purple Dame persona was unrecognizable and, honestly, this was not about her. The face painters or, for that matter, anyone who is passionate enough about something to get into a costume or character are those people in life who have truly come alive. Their liveliness and unwillingness to conform to what society says is cool or fashionable is what, to me, makes life worth living. Purple Dame was definitely alive and I was enjoying every bit of meeting her.

A room directly off the front foyer was radiating purple with Ravens memorabilia hanging from the walls and sitting on the bar. It was impossible to escape football in the house. Even the small brown dog had the laces of a football painted on her back. Purple Dame had pictures with every notable Ravens player in the team's brief history, brief because Baltimore lost their original team, the Colts, to Indianapolis and replaced them with the Cleveland Browns.

The room had a replica of the Super Bowl trophy given to a hall of fame fan of the team that is the defending champion from the previous year. There was even a small split-window VW Bus decked out in the

Ravens logo. She had everything imaginable, including an appreciation of Ravens history. It was interesting to hear about when a team decides to relocate how it impacts the psyche of an entire city. The Colts leaving in the middle of the night in March of 1984 had been neither forgotten nor forgiven.

"Violated, naked, stripped, and sad. Without the Colts people felt like we (Baltimore) were a drinking town with a baseball problem," is how Purple Dame described her feelings.

Over thirty years, and the wounds were still fresh. Purple Dame did, however, give credit to the Colts for providing the city with its football history.

Making all of her historical Baltimore football knowledge even more interesting was the fact that Purple Dame was not a football fan back in 1984. When the Ravens won their first Super Bowl in 2001, Purple Dame worked in downtown Baltimore along the parade route celebrating the team's victory. During the parade she saw a big guy, who was obviously a player, show his love and devotion to the Ravens fans in the crowd. It was apparent to her that the player, Tony Siragusa, could not do enough for the fans. At that moment she understood football players to be more than their impressive physical statures.

The following year she attended her first Ravens game, said she felt like she had three strokes and was hooked; the persona of Purple Dame was born. Being a relatively recent fan of the NFL and specifically the Ravens made it more impressive that

Purple Dame even existed. She had found what made her come alive—the Baltimore Ravens.

Before leaving the interview we asked her what she thought about our trip around the NFL. Her response, coming from someone with such an elaborate fan persona, was surprising. "You guys deserve the cape and mask," she said. "You are like superheroes! Remarkable and completely off the hook." Then Grayson asked if she cared to join us, and much like Al Roker, she dismissed us. "My days of living hippie chic are over," she said.

Camden Yards, where Baltimore's baseball team, the Orioles, play, is next to the home of the Ravens: M&T Bank Stadium. I love walking by baseball stadiums. There is something special, something sacred about a baseball stadium. "Baseball is what we were. Football is what we have become." Mary McGrory, a columnist for *The Washington Post*, wrote about America.

There is a lot of truth in that sentiment, and maybe it is my longing for what this country once was as the reason I love baseball stadiums and driving a vehicle from the '60s. For me, Camden Yards adds to the atmosphere surrounding a Ravens game. There also is Ravens Walk, which is filled with Ravens-related products and is the path that the band takes to get to the stadium.

A Ravens game is a great experience, but Baltimore being the birthplace of Babe Ruth makes it difficult for football to completely escape the baseball roots of the city. Camden Yards is visible in the distance from M&T Bank Stadium, which helps keep baseball in the conscience of Baltimore, even for those in town for a Ravens game.

The Bengals and Ravens game featured an actual Hail Mary pass that sent the game into overtime. The Ravens eventually won 20-17 and our recent string of good games continued. Much like our luck with Hail Mary, that would come to an end soon as well.

CHAPTER 9

The Oilers are Alive!

Tennessee, Jacksonville, and Carolina (24 teams and 17,543 miles)

The fear of death follows from the fear of life. A man who lives fully is prepared to die at any time.

– Mark Twain

For the four months we were on the trip, we were either broke or in the neighborhood of being flat broke, so it was imperative that we do everything we could to save money. Since my original plan of buying a gym membership so we could work out and get a shower, and sleep in Hail Mary was not agreeable to all of us, our lack of resources forced us, on occasion, to stay in the homes of people we may or may not know.

Nashville was one such occasion. Grayson said he thought his sister's friend from high school lived in Nashville. He had little recollection of the friend himself, but that really did not matter at this point in our trip. We had already stayed in enough houses of what would normally be considered strangers, so we were okay with making the call to Grayson's sister who would hopefully call her friend and find us a place to stay. Sight unseen, the friend of Grayson's sister and her husband agreed to take us in for a couple of nights. We were beyond grateful.

We arrived late on a Tuesday night. I still hated getting to people's homes late at night, especially without even knowing them. It just seemed rude, and if I could have done anything about it I would have.

I told Grayson to introduce himself while Eric and I got our stuff out of Hail Mary. Even though I was exhausted and did not feel much like moving, I managed to open the door of the VW Bus and looked up to find Grayson on the front porch of the house. The introduction was inaudible but pleasant.

Suddenly, all hell broke loose. As if she could smell freedom, a medium-sized brown dog shot out from the darkness inside the house and ran toward a busy intersection. With an equal sense of urgency, a female leaped from the darkness following the dog down the street yelling back that the dog could not go outside. Whether the dog could or could not go outside was irrelevant at this point. The dog was outside and, from the looks of it, was enjoying her freedom immensely.

By this time the husband was backing the official search vehicle, which in this case was a black Chevy Tahoe, out of the driveway. We had a fugitive on our hands and the best I could do was establish a perimeter starting at the busy intersection, forcing the dog away from traffic and back toward the house. Everyone was giving chase, but it was apparent that this dog was not about to willingly go back inside anytime soon. About five seconds into meeting our hosts in Nashville we had lost their dog. Not so much lost, as freed their dog. The good news is that fifteen minutes later we had lured the fugitive back into captivity and hopefully put ourselves in the good graces of the husband and wife.

The evening of the game we had an interview scheduled with Titanman, who told us to meet him at the downtown law firm where he worked. After learning more about our meeting location, I thought it would be strangely out of character for a lawyer to transform himself into Titanman. Nothing against lawyers, but that does not seem to me to be the profession that encourages people to come alive and be themselves.

We waited in the lobby of the building of the law office for our interview. A man bouncing with excitement walked into the lobby. From his jovial, almost childlike demeanor he was obviously not someone who fit the mold of being a lawyer. This was a guy who could definitely be Titanman. As we rode the elevator up to the floor of the law firm, he explained he was not a lawyer but part of the office staff. The lawyers, however, encouraged him to be Titanman and they would allow us to film inside the firm's office. To this day I remain skeptical if they encourage Titanman to be himself for his sake or if they need another reason to feel better about themselves.

We walked through the door of the law firm into a world rich with mahogany, but void of life or character. The furnishings were elegant and everything had its place. There were ample offices and conference rooms off of the main aisle. If anything were opposite of living and working in Hail Mary, this would be it.

"We need you to bring it tonight," a lawyer who was on his way out the door told Titanman with a slight smirk. His expression made the comment seem disingenuous and further fueled my speculation of the "support" Titanman received from his co-workers. The comment brought a smile to Titanman's face while he assured the lawyer that he would have it no other way.

Our interview was in a large conference room, and Titanman, at this point, was wearing a Titans jersey but not much else in the way of a super-fan of the team. That, however, would change.

He went into great detail of his life as a Titans fan and the emotion he feels toward the team, especially during a game. His eyes, almost hidden behind his glasses, twinkled with excitement as he proclaimed himself a warrior and the leader of the fans in his section. Games to him are draining both emotionally and physically, he admitted, and tonight's game would be no different. Titanman is the only fan we interviewed who spoke as if he were part of the team.

"Losing to Jacksonville was a hard loss," he told us in a tone that carried the weight of player or coach instead of a fan. "This is our house, and if we take care of business we should be okay. We're excited about getting this team where it needs to be."

His response to Grayson's question about the possibility of retirement further drove home the point that, for Titanman, the line blurred between team and fan. “I want a Super Bowl ring!” he said. Fans usually do not get Super Bowl rings, but if a fan ever deserved one it would be Titanman.

I continued listening intently throughout the interview, but what I really wanted to see was him as Titanman. His costume or, as Titanman probably likes to think of it, uniform, was as complete and extravagant as any other we encountered on our trip. From his Titans shoes to his “Titan Love Shield” to the sunglasses with a red star in the middle, his transformation was complete.

To me, the uniform did not represent him being a fan of the Titans, rather it represented his conversion from a staff member at a stale law firm who probably takes direction, to a leader who provides direction to other Titans fans. It transformed him from ordinary to extraordinary as if the Titans gave him a reason to live and to be excited. As he walked down the hall toward the exit, it felt like we had witnessed Clark Kent going into a phone booth and emerging as Superman.

The bridge to the stadium where the Titans play is a long walk. The Titans were the former Houston Oilers, moving to Nashville in 1997 to become the Tennessee Oilers then, in 1999, the Tennessee Titans. The team had little history in Tennessee and the stadium was virtually unknown to me as a football fan.

I was not excited about the game and considered it as more of something to check off our list, but what I was not expecting and did not know even existed were the relics of the history of the Oilers that are found inside the stadium.

Growing up in Texas I was very familiar with the Houston Oilers and what they meant to the state. Although the team survived mostly in the shadows of the Dallas Cowboys, the Oilers were a beloved team with their iconic coach, Bum Phillips, and the legendary running back from The University of Texas, Earl Campbell.

"Luv Ya Blue!" had permeated a significant portion of Texas in the '70s, especially the southeast part of the state. And although I was not a fan of the Oilers, I missed them being in Houston, because the Texans are like a lot of the stadiums today—really nice and shiny with all of the modern conveniences a new generation of fans expect, but void of history.

Seeing the Oilers logo took me back to a different time in my life and left me longing for the way things used to be—a reminder of what once was. While Nashville fans seemed oblivious or unappreciative of what they were walking past, that logo, which means something to so many people, now serves the functionality of a tombstone marking the final resting place of a loved one that will never be back yet never be forgotten.

The beginning of the game would have made any Titans fan happy, especially someone as devoted as Titanman. The Titans took a 14-0 lead after the first quarter and enjoyed a 17-6 lead at halftime. The Colts, however, scored seventeen unanswered points in the third quarter and led 23-17 at the start of the fourth. Despite the best efforts of the Titans and Titanman himself, they would lose 30-27.

After the game in Nashville we had two days to make it to Jacksonville. With the mechanical issues of Hail Mary seemingly behind us, we did not expect to have any problems making it to the game. I had never been to Jacksonville but always wanted to go because that is where the Georgia vs. Florida football game is played every year. Known for as long as I can remember as the "World's Largest Cocktail Party," it is one of the biggest rivalries in all of college football, and one of only three of the major college football rivalries to be played at a neutral site every year.

The other games are Army vs. Navy, which has recently moved around, but when I was growing up it was always played at Veterans Stadium in Philadelphia, and the rivalry I am most familiar with, Texas vs. Oklahoma, which is played in Dallas at the Cotton Bowl. I have gone to the game in Dallas more than a handful of times and always wanted to see how Georgia vs. Florida compared. If it were not for football, Jacksonville would have the same issues as Green Bay. Nobody would know about it or go there if it were not for Georgia vs. Florida or the NFL. There have been rumblings that the Jaguars are likely to relocate to a different city in the near future, but after watching a game there I hope that does not become a reality.

In Nashville we were at the bottom of the barrel as far as finding someone who would take us in for a night. In Jacksonville, though, that barrel was completely dry. We did not know anyone. Not even someone who knew someone who had heard of someone living in Jacksonville, so it was time to try our hand at shady motel roulette again. As with any type of roulette, it is truly a gamble. There may have been no bigger evidence of this than our motel in Jacksonville.

We were on the third floor again, which seemed to happen to us quite often. Most of the time we ended up on the top floor, which in a nicer hotel would be considered the penthouse. In a shady motel, chances are the room would more resemble an outhouse than a penthouse.

As we were about to be introduced to our accommodations for the night, we looked across the walkway and saw what could be considered a gaggle of ladies of the night outside one of the rooms. I gave the situation one last look and thought maybe there was an actual penthouse and they were in it. To the credit of the gaggle, we never heard any commotion and the next morning we were ready to see what being a Jaguars fan was all about.

I had a friend whom I had met in the parking lot of Rosenblatt Stadium at the College World Series in Omaha in 2011. She lived in Florida and was driving in for the game. Although we had only met briefly over a beer, she had kept up with what I was doing and knew about the trip.

At the Jaguars tailgate, she introduced us to a group of fans in their Jaggin' Wagon. Yes, Jaguars fans actually exist and travel in packs. The Wagon itself was a medical supply van in its former life. Like a dog that had been rescued from the pound, the Jaggin' Wagon was now living the life every medical supply van wishes they could live. The owner explained to us that a group of them had banded together and saved money in a pickle jar to have the Wagon painted black and badged "Jaggin' Wagon" with a Jaguars logo.

"The first thing I did when I got a real job was to get season tickets to the Jaguars," one of the investors in the van said. Which was funny, because apparently the season tickets were a well-thought-out purchase, but the medical supply van was bought on a "whim."

It was not Hail Mary, but it was awesome to see fans celebrate their team with a custom vehicle. These guys were resourceful and committed to the Jaguars, and for that they have my respect. They told us stories that they had taken the Wagon all over the NFL, making them far more adventurous than I was in driving a VW Bus. The Wagon not only got these guys around the country to different Jaguars games, but also served as a beacon for visiting fans to find them. There are fans of opposing teams that go to Jacksonville for one game every year and make it a point to tailgate with the Jaggin' Wagon. Who knew a medical supply van could do so much?

A ticket to the game was going for eight dollars on the secondary market. While large sections of the upper deck in the stadium were covered with tarps with Jaguars logos on them so the stadium would look better on television, the weather in Jacksonville could not have been better for a football game in mid-November. That is exactly why I scheduled November games in Florida.

What was there to complain about if you were a Jaguars fan other than the team's record? If there was something to complain about I could not find it. Inside the stadium was like one big party. I think even the Jaguars would admit that the team is not a perennial Super Bowl contender, but there may be no better entertainment value in the NFL than the Jaguars.

The team is doing what it can to grow its fan base, not only in Florida but England as well. Every year the team plays one of its "home" games in London. If I had not talked to fans from different countries in Buffalo, I would have questioned the sanity of doing such a thing. But after Buffalo I understand how big of a deal the NFL is in different parts of the world and can see the Jaguars becoming the fan favorite in Europe, maybe even the unofficial team of London or, unfortunately, the official team of London.

The Jaguars were playing a very good Arizona Cardinals team and actually led after the first quarter, 14-7. They would not score the rest of the game, however, and lost 27-14. On the plus side, the ineptness of the Jaguars offense meant our seats got progressively better as the game went on and more fans left the stadium. I started in the upper deck and, before the game was over, had comfortably repositioned myself a few rows from the field. The score, or even the teams playing, did not matter. Jacksonville meant good seats for an NFL game and even better people in the Jaggin' Wagon.

Jacksonville was a pleasant surprise. As a fan of a different team in a different league, the Jaguars had been an afterthought of the trip. But being there and meeting fans of the team changed my perspective—the same phenomenon that happened when meeting fans of all of the different teams.

Dapper Don in Buffalo blamed taking the wrong exit off the interstate for the reason for fans of other teams. I started to agree, and found that meeting fans of other teams and spending time in their environment provided a refreshing look at the NFL and humanity as a whole. I had enjoyed the Jaguars experience, but the next game on the schedule was the following night in Charlotte, so our time in Jacksonville and, thankfully, the third-floor room at the shady motel was short-lived.

We were fortunate on this leg of the journey that we were able to stay in Columbia, South Carolina, with a friend of Eric. He was a former Marine who spent time in Afghanistan and returned stateside to become a state trooper in South Carolina. Columbia is only about 90 miles from Charlotte, so having the state trooper, Sal, on our side saved us the mental and financial cost of a motel room.

After our experience in Jacksonville, the two-story home in Columbia was a much needed and welcomed sight. That night we went to downtown Columbia to eat a hamburger with Sal and his sister. The hamburger also was a welcomed sight. We had sustained ourselves for the most part on chips from the gas stations we stopped at along our path, which were spelled rarely by home-cooked meals.

After the hamburger we headed back to the house in Hail Mary. Sal wanted the VW Bus experience and was now riding shotgun—white-knuckling it all the way back to his house, unbeknownst to me. Apparently he felt like his life was in danger. I was busy trying to navigate through the cold and rainy weather without windshield wipers or being able to defrost the windshield.

There were two things that gave us the most trouble other than the obvious maintenance issues—the cold and the rain. At the time, we still had not connected the heater tubes Bruce in Florida had given us, and we were not going to have windshield wipers for the duration of the trip. In an ideal world, we would have been able to replace the motor for the wipers, but that apparently is a long, convoluted process; something we never had the time to undertake. So we found ourselves driving through a cold, dark and rainy Columbia, South Carolina, night with a former Marine riding shotgun, Ooh Rah!

I am not going to lie and pretend I was completely confident in my ability to safely navigate us back to Sal's house, but sometimes in life you have to fake it—not just for your sake, but for the people around you.

When we got back to the house and everyone heaved a sigh of relief, Sal said that the ride in Hail Mary was the third scariest of his life. We finished behind every time, as a Marine, he went down a mountain in Afghanistan in a Humvee, and the time as a state trooper he was going over 100 mph the wrong way of a highway chasing a drunk driver. Third is respectable, but I do not like to finish third in anything, and I was all for moving up in the rankings if Sal wanted to join us.

Knowing how the rest of the trip went, I am extremely confident that had Sal been in Hail Mary for the final two weeks of November we would have at least moved into second if not first place.

I kept wondering why someone has not taken my idea and converted a VW Bus into a tailgate vehicle. We had seen a delivery truck and a medical supply van used for tailgating, but why not a vintage VW?

The first Carolina fans we interviewed changed all that. They had a VW Bug that was black and Carolina blue with the Panthers logo prominently displayed on the sides and back. Behind the bug was a trailer that held all of their tailgating gear. I did not know you could pull that much stuff with a VW Bug, but apparently it is possible.

We had been waiting on them, and they pulled into the parking lot and stopped the car. Needing to move it to a specific parking spot, they could not start the engine. For thirty seconds, the bug would act like it wanted to start but not completely turn over. There were points during our trip that having Hail Mary act as if she wanted to start but not completely turn over would have been progress for us. Needless to say, I felt their pain and was prepared to offer my help in pushing the VW Bug into its place or tapping the starter if necessary. Eventually, like all good VWs, it started and got to where it need to be, late.

Carolina's Bank of America Stadium is nice and has a really good pregame atmosphere. I am not sure why certain teams have better environments than others, but I believe it has a lot to do with how much the city embraces its football team. How much that city is identified by its football team impacts the energy in and around the game. Places that have lost teams or spent decades on the outside of the NFL looking in know how valuable and irreplaceable a team can be to a city. It could have been that the Panthers were playing Tom Brady and the Patriots on *Monday Night Football*, but I would like to think Charlotte, being football-starved for so long, embraces the team regardless of the opponent.

One of the really unique aspects of the Carolina Panthers experience is how the players walk by the fans to get to the stadium. The fans know if they just stand at the fence guarding the walkway that eventually they will see the entire team. Unfortunately, we did not have time to wait because we wanted to see everything in and around the stadium and possibly get another interview for the documentary before the game.

We walked around to the different parking lots, absorbing the environment. Standing next to us was a guy with a Carolina blue colored wig that looked like a Don King starter kit. When I actually took notice of him I saw he was dressed in a cape, draped over a jersey with a plush toy black panther laying on his shoulder. He was accompanied by a friend who had painted his face and, instead of the wig, had a custom-made cat mask covering his head starting above his sunglasses. If these two were superheroes, this guy was clearly the Robin in the relationship. I thought Batman and his sidekick would be good interviews and Grayson made the introductions.

They were skeptical of our intentions at first, but after a little banter they relented and gave us an interview. One of the most unforgettable moments of the trip was standing in the shadow of Bank of America Stadium listening to these fans sing the Carolina Panthers fight song. People passing by stopped to take pictures of the dynamic duo. We were all in the moment and the smiles on their faces as they openly proclaimed their allegiance to the Panthers through a song is why football is so important. This was probably the real reason Batman gave us the interview. He enjoyed the spotlight and putting his love of the Panthers and Carolina on public display. These were the moments I was hoping to experience on this trip and it was turning out better than my wildest dreams.

Life was good. We had not had any issues with Hail Mary since late October with the flickering red light in Florida, and were well on our way to completing our tour in sixteen weeks. I was beginning to see the end of the trip, and realized the holidays were fast approaching. While Thanksgiving would be spent away from our families, having made the overnight drive from Dallas to Green Bay meant we would be home for Christmas and for good.

As a group, we were finally beginning to hit our stride. We had been streamlining our process since we began the journey in September, and everything from finding motels, to packing our bags, finding parking at the stadiums, and finding fans to interview was all done with less effort and in less time.

Hail Mary was hitting her stride as well, and maybe, most importantly, she was actually going to finish the race. This was being overly optimistic as it turned out, but this entire trip and filming the documentary was born out of optimism. Trying to make it to every NFL stadium in sixteen weeks in a 1967 VW Bus reeks of optimism, but when you own an air-cooled VW, it is always important to temper any optimism with a healthy dose of reality, which says a vehicle—any vehicle—that is nearly fifty years old will eventually have issues. The fact that we had made it this far was nothing short of a miracle.

Looking at the upcoming schedule, other than driving from Atlanta to New England in two days, there was nothing to keep us from being optimistic. Hail Mary would soon temper that optimism.

CHAPTER 10

Traveling Circus

Atlanta, New England, and Washington
(27 teams and 19,304 miles)

Do not take life too seriously. You will never get out of it alive.

– Elbert Hubbard

I had lived in Atlanta for twenty-one months while I attended the MBA program at Georgia Tech. I was even an Atlanta Falcons season ticket holder. At that time, the city of Atlanta was abuzz with Michael Vick and I was caught up in the excitement as well. I wanted to make the most of my time in Atlanta and could not think of a better way for a football fan like myself to do so than going to the Falcons games.

The Georgia Dome is your typical domed stadium, and having been to more than a handful of games there I was not terribly excited about going back. It was still football, but the newness was not there for me. Returning to Atlanta brought back fond memories I have of the city and Georgia Tech. We were going to stay with Eric's sister and her family in Tyrone, Georgia, just outside of Atlanta.

On our way to Tyrone, we passed through Atlanta just in time to find ourselves in the midst of rush-hour traffic, which started to break as we approached our exit. The cars at the exit were backed up almost to I-75 from the red light at the end of the exit so I began to slow down. Since the episode outside of Buffalo when our brakes went out, I had replayed that feeling continuously in my mind. As you can imagine, it was not a good feeling and one that I did not care to relive. I pushed down on the brake and slid Hail Mary into neutral, preparing to come to a complete stop. She had other plans, however. We had slowed down considerably since leaving the freeway, but it was painfully obvious that our brakes had once again let us down. Cars were about eight deep from the red light at the end of the exit. I mashed on the horn to alert the other drivers only to remember Hail Mary did not have a horn, then I put on my turn signal and forced my way to the side of the road where she stopped.

There are several times during this episode of my life where I did the wrong thing, and this happened to be the first. I did not want to have to tow Hail Mary again, and since we were only a few miles from where we were staying for the night, I thought if I kept her in first gear and went really slow that we could make it to the house and assess the damage there, maybe even wait until the morning.

That was a bad idea on so many levels, but somehow I found support from my traveling companions. Although it was clearly a bad decision, it was this type of bad decision that had led to some of the most exhilarating soul-enhancing events of my life.

I started Hail Mary and gingerly tapped the gas to get her moving in the right direction. It only took me a few seconds to realize my lapse in judgment and I soon found myself forcing Hail Mary across three lanes of traffic so I could keep moving and not run into any of the cars in front of us. The light was stale red, but it did not matter. Like a bull racing toward the red cape of a bullfighter, she was going through the intersection whether it was clear or not.

After turning right at the light and making it safely to a major road, I immediately considered a Plan B, taking into account the recently acquired understanding that my original idea was about as likely to work as Hail Mary turning into a time machine and teleporting us back to five minutes before so we could have her towed to the house. A few hundred yards from the intersection there was a strip center with a laundromat and a U-haul rental center.

I could feel Hail Mary wanting to stop shortly after turning into the strip center, but wanting and doing are two entirely different things. Grayson jumped out of the back seat and positioned himself in front of Hail Mary, hoping to stop her and push her somewhere safe so we could get her towed. But the parking lot to the right of the strip center had a slight downward grade to it so, despite Grayson's best efforts, Hail Mary and the parking lot were both working against him. Seeing that he would not be able to stop Hail Mary, Eric and I pleaded with him to get out of the way—the last thing I needed was for him to slip, fall and be run over. That, however, was probably my second mistake;

I should have told Eric to get out and help Grayson so I could steer her to a safe spot.

Grayson reluctantly removed himself from the front of the VW Bus and I turned the wheel to the right hoping for level ground, not knowing what lay ahead would provide a direct challenge to my mortality.

There is always that most frightening or thrilling point of every roller coaster ride, where you slowly crawl up to the top and then just before you are thrown to the bottom you get a good look at how far down you are about to go. Well, we were at the top of the roller coaster about to be thrown to the bottom at an ever increasing rate of speed. I should have told Eric to jump out, but I did not, fearing that we were already going too fast for him to exit safely. If Hail Mary was going to crash I wanted to use the passenger side to prevent me from being injured or, at the very least, minimize my injuries, but as long as Eric remained in the passenger seat I would not be able to do that.

Instead of jumping out, Eric grabbed the handle in front of the passenger seat above where a glove box is on a modern car. Grayson was now to the right of us looking much like that teenager working on the roller coaster who gives you the thumbs up as you begin the ascent up the mountain. He understood the gravity of the situation and gravity was exactly what was going to propel us down the road directly to the crash site.

At this point I understood we were going to wreck. Eric may or may not have understood it, I do not know because he never said a word. In his defense, once we started going down I did not have much to say either. To the left of us was a long exposed concrete wall a few feet high—just high enough to cause serious damage to Hail Mary's nose. To the right of us were all of the dormant U-haul trucks parked for the night. Since Hail Mary would probably lose a front-end collision with a small dog, a large U-haul truck was out of the question. Staring straight at us was more of the exposed brick wall that was on our left. By my calculations we would reach our maximum speed just before impact, which would make for a spectacular crash.

The funny thing is, in Buffalo, when our brakes went out, I very briefly questioned if this was how my life was going to end. In Atlanta, despite being surrounded by a cement wall and U-haul trucks, I never once thought we were actually going to die. I did think it might be the end for my beloved Hail Mary. I will not ever tell her that, but I was prepared to part ways if it meant saving Eric and myself.

Hail Mary, Eric, and I were all-in at this point. We had pushed all of our chips into the middle of the table, turned over our cards and hoped to live to fight another day. Eric still had not removed his hands from the handle in front of him nor said a single word. Again, this is understandable since I may be driving him directly into a premature death. There were no good options at this point other than to ride Hail Mary all the way down.

I did actually have a plan when we entered the strip center and it was better than Plan A, which was just drive real slow until we got to the house. As we were racing down the backside of the strip center, I began to evaluate my options: I knew I could not turn right because it was going back toward the strip center, as well as where all of the U-haul trucks were parked, and I could not tell if the line of trucks ever stopped. The cement wall in front of us was not going anywhere, so staying straight was an even worse option if that was possible.

Beyond the cement wall ahead of us were shrubs and bushes separating the strip mall parking lot from I-75, and beyond the cement wall to the left was more dense vegetation. If I could somehow get Hail Mary into that vegetation, she would have no choice but to stop. I did not know if the cement wall to our left ever ended, but we were about to find out. In the few seconds during which all of this transpired, I had made up my mind to turn left where the road ended.

The good news is our seat belts worked, something else that, along with the windshield wipers, I never tested before taking this trip. Hail Mary took the curb about like Evel Knievel jumping the fountains at Caesars Palace. We made it through the first obstacle and now found ourselves in the vegetation I had coveted earlier. There was a small tree directly ahead of us, so I steered Hail Mary to the right—lining it up to hit on my side and not on the passenger side. After conquering the tree, the VW Bus grudgingly came to a stop. There were a few seconds where I did not say anything, just held on to the steering wheel trying to collect my thoughts on what had just happened, hoping Eric was okay and that Hail Mary had not sustained too much damage. I also contemplated how to explain all of this to our producer at NFL Films.

Eric broke the silence and asked if I was okay. I told him that I was good and asked about his condition. Relieved, he said that he was good, too.

The bumper had been bent from the tree, so getting out my door was difficult. The passenger door was okay so we both climbed out to find Grayson, who looked like he had seen a ghost as he stared at both of us in amazement. We walked around Hail Mary to assess the damage and to see if she could be salvaged. A paint chip on the passenger door and a small dent on the front bumper from the tree was all the damage we could find.

Ironically, Hail Mary fired right up and, as I pushed the gas, Grayson pushed her out of the thicket that had warmly embraced her moments before. We pushed her to a parking spot and called a tow truck. There was not much left to do, so in the middle of the night at a laundromat/U-haul strip mall off I-75, Grayson and I played catch until the tow truck arrived.

As I said earlier, an entire documentary could be filmed about the tow truck drivers we, unfortunately, had to come in contact with during our trip. Nothing against tow truck drivers, specifically the ones we met, but you really do not want to have to use them. It was not a particularly good sign that we had more tows than months spent away from home.

Eric's sister picked him up from the strip mall, leaving Grayson and me to ride to the house in the tow truck. The tow truck driver was in his forties, had a thick southern accent, and wore a University of Georgia cap. We gave him the address of the place where we needed the vehicle towed, and he quickly glanced at us to make sure he heard us correctly. It is always amazing to me what people will say to you when confined to a tow truck. "Gets a little dark over there," is how he characterized our destination.

What he really wanted to ask is: Why are two white guys going to a predominantly African-American, albeit affluent, neighborhood? That effectively created an uneasy feeling between Grayson and myself, and the tow truck driver. We were not rude, but after his comment we only told him what he needed to know. We had already learned everything we needed to know about him.

We towed Hail Mary to the house, and the next morning to a local repair shop. We did locate an air-cooled VW mechanic, but he was about an hour away and our AAA did not cover a tow of that distance. AAA was getting tired of us and we felt it best not to press our luck, after all, we may need them again in the near future.

The next afternoon everyone was away from the house we were staying at, so Grayson and I decided to play basketball in the driveway. About thirty minutes into the game I noticed a police car slowly driving past the house. The cop gave a good long look at us and, although I noticed him, I was not concerned about it. I had not played basketball in years so my shot was a little off, but I did not think it warranted being arrested. The cop made another pass in front of the house and, again, I thought that while odd what we were doing was probably only offensive to the game of basketball itself, we were not endangering society as a whole.

Finally, like a nervous teenager circling the block before he gets the courage to ask a girl to prom, the cop finally stopped his car and began to walk toward us, questioning what we were doing at the house.

In Cleveland, I had unknowingly walked into a field sobriety test after the game and, if I was not mistaken, had just been racially profiled. Both firsts in my life.

A neighbor started walking toward the house as well, as if to corroborate the cop's idea that we did not belong in the neighborhood. With no getaway car and opting to play basketball instead of looting the house, in the neighbor's eyes we were apparently the worst burglars since the Wet Bandits in *Home Alone*. Fortunately, Eric's brother-in-law pulled into the driveway at the point where I was starting to think our chances of getting out of this basketball game unscathed were about fifty-fifty. He, an African-American himself, began to laugh at us and assured the neighbor and the cop that our story was accurate and that all we were really guilty of was bad basketball.

The Falcons game itself was not nearly as exciting as our brief time in Georgia. How could it be? We had looked death in the face and been racially profiled. I am not sure the Falcons have ever played a football game as colorful as our two days in Tyrone.

The second half of the game saw the teams score three points between them. And although the Falcons defense held the Saints future hall of fame quarterback, Drew Brees, to just two touchdown passes, they still lost the game 17-13.

The Georgia Dome was better than the game and better than I remembered. It, too, is like a dead stadium walking. Ground has already been broken on a new stadium next to the Georgia Dome that is scheduled to open for the 2017 football season. I would like to be excited for the Falcons and the city of Atlanta, but when they tear down the Georgia Dome they will be tearing down the memories I have of taking my oldest son to his first professional football game, and I cannot ever be excited about the senseless implosion of memories.

We left Atlanta on Friday and had every intention of making it to the New England game on Sunday night with Hail Mary. She, again, had other ideas. Maybe she heard us discussing the weather report for the game and decided to sit that part of the trip out.

Back when we were in Pittsburgh for a *Sunday Night Football* game, we saw the bus NBC uses to promote the schedule. It had every *Sunday Night Football* game for the entire year listed, with a picture of one of the stars of each team. I quickly glanced at the schedule and referenced the Broncos vs. Patriots game in November while making the comment that it was going to be cold at that game. The other two agreed, but it seemed to be a hollow gesture at the time.

We had no idea of how cold it would actually be until we started getting weather reports a week or so before the game. It turned out to be the coldest home game for the Patriots in the last twenty years. The wind chill would be as low as four degrees.

I was concerned about two things when I made our travel schedule. Try not to drive at night with Hail Mary and to avoid the cold weather of the Northeast. The first concern went out the window our first week on the road and, up until now, we had done our best to avoid cold weather—other than the snow flurries that greeted us in Minneapolis. The four-degree wind chill meant we were staring the cold weather of the Northeast squarely in the face and we were much more likely to blink than Old Man Winter. Maybe Hail Mary was the smartest one on the trip.

It was supposed to be a long day of driving for us because I always like to get to our destination before our luck with Hail Mary runs out. We made a routine stop for gas and, after filling up, headed back out on the road. Shortly after getting on the highway we would be reacquainted with the glory that is VW Bus maintenance.

It started when I felt something under my seat, like when a tire goes flat, yet we were somehow still moving. Being that my seat was directly on top of the tire I could feel it, but nobody else in the vehicle could. I pulled over at another gas station fully expecting to find a flat front tire—an issue because a 1967 VW Bus uses an uncommon tire size and an even bigger issue for Hail Mary because she has two different sized tires on the front and back. The front tires are smaller than the back tires because she is slightly lowered and the smaller tires prevent her wheel wells from rubbing against the tires when she hits a bump.

I was elated to find that all four tires were still inflated and that it appeared we would be good to keep driving to Massachusetts. The elation was short-lived, however. Once we got back on the highway, the flat tire syndrome came back. We were just outside of Greensboro, North Carolina, and decided to take advantage of being in civilization by having Hail Mary looked at by a mechanic.

Even though it was closing time and the mechanics working for a national chain were cleaning up to leave for the day, they surveyed the situation and realized there was something drastically wrong with Hail Mary. They told us to not drive on it, to go to a local motel and bring it back in the morning so they could take the tire off. The mechanic warned us that we ran the risk of the entire wheel falling off if we insisted on driving any farther. It was obvious that they had a better offer on a Friday night than sitting around working on an old VW Bus and maybe that had something to do with their grim prognosis of Hail Mary, but we could not take a chance on them being right and me having to steer us to safety on three wheels. Although we had been able to avert certain pain, if not death, with no brakes while speeding toward a brick wall, surviving the loss of a wheel while driving on a major interstate at a substantial rate of speed would be asking a lot, even for the mojo of Hail Mary.

The next morning I left the others at the motel and took Hail Mary to be repaired—they would take a cab to the mechanic after check out. I arrived before the mechanic opened and impatiently waited.

One of the guys from the previous night promised he would be at work first-thing the next morning, but evidently his better offer from the previous night had prevented him from fulfilling his promise, because he was nowhere to be found.

I noticed a guy chain smoking inside his truck in the parking lot, emerging from his mobile, smoking sanctuary when the doors to the mechanic opened. His slender build was draped with the outfit of a mechanic. His trucker cap was on backward and a long black ponytail swayed from side to side as he walked. Truthfully, he looked to be the type of person who stayed dirty, almost like he slept in a coal mine every night. I thought to myself if he was the mechanic we were in trouble.

I walked into the lobby, introduced myself, and briefly described my issue with Hail Mary. If the man behind the counter could have shown less emotion or interest in helping me, I do not see how. I surrendered my keys and took a seat in the waiting room where I found that one staple of every automotive waiting room, coffee. While automotive waiting room coffee is never good coffee, it is free, and contemplating the inadequacies of the coffee somehow helps to pass the time. Maybe it is the small, white foam cups or the chalky powder posing as creamer or just the fact that you attempt to determine the age of the coffee like it was a fine wine that briefly takes your mind off of your automotive shortcomings.

Soon Hail Mary found her way onto the lift, and I meandered out to the forbidden land of the garage to meet the pony-tailed, chain-smoking, consummately dirty mechanic. He was friendly enough and had a VW story of his own to tell. I really cannot remember the specifics about that one, because the story I remember the most was of his days in a traveling circus. That is right: A traveling circus!

Now, thanks to Hail Mary, I was running out of things to see and hear because I am pretty sure after the juggling torches/guess my weight/mechanic, I had seen and heard it all. Somehow the strangeness of it did not surprise me, and I guess the expression on my face indicated that I wanted the mechanic to elaborate on his glory days in the circus.

His story started with a half lion, half tiger or what is known in the traveling circus world as a liger. He related to me the tragic story of one of his co-workers who met his demise at the paws of a liger. The worker, he said, had his back turned to the liger cage which is something they probably cover in the *How to Take Care of Your Liger* manual, but I cannot say for sure. Apparently unprovoked, the liger reached through the cage and with one swat of his paw ripped the worker's spine from his back, killing him instantly. I can neither confirm nor deny this tragic tale, but I can confirm the existence of ligers, at least on Wikipedia.

Hail Mary was deemed ready by the ex-traveling circus member that afternoon. We were eager to get back on the road, and restart our long journey to the Patriots game. After being on the road for maybe an hour, our trip took another detour outside of Durham, North Carolina, when the flat tire syndrome returned. This time we knew what it was and the severity of the issue. Evidently our mechanic in Greensboro knew more about ligers than air-cooled VWs.

Our trip to New England, just like the weather for the game, was turning south. The best we could do was look for a mechanic that specialized in VWs. Such a mechanic was not far from us, but the chances of it being open on a Saturday evening was a long shot. We called only to get a recording saying the shop would reopen on Monday, but Monday was too late to help us. We would miss not only the Patriots game, but the Redskins game as well. There was no way to make up one game, let alone two, this late in the season, and the last thing I wanted to do was potentially face colder weather in the Northeast later in the winter.

We had reached a certain comfort level of knowing that whatever happened to us or Hail Mary we would make it. There was also a comfort level of leaving Hail Mary on the doorstep of a repair shop with instructions—much like leaving a basket of kittens on the porch of a nice house with an apologetic note. I scrambled to find an envelope and hastily wrote instructions and contact information in what had become a driving rain. Must every breakdown be in the rain? Maybe the rain was a metaphor for the condition of Hail Mary.

Grayson and Eric had arranged for a taxi to take us to the Raleigh airport so we could rent a car and continue our trip around the NFL. We parked Hail Mary as far to the side of the road next to Hicks VW as we could. Since she was free from any apparent danger, I slipped through the locked gate and made my way to the office door with the keys and instructions, hoping a dog or, even worse, a liger did not jump out from behind an old VW Bug.

We loaded Hail Mary's contents into the waiting cab. As we were leaving I remember thinking this may not work out for us. Maybe Hicks VW will be upset we broke in, or maybe they will not be able to fix Hail Mary, or maybe these recent issues are a result of the crash at the Atlanta strip mall. I was afraid we had driven our last mile in Hail Mary, but would not know for sure until our newfound mechanic had a chance to survey the situation, which would be Monday at the earliest. Now our focus turned to renting a car, getting to Foxborough for the Patriots game in the bitter cold, and meeting up with an NFL Films crew in twenty-four hours.

The producer at NFL Films was disappointed to hear that Hail Mary would not be accompanying us to the game Sunday night, but suggested we take pictures of Hail Mary to put in the rental car. We had plenty of pictures of her, and rightfully so since she was the fourth member of our team, perhaps even the most important member.

Getting to Gillette Stadium was difficult because of the lack of roads around it, and the line of traffic seemed to go on forever. We had to meet the NFL Films crew at a certain time near the stadium, so Grayson quickly looked for an alternate route through an adjacent neighborhood. We emerged through the maze and traffic to find the hotel near the stadium where we were to meet with NFL Films.

As always, the NFL Films crew sprung from the minivan to offer us direction in what they needed to film. This game, however, was an extraordinary situation. The NFL Films cameraman approached the window to the rental car and offered us his take on the weather. "This is ridiculous," he said.

We shared his sentiment, so we all had the common goal of making this as easy and brief as possible. He secured us a parking spot that normally costs eighty dollars on the promise that after filming we would find parking somewhere else or pay the attendant. I think everyone except the parking lot gatekeeper knew we were not going to move our rental car after filming. Maybe he did know, but the cold weather had effectively frozen his desire to care.

I was the only person in our group with a ticket to the game, the escalating ticket prices on the secondary market along with the decreasing temperatures prevented the other two from going to the game, or maybe even wanting to go the game. If money were not an issue, the weather would still be sufficient to deter even the most hardened football fans from Texas from going to the game.

I made my way to my seat in the upper recesses of the stadium, which was near capacity at the start of the game. The Broncos, behind Peyton Manning, jumped out to a 24-0 halftime lead over the Patriots. I had personally witnessed beer after beer, purchased with the best intentions, freeze before the person made it back to their seats.

My section began to clear out even before the seemingly insurmountable halftime deficit of the Patriots. I now sat in my seat in my nearly empty section contemplating where everyone had gone and began to question why I was still sitting there. If Patriots fans did not stay and this was their team and, more importantly, their weather, how could a Cowboys fan from Texas be expected to sit through this?

I made a deal with myself that I would spend halftime in the restroom to warm up and re-emerge for the second half kickoff. When I opened the door to the restroom, it looked like my entire section had lined up against the wall. It was not the typical line to use the restroom—this was a line of Patriots fans seeking refuge from the cold weather and, possibly, from the Broncos.

The Patriots began to rally in the second half and the fans listening to the game on the speakers in the restroom started to find their seats again.

I decided to walk around the stadium between the third and fourth quarters. From the walkway I could see the parking lot where the rental car was spending the game, and also saw a tow truck driving the lot like a great white shark circling its next prey. We did not have the required parking permit hanging from our rearview mirror, which, to me, made the car stick out like a bloody carcass to that circling great white shark.

I thought if all the issues with Hail Mary were not going to stop us from seeing every stadium in sixteen weeks I would be damned if a tow truck would get in our way. I made the decision to forgo the rest of the game in favor of moving the rental car and depriving the great white of an easy meal. Fearing that it was too late, I hurriedly skipped down the stairs and ran through the parking lot to find the car resting peacefully among the ocean of cars whose owners paid for parking. I left as quickly as I could to find warmth and the place we were staying in Rhode Island, and rejoined my group in time to enjoy overtime with the luxury of a heater. In the end, the Patriots came all the way back to beat the Broncos, 34-31.

The next morning we started out early for the Redskins game that night. We had been invited to a tailgate at FedEx Field to interview some of the fans for the documentary. For most, being a Cowboys fan means you have to hate the Redskins—it is not optional, it is mandatory—or your allegiance to the Cowboys could be questioned. I do not hate the Redskins and this trip only served to lessen my negative emotions toward any team.

Truthfully, I would have been more excited about going to the game if it had been at RFK Stadium. I had watched countless games being televised from the old stadium, and would have much preferred to pay my respects in person to the home of "The Fun Bunch" and "The Hogs," monikers given to the wide receivers and offensive lineman of the Redskins when they were in their prime during the '80s. As a Cowboys fan, I did not like John Riggins or Joe Theisman, but I respected them and understood that without the Redskins there are not any Cowboys. Rivalries are what make sports great and this one, to me, was and always has been the best in the NFL, and RFK Stadium was a classic venue in what I consider the golden era of the NFL.

Except for the huge letters on the outside indicating that it is FedEx Field, you could easily mistake it for MetLife Stadium. There was not much architecturally awe-inspiring about it either. MetLife has held a Super Bowl, which in itself is not enough history to separate itself from FedEx Field. Rice Stadium in Houston has held a Super Bowl but football fans do not clamor to see a game in that stadium. Maybe I was somehow expecting to see RFK, knowing that it was not possible but still longing for the days of the once great stadium. Whatever the case, as we have done throughout the trip, we would make the most of it.

We arrived at the tailgate and were having a good time meeting fans and interviewing some of them for the documentary. I do not know what it is about alcohol and a camera that makes some people lose their minds. It had not happened to us all trip, and now we were at the second to last game of November and we finally met that guy. That guy who, with a small amount of alcohol acting as a gas can, ignites his personal fire of stupidity. During our first interview, he was making a complete idiot of himself in the background. I could have let him go and had that be what people who watch the documentary think about Redskins fans.

For some reason, the camera did strange things to us as well; it gave us power. It was not that we demanded it, more like people just gave it to us. I decided to exert my power and influence over the intoxicated fan and informed him it was not live television, and that I would appreciate it if he simply moved on. Honestly, the lens we were using prevented him from even being in the shot so it would not have mattered much.

For the next forty-five minutes, I had successfully converted the idiot on camera to the Redskins fan who was stalking me. "It isn't live television. I know it's not live television," he taunted.

That was an unpleasant experience, and as a Cowboys fan truly tested my patience. If we had not been through everything we had already experienced on this trip before we got to the Washington game, I might have taken a different course of action. My personal heckler was not worth my time or attention and as soon as we both realized that, he quickly found another tailgate to torment.

There was one Redskins tradition I had to see. RFK Stadium was obviously out, but Chief Zee was still alive. Chief Zee was the legendary fan of the Redskins who dresses as a Native American, something he has been doing for at least as long as I have been a football fan.

The Cowboys had the equivalent to Chief Zee in Crazy Ray, and the two had epic battles taunting each other and cheering on their teams during games. Crazy Ray passed away in 2007 and Chief Zee passed away during the writing of this book in 2016. I am sure Crazy Ray was waiting at the Pearly Gates and John Facenda was narrating his reunion with Chief Zee.

We finished our interviews, and I turned to my left to see what else the parking lot had to offer in the way of fans to interview, hoping not to make eye contact with "It's not live television" guy.

Then I saw him. The man, the myth, the legend: Chief Zee! Not off in the distance, but maybe ten yards away. It was like I had seen Elvis. I could not believe it and was even a little star struck. We had to get his interview. He was cordial enough, and agreed to a brief interview. We got what we could from him and then let him make his way to the stadium. I had not seen it when I first noticed him but he had a motorized wheelchair he used to navigate the vast stadium parking lot. My last image of Chief Zee was him riding off toward the stadium, headdress and all looking at me filming him saying "God bless you." That was Chief Zee and it could not have been any better.

The game-time temperature flirted with the freezing mark, which was balmy compared to the night before at the Patriots game. Grayson and I sat in different sections but met up at halftime. He complained about how cold he was, and I, having sat through most of a game with a single-digit wind chill, convinced him that it was not that bad.

The Redskins were never really in it, losing 27-6 to the 49ers. Once again I felt cheated out of the Redskins experience. Except for Chief Zee these were not the Redskins I thought I knew. The stadium was half empty and the majority of the people in the stands were 49ers fans. There was no "Hail to the Redskins" playing as fans dressed as hogs jumped up and down causing the stands to shake visibly.

As a fan of football from the late '70s and early '80s, I wanted more. I wanted the history of the Redskins, which seemed, at least for this night, to be as lost as my days of carrying my NFL lunchbox to elementary school.

A good friend of mine had been following our progress around the county. His wife, whom I knew fairly well, was from the DC area, and since her parents still lived there my friend paved the way for us to stay at their place following the game that night. I had never met her father or stepmother, but at this point it saved us fifty dollars and that would probably be needed to help pay for Hail Mary's impending repair bill.

After the game, we drove to the townhouse where our host was waiting at the door for us. He was slender, with a goatee and Redskins cap that complemented his burgundy turtleneck. He immediately inquired about Hail Mary, almost as if we were family and she had been in his thoughts and prayers. I told him what had happened and neither one of us could hide our disappointment, but I let him know that earlier in the day we had talked to the VW mechanic and Hail Mary would be ready tomorrow. That seemed to appease him or at the very least got us in the front door.

The townhouse looked relatively small from the outside so I was expecting us to be a bigger intrusion than we were. When we made our way inside it was obvious that we could live there a lifetime and never see much of each other. He offered us some bottled water and blankets that we gladly took on our way to the basement. The basement was completely furnished with a living area and a bedroom.

Our host was ready to go to bed so we quickly said goodnight to him, acclimated ourselves to our new surroundings and fell asleep. Our plan was just to wake up whenever and start driving to pick up Hail Mary. The next morning we learned at around six o'clock that our host had other plans for us.

I was sleeping on the couch and heard someone coming down the stairs to the basement. From the silhouette, I could clearly see that it was our host. "You guys up yet?" he asked.

I raised my head. Up yet? No, but we were now. I got the feeling our staying there was not completely signed off on by his wife. Feeling uneasy and not wanting to be there any longer than necessary, I urged everyone to get ready to leave. After gathering our belongings we made our way to the top of the stairs not knowing what to expect. To our surprise, our host had a fresh pot of coffee and a warm fire to greet us. He was still wearing his Redskins cap and burgundy turtleneck from the previous night, and it struck me that he was obviously the type of fan we needed for the film.

At first he was reluctant to give us an interview, but soon began to warm up to the strangers from the basement. The interview turned out to be four guys, sitting around a fire, drinking coffee, and talking football. Despite our abrupt awakening, I could not imagine how things could get any better. Our host ended up being one of my favorite interviews throughout the trip. He shared my sentiment about RFK Stadium and a love for football. I can sit around and listen to old coaches, no matter if it is football or baseball, talking for hours and not get bored; the same feeling I got from all of us sharing our football stories.

I am not sure if he enjoyed our company as much as I enjoyed his, or if he understood how much we appreciated him giving us a place to stay for the night. Either way, it was time to move on and pick up Hail Mary.

I had spoken to someone on the phone about the repairs, but never about the actual cost of the repairs. At this point our most expensive repair was $600 for the new alternator, so when I was talking on the phone and authorizing additional work to be done that was my point of reference. I thought nothing could cost more than an alternator. Her current issue should be a simple fix, so there was no way it would cost us more than $600. The other places that tried to fix the issue only charged a couple-hundred dollars—that should have told me something, but I was oblivious. We just wanted to finish the tour in Hail Mary by any means necessary so I was willing to pay something similar to a new alternator.

To me, the North Carolina accent with its long draw—similar to a Texas accent—is what makes the state what it is. Everyone we met in North Carolina could not have been nicer, but we had left Hail Mary on the doorstep with a "please fix me" note, so it was pretty obvious we were at the mercy of the VW mechanic. I had flashbacks to *National Lampoon's Vacation* when Clark Griswold is paying for repairs after launching the family truckster fifty yards in the Arizona desert. In the film, he asked the mechanic how much for the repairs to which the mechanic replied, "All of it boy."

That, fortunately, was not the case. The mechanic did not take advantage of us, but when he gave me the bill of over $1,300 it took the wind out of my sails. I had $1,600 in my account, thinking we were looking good until the end of the trip. Now we had a VW Bus that looked and sounded great, but I did not know if I had enough money to make it to the end of December.

CHAPTER 11

Sad Goodbye

Detroit and Indianapolis
(29 teams and 20,117 miles)

You may not win the Super Bowl. Your kids may not go on to be doctors and lawyers and everything may not go perfectly. That doesn't mean it was a bad plan or the wrong thing. It's just like a football season. Everything's not going to go perfect.

– Tony Dungy

The plan was to drive to Cincinnati and stay with my friend Patrick again until Thanksgiving Day. We would drive to Detroit for the game then back to Cincinnati to wait for the Indianapolis Colts game the following Sunday. Staying with Patrick would save us some money, something I desperately needed to do at this point, and also allow us to spend some time in one place.

Up until now, with the exception of Minnesota, we had not stayed in one place for longer than two days. Because of this, December would be the easiest but most difficult month of the tour. We only had four games after Thanksgiving, and that meant we had to stay in one place for up to a week at a time. Remaining in one place a week at a time sounded ridiculously difficult at this point, not to mention expensive since even the shadiest of motels gets kind of pricey a week at a time.

We still had to make it to December via Detroit, but we were feeling pretty confident that $1,300 in repairs would buy us another five weeks with Hail Mary. Her heater was now fully functional, but we still were not going to be able to wear shorts and tank tops while driving to Detroit on Thanksgiving. Although the heater provided some relief, we still wore heavy jackets, hats, and gloves in Hail Mary. We were driving through snow on the ground and some falling from the sky, but compared to New England, and even Washington, this was comfortable.

Detroit is one of two teams that traditionally play a home game on Thanksgiving; with Dallas being the other team. My family being Cowboys fans meant we ate during the Lions game. It was on, but I always viewed it as the second- or third-best game of the day behind the Cowboys and the rivalry game between the Texas Longhorns and Texas A&M Aggies. My almost indifference toward the game may come from the fact that the Lions rarely field a Super Bowl contender and is one of the few teams to never play in a Super Bowl. That may have something to do with it, but my angst toward the Lions stems from, in large part, the history between the Lions and the Cowboys.

I am not sure why playing the Lions in Detroit has always given the Cowboys issues. From 1981-1991, the Lions hosted the Cowboys five different times, winning four of those games. Recent history has been better for the Cowboys, but not much. Since 1992, the Cowboys have only won three of the seven games played in Detroit.

The most hated team in the NFL are my Dallas Cowboys, something that was never more evident than when we were sitting in the Saints suite in New Orleans after their game against the Bills.

We watched the Lions and Cowboys game in Detroit on the television screens. The Cowboys were winning, but the Lions had time for one last drive. The Cowboys defense folded like a lawn chair in a hurricane, and the Lions offense went down the field and scored a touchdown to win the game. The suite broke out in cheers except for this guy.

Why are these people cheering? I wondered. Neither of the teams are in the Saints division, and it is still too early in the season to scoreboard-watch for the playoffs. I determined it was out of pure hatred for my Dallas Cowboys.

To the larger point about Detroit, my Dallas Cowboys had done like they always had and found a way to lose in Detroit. For that I held a grudge but, like most of my animosity toward other NFL teams, that would soon change.

I wanted to visit the Pontiac Silverdome, the site of Cowboys tragedies from years past, but that stadium no longer exists. The stadium is technically still standing, but the roof is gone and although once great, it, like much of Detroit, has been left to rot and decay.

I was not sure what to expect from Detroit. I had heard and seen all of the pictures depicting the demise of Detroit and found it hard to believe that anyone still lived there, let alone enough people to support professional franchises in all four major sports. The reality of it is that the area around Ford Field is one of the best environments in the NFL. Comerica Park, with two majestic tigers guarding the gates where the Tigers play baseball, is adjacent to the stadium. The Honolulu blue is everywhere, and football is obviously a time for the city to put all of their doom and gloom behind them and celebrate. I walked into the stadium and got an instant sense of wow. It was much nicer than I expected and I became lost in the greatness of Detroit. Before I was even aware of it, the atmosphere of the stadium and the Lions began to overtake my memories of countless Cowboys losses.

My grudge against Detroit began to waiver in favor of the people of the city and the Lions fans. It was Thanksgiving and my mind was flush with family memories of watching football together. There was also something about Detroit and Thanksgiving that had the sense of family prevalent in the atmosphere around the stadium.

We managed to find an older gentlemen wearing a Detroit Lions stocking cap with a fuzzy ball on top and asked him what having a game on Thanksgiving meant to him personally.

"It means my dad taking me to Tiger Stadium. That was a long time ago," he replied with tears welling in his eyes. His love for his father through this game hit a soft spot with me, since my father and I can always find a way to talk about sports, and it is always an interesting and rewarding conversation.

Back in September, I had, without thinking, blurted out that we were going with "No Shave November." I had never grown a beard and, like our struggles of keeping Hail Mary on the road, I struggled to keep the hair on my face.

As I walked up the stairs to my seat in Ford Field a fan sitting on an aisle seat stopped me. "I like what you're doing," he said. At first I thought he was talking about us going to every NFL stadium in sixteen weeks, that somehow he had seen me and recognized me, but from where? "Brett Favre. The Favre thing with the beard," he said, quickly ending my excitement. "That's it. You got me," I replied with a smile.

In his defense, the Lions were playing Green Bay and quarterback Brett Favre is a Packers legend. Favre and I are both extremely attractive with beards. That is not entirely true but there is a definitely a resemblance.

This game meant November was over for us, as were my days of being mistaken for Brett Favre. The Aaron Rodgers injury we had witnessed against the Bears in Green Bay had effectively ended the Packers season, and they were simply playing out the schedule. There may have been no better example of that than the Thanksgiving Day game against the Lions. The Packers led 10-3 early in the game, but Detroit would go on to score thirty-seven unanswered points to win 40-10.

I spent most of the drive back to Cincinnati missing my family on Thanksgiving. It had been a long time since I had been home. We only had four games left, but those four games would take as many weeks to complete, and we had to go all the way to Seattle. On a day like Thanksgiving, and knowing what was ahead of us, the light at the end of the tunnel seemed no closer than when we were struggling with the September heat in Texas. I say knowing what was ahead of us, but nobody could predict what was truly ahead of us.

The Saturday after Thanksgiving we had taken Hail Mary out in Cincinnati. When we returned to Patrick's house, the clutch fell to the floorboard. I had nothing at all in the way of a clutch, so if it was not fixed, we would not be able to shift gears or go in reverse. More importantly, if it was not fixed soon, we would not make it to Indianapolis the next day for the Colts game.

I called Brian at Drew's Off-Road. Fortunately he was open, but only until noon or so. We had to hurry so we quickly called AAA for what looked to be our last tow of the trip.

Brian believed he knew what the issue was but, unfortunately, that issue required us to pull the engine out of Hail Mary. Since I enjoy seeing all of the parts and understanding how everything works and fits together, I was more than content with him removing the engine. Through the whole thing I was confident in Brian's ability to get us on the road to Indianapolis.

With the engine out of the VW Bus, Brian began to tinker with various parts, and with every twist or turn of a part I pretended to better understand the intricacies of the air-cooled VW engine—as if at the end of the trip I would be able to open my own repair shop. I remain, however, as clueless as the day we left my driveway in Hail Mary.

With a hint of regret, Brian informed us that what he thought was the issue was not the issue, and we had not really needed to take out the engine, at all. After getting the engine back in place, Brian checked the clutch cable and deemed it to be the root of our current issue. He went into the store to grab another cable off the shelf and returned empty-handed—they were out of clutch cables, and we were out of luck.

In our moment of despair, the voice of John, our mechanic in Austin came to me like Obi-Wan Kenobi to Luke Skywalker.

"Take all of the parts you can think of," his voice said as he went through a list of parts I needed to have on-hand for the trip, and a clutch cable was included in that non-exhaustive list.

I excitedly rummaged through our Husky trunk that served as storage for the extra parts like a magician going through his bag of tricks. There it was at the bottom: the silver cable that would help get us to Indianapolis and, hopefully, all the way to Seattle. Brian replaced the cable and took Hail Mary for a stroll around the back lot to make sure it had the right amount of tension.

As long as I live I will never forget what he said next. His words would come back to me in fewer than twenty minutes of being on the road. "Something about your brakes feels weird," he said with a puzzled look on his face. "Will they go out?" I asked in a near panic.

He assured me that they would not, but they did not seem right. Drew's Off-Road was past closing so we headed back to the house in Cincinnati, not thinking too much about our brakes. With just a few miles left of our journey for the day, we drove along a major thoroughfare then took the exit back to Patrick's house. Hail Mary sensed that our path home was riddled with traffic lights and that this was the perfect time to stage one last revolt.

I approached the first stale red light and the unforgettable, but unfortunately not entirely unfamiliar, feeling of the brakes going out rushed from my right foot all the way through my body. There were no cars ahead of us and, once again sans horn, Hail Mary barreled through the intersection unscathed. I do not know if other cars saw us and stopped or if we were like a game of Frogger and missed all of the cars. I did not have time to contemplate the degree of our good fortune and was becoming more emotionally bankrupt with every passing moment.

Ahead of us was another stale red light on which we would roll the dice once again, slipping through without even the smallest benefit of alerting others of our arrival into the intersection. Once more we emerged on the other side of the light unharmed. After the second red light, there was a modest hill we had to climb, but there was no way we would make it up the entire hill in our current situation. Consequently, we would be rolling back down into the intersection within the next few seconds if our trajectory did not change soon.

Learning from the episode at the strip mall in Atlanta, I decided to turn up a street to help Hail Mary slow down. She slowed down and began rolling back toward the busy street where fate, luck, God or maybe all three had intervened just seconds before to keep us safe.

I told Eric to get out of the bus and keep her in place while I got something to put behind the back tires to prevent her from being destructively reckless. He took my advice, leaving the passenger side door open. I looked back and saw a telephone pole that would have tested the structural integrity of the door and probably won. I calmly asked Eric to shut the door as Hail Mary continued progressing down the hill toward the street.

With the help of some people who may have witnessed our red light adventure from the beginning, Eric was able to hold Hail Mary in place while I found rocks to put behind the back wheels.

If Hail Mary was going to go out, she was going out with a bang. This last episode was the end of the road for her as far as this trip was concerned. She had finally convinced me that she had had enough of seeing the country and just wanted to be back home. We all wanted to be back home, and if it was as simple a matter as running out of brakes, we might have been content with being four games shy of completing the trip. For the rest of us, it was not that simple, and if Hail Mary was an unwilling or incapable participant we were still going to complete the trip.

We made arrangements to have Hail Mary towed back to Patrick's house where she would spend part of the winter before being towed back to Brian at Drew's Off-Road; her home until we could pick her up in May of the following year. The plan now was to rent a car in Cincinnati and drive it to the game in Indianapolis. Then we would drive the rental car to Austin and pick up my daily driver to finish the tour. It may have added hours and hundreds of miles to our trip, but when you are covering over 25,000 miles in sixteen weeks what is a few hundred more?

We put the stickers on the back of Hail Mary, said our goodbyes and took the invitation to Steve Sabol's memorial in the rental car with us.

I can remember backing slowly down the driveway and watching Hail Mary, almost as if we were leaving a loved one after the holidays. It was not a great feeling, and I was truly sad driving away knowing it would be months before I would see her again. To tell the truth, I was just as excited to get Hail Mary back home as I was to go to the final four games of the trip. Since the day I bought her, she has been a part of my family and my soul.

Putting all of that behind me, we made the short drive to Indianapolis. It was a little less than 300 miles, which for us was considered a short trip. We had passed the stadium during one of our drives through

Indianapolis on our way to a game in a different city. It was apparent from afar that the stadium would be a unique experience because of the exterior's almost barn-like qualities. When we had passed it a couple of months earlier, I tried to imagine the day when we would go to the Colts game at that stadium; not so much for the experience that the stadium offered, but because that meant we would have made it to December.

Football fields, as I stated earlier, are all the same. They have the same measurements with different surfaces and different paint and logos to mask their overall uniformity. What makes baseball such an appealing spectator sport to me is that all of the fields are different. No two baseball stadiums are the same, each feeling different from the next. Other than the distance between the bases and the pitching mound to home, baseball fields can vary greatly. But when it gets down to it, all football fields are essentially the same. What separates one field from another is either the history of the games played on the field and/or the actual stadium surrounding the field. There is no better example of this in the NFL than Lucas Oil Stadium.

On our walk toward the stadium, I struck up a conversation with one of the myriad of Colts fans wearing Andrew Luck jerseys. I do not remember why or how my conversation with the young, twenty-something, clean-cut, typical Midwesterner started, but the more we talked, the more passionate he became—not about the Colts, but rather about the stadium and the Midwest. I stopped and told Grayson and Eric that we needed his interview for the documentary. His fire and passion were evident through his plea for tourists to understand where they were and what they were seeing.

"People don't understand what they are looking at. This is the heartland of America!" he said as if planting a flag for all the Midwest. Part tour guide, part Colts fan, he turned his focus to the stadium itself, explaining how it was designed to look and feel like a barn because that is a symbol of the Midwest. After the loss of Hail Mary earlier that morning, his pregame speech served to rekindle my excitement about going to the stadium.

There is a true sense of grandeur when you walk into Lucas Oil Stadium. It emphasizes the rich history of motorsports in Indianapolis, filling the walls and ceilings with a liberal supply of colorful decorations from the world of Indy Car and NASCAR. As I walked toward the stands to get a view of the field, I saw a large glass wall beyond the opposite end zone that perfectly frames downtown Indianapolis. The light permeates the window and saturates the stadium and field.

As we continued walking to our seats we saw banners of fans hanging in the concourse, along with a huge sculpture jutting from the wall of the torso of a generic Colts player extending his hands as if diving for an imaginary ball.

I am opposed to teams moving, and as someone growing up with the Baltimore Colts I was of the opinion that this was a "new" team, void of history.

The Colts ripped out the hearts of Baltimore when they moved in 1984, and for that I had some underlying ill will toward them. Like a bad divorce, eventually you get over it and it was obvious that Indianapolis was a very special place for football. In the basketball and motorsports state of Indiana, the Colts had created a palace while paying tribute to what makes the Midwest so great.

The Colts were playing the Titans, and I could not help but think of our friend, Titanman. He would not be leading fans in his section today, but he undoubtedly was watching the game. Much like the game in Nashville between these two teams, the Titans had a chance to win only to falter in the fourth quarter. The Colts and the Midwest rejoiced in the 22-14 victory and we were soon on our way to Austin.

CHAPTER 12

A Grand Experience

Arizona, Oakland, and Seattle
(32 teams and 23,933 miles)

Football is unconditional love.

– Tom Brady

Hail Mary had managed to turn two-hour trips into five-hour odysseys for most of our three months on the road. Now, even without her being physically with us, she had turned an 1,100-mile trip to Scottsdale, Arizona, into a 2,100-mile trip to Scottsdale via Austin.

The difference between traveling in Hail Mary and a modern vehicle is almost comparable to the difference in driving and flying. If we were going directly from Indianapolis to Scottsdale in Hail Mary, there would be little guarantee that we would make it. Now we were driving twice as far and could make it in a few days as opposed to possibly never. Even having said that, I would have preferred to be still traveling with her.

I was looking forward to seeing Arizona and taking a detour along the way to Sedona and the Grand Canyon. Something about Arizona had always appealed to me even though I had only been there a couple of times and never for very long.

The Cardinals were a divisional rival of the Cowboys when they were in St. Louis. As a kid, I had a soft spot for the Cardinals and some of their players like Jim Hart—probably because my father is also named Jim—Ottis Anderson and Pat Tilley. What I really liked was their helmets, especially their logo. It was a cardinal, but not like the realistic cardinal of the St. Louis Cardinals baseball team that gave you a pleasant, light, airy feeling, much like a butterfly. The football St. Louis Cardinals logo had a bold, aggressive cardinal, much like a hawk or a bald eagle. It had a harsher look than the open grass and sunny fields look of the baseball team. Growing up, it was that logo that made the Cardinals mini-pennant one of the best-looking on my wall. One of a few teams to have white helmets, the red of the cardinal popped off the helmet and popped off the pennant when I would look up at the different teams on my wall.

The Cardinals never really had a great team. They had good teams with possibilities, but as a Cowboys fan it was okay to have a soft spot for them because they never posed a significant threat to my real team.

The first game I ever saw in person was the Cowboys playing the Cardinals in Texas Stadium. My family and I were a few rows from the top of the stadium for that game, which meant after thirty-five years my seats to games had improved by only a few rows, if any. On the bright side, we were close to the fifty-yard line.

I remember seeing those bright red uniforms with the white helmets of the Cardinals that gave context to that pennant in my room. They could never replace the classic white and blue uniforms of the Cowboys with the silver helmets and the iconic blue star, but it was still a cool uniform to me.

The Cardinals moved to Arizona for the 1988 season. Despite being more attached to the Cardinals than the Colts, or at least as attached as a die-hard Dallas Cowboys fan could be, I did not hold the same ill will toward the Cardinals for moving from St. Louis as I did for the Colts moving to Indianapolis. Maybe because the Colts moved first, and by the time the Cardinals moved I had learned to accept the dark side of professional sports. That could have been it, but more likely it was that the Baltimore Colts had beaten my Dallas Cowboys in a Super Bowl. The game was played in 1971 so I was not even born yet, but that did not seem to matter.

My older brother bought a Colts helmet when we were younger, and I could not understand why he would not want a Cowboys helmet like mine. Did he not understand the history? I was five years old and knew I could never wear any helmet other than the Cowboys. Even if he was not a Cowboys fan, the next best helmet would have been the Oilers—they were at least in Texas! As a toddler wearing Toughskins, I knew Houston was a lot better than Baltimore, wherever Baltimore may be. The Oilers being ahead of the Colts in the fan pecking order was obviously lost on my brother.

We arrived in Arizona early, our ability to tell driving distances through time was apparently still a little off from all those days spent with Hail Mary. Off of Highway 70 in San Carlos, Arizona, there is the Apache Gold Casino, drawing people in with all of the glitz and glamour of a truck stop in Las Vegas. To us, it was one of the nicest places we stayed the entire trip. Seeing all that the casino had to offer crossed our minds, but since we had visions of actually staying in Las Vegas, whatever money we would lose in Arizona would be taking money away from the casinos in Vegas.

The room was not extremely luxurious by most standards, but it was not the cheap furniture sitting on top of cheaper linoleum designed to look like wood we had grown accustomed to, so we were happy.

With time to kill, Grayson and I considered going on a Shamanic counseling and healing retreat led by a member of one of the Indian tribes in Arizona. We thought a journey into our souls would be an interesting experience, as well as something else we could put in the documentary. Although I think Eric was indifferent to the experience, he would have gone with us to capture it on camera.

I sat outside in an open field and called the phone number we had found on Craigslist, since all the good Shamans are on Craigslist.

The Native American—who would have led us—answered, and I asked about the spiritual journey, how long it took to find the meaning of life and, maybe more importantly, what this newfound knowledge was going to cost us? It was a daylong trip and was almost $200 each. Once again we considered that the money we lose in Arizona could not be gambled away in a Las Vegas casino. I think it would have been a great experience and one for which I would gladly return to Arizona, but we needed our money to last the next three weeks. Besides, after three months and one week on the road in a VW Bus, I had a pretty good grasp of the meaning of life or, at least, my life.

The University of Phoenix Stadium is part of a shopping center and located next to the Gila River Arena where the professional hockey team plays. It sits on a large, mostly flat, area of the desert that helps give the giant silver stadium the appearance of an alien spaceship.

At the time, the Cardinals were a winning team threatening to make the playoffs in perhaps the toughest division in all of professional football, yet there were not that many people tailgating for the game. Their opponent, the St. Louis Rams, seemed to have as many fans—if not more—than the hometown Cardinals. It seemed odd because St. Louis is not that close to Arizona, they were not having a good year—even by their standards—the team does not have the national following like the Cowboys, Steelers or Browns, so why were there so many Rams fans at the game in Scottsdale?

The answer should have been obvious to longtime NFL fans, but it was not. They were not fans of the St. Louis Rams, but rather fans of the Los Angeles Rams. Despite their team abandoning them in the mid-'90s, these fans never abandoned their team and came to the Rams game in Arizona every year. Not only that but they have started a movement on Facebook to reclaim what they see as being rightfully theirs, the Rams. The movement to bring the Rams back to Los Angeles has over 48,000 likes, and the fans we talked to view the team as simply being on a twenty-year vacation. Their loyalty and devotion rival that of any team in any sport, and validated my opinion that the Rams belong in Los Angeles and that they have always belonged in Los Angeles—never more evident than on our trip to Arizona.

One of the fans we met could have walked into the Rams locker room and been mistaken for a player. More like a kicker or a punter, but the point is he wore the helmet, shoulder pads, jersey, padded pants, cleats, wristbands, and even gloves. He told us he was born during a Rams game; specifically that he was born toward the end of a Rams game that forced his father to choose between seeing a last-second field goal or seeing his son being born. We never got confirmation on how that worked out for his father, but the Rams won the game.

The other fan we met wore a glorious Eric Dickerson Rams jersey. The body was white with blue numbers that illuminated in the Arizona sunshine. Even more glorious than the jersey—incidentally one of my favorites in football history—was what he wore on top of his head: A watermelon that had been neatly carved out to prevent it from moving was perched atop his head like the crown of a king.

The Melonheads are a group of rabid fans that attended the Los Angeles Rams games wearing watermelons on their heads. I am not sure of the symbolic meaning behind the watermelon, and while some questions are best left unanswered, my thinking is that these fans were at a tailgate where vast amounts of alcohol were being consumed. They also had a bounty of watermelon and, in an intoxicated state of euphoria and enhanced creativity, decided to carve the watermelons into hats. A black marker is used to write a tribute to their favorite Rams player, making each watermelon unique.

The Cardinals still wear, for the most part, those jerseys and helmets that I liked so much as a young football fan. The actual Cardinals logo has been changed slightly to give it an even more intense look. Unlike the Dolphins, which aborted all tradition in their recent logo redesign—I still shake my head at that one—the Cardinals simply tweaked their traditional logo.

On the outside of the stadium, the Cardinals have an emotionally moving tribute to one of their most beloved players of all-time, Pat Tillman. A free spirit who went to Arizona State University, Tillman was drafted by the Cardinals in the seventh round. His loyalty to the Arizona Cardinals was immeasurable, which he proved by remaining with the team despite receiving a more lucrative offer from the St. Louis Rams.

After the September 11th attacks, Tillman left professional football altogether to enlist in the Army, and lost his life fighting in Afghanistan in 2004. Although he never attained the status as a professional football player that he had achieved in college when he was elected to the College Football Hall of Fame, Tillman left an indelible mark on the entire NFL, not just the Cardinals. His commitment and sacrifice to the team and our country is memorialized with a statue and pool at the front of the stadium. If I ever bought a jersey for another player of a team other than the Cowboys, it would be Pat Tillman's.

I found myself looking at the statue and across the pool and thinking about what kind of statement I was making with my life. I thought of my children back in Austin and hoped they would find some inspiration from me living my dream that would convince them to be who they are. While I cannot measure up to the sacrifice and example that Pat Tillman set for all of us, hopefully, at least for my family, this trip, the documentary, and possibly this book, will serve to inspire them to live their dreams. "Pat Tillman provided an example we should all cuddle up to," a Cardinals fan we interviewed summed it up perfectly.

NFL Films met us at the Arizona game, and we walked around inside the stadium with the cameras, as well as other fans, fixated on us. The puzzled look on their faces almost screamed: "Who are those guys and what makes them so special?"

Our seats were in the upper deck, seemingly miles removed from the field, but with the help of NFL Films we were able to sit in the lower area a few rows from the field. Not for the game, but just long enough for them to get us and the field in the same shot. After we finished filming, I took one last look, exhaled and realized that the game was probably totally different at this level.

Except for Dallas and Jacksonville, all of our seats left something to be desired. Regardless, I was living not only my dream, but the dream of a lot of people, and for that I was truly fortunate.

The Cardinals never trailed in the game and won 30-10. I hoped the Los Angeles Rams fans were, at least, content with seeing their team play in person despite the outcome. They were great fans and deserved better than one game a year—they deserve a team. In 2016, the Rams returned to Los Angeles, effectively leaving St. Louis without a team—again.

I was excited about Arizona for both the Cardinals game and visiting Sedona. Although we had missed out on the Shamanic counseling and finding the meaning of life with a Native American off of Craigslist, Arizona had been perfect.

The Grand Canyon was on our way to Las Vegas and something I had to see. Since winter is an off time for visiting the largest hole in the ground, the road leading to the park was mostly desolate. I kept thinking the closer we got to the Grand Canyon the more likely it seemed the world was about to end—not in an apocalyptic sense, but in the sense that the road ends and there is a big hole in the ground for as far as you can see.

It was twenty-five dollars to get into the park, money I had earmarked for Vegas, but I had to see this. My only impression of the Grand Canyon was Clark Griswold looking out across the horizon with his wife Ellen after he had just robbed a motel. He spent a few seconds impatiently soaking it all in before hurriedly leaving. In the movie, his antics were intended to be funny, so I was expecting a little more from my experience.

When we were in Nashville we discovered a fantastic beer called Hap & Harry's. I enjoyed it so much that we purchased a couple of six packs and rationed them during the rest of the trip. The Grand Canyon, however, was a cause for celebration and consequently a Hap & Harry's moment. There was still snow on the ground, and I walked with a triumphant purpose toward the end of the Earth with Nashville's finest beer in one hand and the football in the other. Needing to enjoy my refreshment of choice at the optimal temperature, I set the Hap & Harry's down in the snow next to the railing of the Grand Canyon fearing that I may never see the beer again.

The Grand Canyon is difficult to put into words. I think the people who named it probably did what we were doing. Enjoyed a beer while looking out, and contemplated a name. They either ran out of beer or had a limited vocabulary, so they settled on "Grand." The canyon is everything the word Grand is meant to convey and then some.

We walked along the railing and took in everything our surroundings had to offer. People were scattered around the edge posing and taking pictures with the Grand Canyon as their backdrop. We, as you might expect by now, played catch at one of the very few places in the world that offers such a high stakes game. One errant pass and the football would require a jackass to retrieve it, and if we lost our football this far into the trip, and at the Grand Canyon no less, we would be the real jackasses.

There was a little bit of a Clark Griswold moment in our time at the Grand Canyon, but there is not that much to do there and, although it was visually impressive, we had places to go and football to see.

We were headed to Vegas for a few days, and the Cowboys were playing an important game against the Bears that night. I had visions of grandeur of watching the game from one of my favorite places on Earth: the Race and Sports Book at Caesars Palace. Although the reason we were going to Las Vegas was not a direct result of us being gamblers, it helped, and we needed a cheap place to stay while we waited for the game in Oakland on the following Sunday.

There are no cheaper rooms to be had than in the city that never sleeps. I thought we had died and gone to heaven when we booked the "luxurious" Hooters Casino Hotel for less than twenty dollars a night, tax included. It is a block from the strip and across the street from the MGM Grand.

We drove all day and part of the night. I could see the lights of the city when the Cowboys game started. Through the radio, Danny White, the ex-Cowboys quarterback, provided the play-by-play—*The* Danny White. Since he is not exactly a beloved figure in Dallas and not part of the Cowboys radio network, why was he doing the game? I felt sorry for him, really. He was always one of my favorite players and led the Cowboys to three straight conference championship games, but suffered the same fate as most people who replace a legend; never living up to their predecessor and, in this case, Danny White was never Roger Staubach, and he was never going to be, no matter how many games he won.

While I hate to be the one to deliver that piece of bad news to Danny White, he was delivering equally bad news to Cowboys fans that night. The Bears were winning the game in what could only be described as weather conditions similar to those we faced in New England, and the game was essentially over by the second quarter.

We made it inside the Hooters Casino Hotel, but not to our room. I went into the bar to join what was essentially the viewing party for the end of the Cowboys season. I had kind of expected the Cowboys season to be over without a Super Bowl, but did not expect it to end quite so suddenly or in the second week of December.

As sports fans, we are eternally optimistic that if our team is playing in a game, we could win. "If everything goes right, we can win this game ... If the ball bounces our way, good things can happen ... If our quarterback throws for five touchdowns and runs for five more, then I like our chances," according to fans of significant underdogs.

You have to actually be in the game to win it, and the Cowboys loss meant their season would end after three more games. The Cowboys one-sided game also meant the Race and Sports Book at Caesars Palace would have to wait for another day.

I love to play no-limit Texas Hold'em, and playing in the World Series of Poker in Vegas is something I have aspired to do in my life, even before I go to a Super Bowl in person, something that was confirmed by the New York Jets fans we met back in October.

I occasionally play in the low-stakes tournaments at the Luxor, and have played in other tournaments, including Hooters, but for some reason I am comfortable at the thirty-five dollar tournaments at the Luxor. The last time I was in Vegas I finished third in a tournament and walked away with a hundred bucks or so. While I am not ready to retire on my winnings or play the high stakes games, it is not bad to get paid for doing something you love to do. Since I was low on money for this trip and we had no free places to stay for the rest of December, I was not sure I would be able to afford even the low-stakes tournaments.

Grayson had done well playing blackjack, however, and loaned me enough for the entry fee at the Luxor. Eric accompanied me to the casino, and I told him if I won he would get the hamburger he wanted from Gordon Ramsay BurGR in Planet Hollywood, and I would, in turn, get my corn dog from Hot Dog on a Stick—the best corn dogs in the world—which reminded me of going to the mall when I was a kid. Most of them have since closed down, but the Luxor is home to one of the last remaining holdouts.

At a low-stakes poker tournament, it is important to try and determine who can play, as well as who knows the odds of making a hand and who does not. Since it is impossible to tell by just looking at someone if they know how to play poker or not, you have to pay attention to how they bet and the hands they turn over. Some people wear sunglasses to make others at the table think they are professionals, but since professional poker players are not found loitering at the thirty-five dollar tournaments, wearing sunglasses is usually a tell that they, in fact, cannot play but have watched it on television. And there is always a loud-mouthed player the dealers seem to know. I am not sure how they know them, but maybe they live in Vegas and frequent these types of tournaments. These players need to be handled with caution because they have played enough, bluffed enough, and won enough that they can smell the true, amateur, "I saw this on television and wanted to give it a try" players.

Eric had bet on a basketball game and was watching his money slowly leave his pockets at the Sports Book across from the Poker Room at the Luxor.

One by one, the other poker players took themselves out of the game through either desperation or stupidity. I benefited from their inadequacies and after about an hour of playing, found myself at the final table—miraculously in the final four. Eric had lost interest in the basketball game by this time and watched the tournament from behind the glass that segregated the Poker Room from the Sports Book.

I was down to my last few chips and decided—with two clubs, one of them being the ace—it was time to go all-in. Not yet in the money, there was not only my tournament life at stake, but Eric's hamburger and my corn dog, as well. Two clubs came on the turn and another on the river. Flush! I had survived! I did not advance, but I survived and was in better shape to make a run for the money and that all-important corn dog.

The tournament was now down to two players, me and someone who, like me, enjoyed the game but did not see a need to speak that much. I had the best hand and the most chips so I pushed everything to the center of the table and went all-in. My opponent, to his credit, had a good hand as well. The dealer turned over the five cards and announced me as the winner. I got up from the table, victorious with both hands in the air. "Wait a minute—he has a straight," the dealer clarified.

The loss crippled me, and I went out the next hand in second place. But winning enough of a surplus to afford the hamburger and corn dog was victory enough for me.

I am always happy to be in Las Vegas, but this time I was happy to see it in our rearview mirror. We were two games and two weeks away from finishing the tour, and it could not come soon enough.

The Raiders, the next team on our schedule, is one of those classic teams in professional football.

Steeped in history with an eccentric late owner, Al Davis, and a colorful cast of former players like Lyle Alzado and Lester Hayes, the Raiders to me were similar in a way to the Cowboys, but at the same time their polar opposite—America's Team, but not in the same way as the Cowboys.

The Raiders are villainous and often considered the dirtiest team in the NFL, a reputation that seems to be embraced by the organization and is reflected in the culture of the team. The Raiders played to win and do not care what harm they inflicted on their opponents or themselves.

Those dirty play characteristics are reflected in the reputation of the infamous Raiders fans in what is known as the Black Hole, a legendary place in the football world much like the cantina in *Star Wars*. The place is aligned with the "scum and villainy" of NFL fans, and once you enter the Black Hole your survival is in some doubt. This fear, of course, is the perspective of someone from the outside looking in. The media portrays the Raiders and their fans in this light partly because that is how they want to be seen by the rest of the NFL, and maybe because they are from the rough part of the Bay Area. If the Cowboys were not my team, it would probably be Oakland. I somehow identified with the image of the Raiders.

N.W.A., the most popular rap group among the Caucasian suburban dwelling youth of the late '80s and early '90s, had further helped convince me that I identified with the street images of California. I had the Marcus Allen *Sports Illustrated* poster on my wall and was desperate for him and the Raiders to beat the Redskins in Super Bowl XVIII, and before that, I was a Raiders fan in Super Bowl XV when they played the Eagles. Both times the Raiders were my rootable team and did not let me down.

The Raiders have three Super Bowls, two as the Oakland Raiders and one as the Los Angeles Raiders. Their indecisiveness on what part of California to call home is part of their schizophrenic persona and strangely part of their appeal. The Raiders are an oddly entertaining franchise—sort of like the Kardashians. You do not know why you watch, but you find yourself doing just that so you know how things turn out. Football is better when the Raiders are relevant, something they have not been for over a decade.

Oakland was close enough to see if Bonnie, our Texan-hating host from the first week of our trip, would let us sleep on her amazingly comfortable chairs in the living room for a night or two. She was gracious enough to allow us to return to her home. Since we owed her for giving us a place to stay again, we offered to take her out for dinner.

She picked an Italian place in a strip mall located next to a K-Mart not far from her house. It was a quaint place with an elegant ambiance and few tables, further adding to the understated panache radiating from the walls of the strip mall exterior.

Eric decided to walk to the K-Mart while I waited for our name to be called for a table. A few minutes later Eric returned and asked if I knew who Lester Hayes is—unknowingly questioning my legitimacy as a football fan growing up in the late '70s and early '80s. I quickly confirmed that I did, indeed know who Lester Hayes is, and inquired if he had died. Eric assured me that he was alive and well, and signing autographs at the K-Mart. I immediately went inside the restaurant and found Grayson at the bar with his girlfriend and Bonnie. I apologized for the interruption, but we needed to get back to work and interview *The* Lester Hayes.

We started the interview by asking him about the fans in Oakland. Truthfully, I think we could have asked him a question concerning global warming and its impact on the polar bear population and he would have given us the same answer.

He closed both hands as if making two fists then, putting them side by side, raised them to the height of the camera ensuring his two Super Bowl rings were at an advantageous angle to adequately sparkle under the best lighting a value store like K-Mart has to offer.

"Guys, it's like this," he said as he was raising his hands, "I'm a champion!" He almost gave the impression that he was reinforcing the fact he was a Super Bowl champion to himself as much as he was educating us and the camera on his successful career as a Raiders cornerback. The remainder of the interview was an inspirational speech delivered from the perspective of an impassioned preacher without the context of God.

I still could not believe our luck. This was Lester Hayes—*The* Lester Hayes that caused the NFL to ban

Stick 'Em because of his liberal use of the product to enhance his ability to grab and hold on to the jerseys of the opposing team's wide receivers, thus preventing them from successfully getting open down the field. Lester "The Molester" Hayes was in a K-Mart fielding questions from us in what ended up being my favorite interview of the entire trip. I was amazed at how many people walked by and did not realize who he was and what he meant to the Raiders mystique. He was, and will forever be, the quintessential Raiders player to me.

I do not know how it happened, but the Black Hole tailgate extended us an invitation to join them for the Raiders game. If legend is to be believed, these were going to be some of the most intense fans in the NFL and, as I said before, our safe return would be in doubt.

We took the train from Concord to O.co Coliseum, and it was like we had been let out on a completely different planet. You could see the stadium from the tracks, and it looked like one continuous façade of concrete with small signs intermittently placed in perhaps a half-hearted attempt to conceal the sterile, lifeless gray environment.

The reputation of the area surrounding the stadium was infamous for its crime and violence, and I remember being at the stadium and looking beyond the tracks and thinking how close we were to a completely foreign way of life to me. It was like those N.W.A records had come to life. The reputation for violence in the area around the stadium was later confirmed by a member of the Black Hole tailgate who warned us not to go three blocks on the other side of the tracks or we would be killed. Although we never felt unsafe at O.co Coliseum, we took his word for it and did not venture to the other side of the tracks.

While the reputation of the neighborhood around the stadium may be true, the reputation and myths about going to a Raiders game and the Black Hole tailgate could not be more wrong. We made our way to the tailgate and were greeted with smiles and offers of food and anything we wanted to drink. Our uneasiness about joining the Black Hole quickly disappeared. The tacos we ate were incredible and could only be matched by the hospitality offered to us by the people of the Black Hole.

We met with different members of the tailgate and learned their stories and history with the Raiders. There was one fan, however, who was born and raised in Philadelphia. Although he still lives there, he travels to the West Coast a couple of times a year for a Raiders game. The obvious question was: How does a guy from Philadelphia become and, more importantly, survive being a Raiders fan? He told us that he had watched Super Bowl XV between the Raiders and Eagles—just as I had done over thirty years ago. His room at the time was an Eagles fan cave, but after watching the Raiders beat the Eagles, he decided he was converting to the dark side, and has been a die-hard Raiders fan since. Members of the Black Hole attended his wedding, and they keep in touch throughout the year. A different picture of the Black

Hole was beginning to emerge from these types of stories. One not of violence, but of a family.

The next interview may have been our best fan interview the entire trip. The leader of the Black Hole tailgate introduced us to a very timid, but very talented, Raiders fan. He was an artist, and he would bring one of his poster-sized drawings of a different Raiders player to every game. Sometimes the player would, before or after the game, pass by the tailgate and sign the drawing. He did not want to be on camera, but we wanted to hear his story and wanted the rest of the world to possibly hear it as well.

Our equipment was very unassuming. A midlevel DSLR with a Rode mic and two small lapel microphones were all we carried, well, that was all we could afford, but were perfect for moments like this, when we wanted to hear the personal stories of fans, but did not want the look of our camera to somehow intimidate them.

After a lengthy discussion, we convinced Mandeep that he could trust us and to tell us his story. For this particular game, he had drawn a picture of Sebastian Janikowski, the Raiders kicker who strangely enough is one of their most popular players. It was an intricate drawing of the kicker from the torso up, screaming like he had just made the Super Bowl-winning field goal.

Throughout the interview, Mandeep held on tight to the drawing and held it in front of his body, almost as if to protect himself from the camera and us.

At one time he had been an outsider, he said. To hear him tell it, he has been one most of his life, describing himself as an "outcast," and that the outcast image of the Raiders is, in part, what drew him to the team and helped him identify with them. He gave the impression that he did not have much of a support structure at home and very few friends. He did have a passion for the Raiders, though, and that led him to the Black Hole tailgate.

The story we got from him and others we talked to that day was that Mandeep would go to Raiders games and walk by the Black Hole, always remaining on the periphery. Eventually, one of the members of the Black Hole did as they had done with us and extended a warm greeting and a smile. Since that day, the Black Hole has become Mandeep's family. The members of the tailgate have filled an emotional void in his life, giving him a sense of belonging and of importance in life. He may never feel comfortable enough to put down that poster-board-sized drawing he figuratively keeps in front of him, but the Black Hole tailgate is a start. For us that day and for Mandeep every Raiders home game, the Black Hole tailgate was a sanctuary, a home, and a family.

This game marked the first week of the fantasy football playoffs, and fate presented another opportunity to watch, in person, the best player on my fantasy team—Jamaal Charles. Whether it is actual skill or pure luck, my team is a perpetual contender and, more times than not we are still playing well into December. We were decisive underdogs going into the game and had an extra $100 on this particular week. At that point of the trip, that was a lot of money—enough for two whole nights in a shady motel!

Charles scored on a forty-nine-yard reception the first play of the game running straight toward the end zone where our seats were located. Surrounded by Raiders fans, I could not even cheer—it was not that the section we were sitting in was filled with fans of questionable moral character, but it was still pretty early in the game, so I thought it best to not endear myself to Raiders fans just yet. Since we were in Oakland, I did not want to find myself on the wrong side of either the tracks or Raiders fans.

The game only got worse for the Raiders but better for Charles, the Chiefs, and my fantasy team. Charles scored five touchdowns on the day and didn't play in the fourth quarter. The Chiefs won the game "going away," as they say, 56-31.

I liked the Raiders, the fans of the Black Hole tailgate and our entire experience at O.co Stadium. And, despite the prosperity of my fantasy team, I never cheered once for Charles and the Chiefs but two nights in a shady motel were mine!

As it turned out, Grayson has a younger cousin who lives in Portland, Oregon, which on the surface of it made it a good idea to contact him to see if we could stay with him for the week leading up to our last game in Seattle.

I had never been to the Northwest despite hearing positive things about it. Most comments I heard drew favorable comparisons between Portland

and Austin, and I needed a little Austin heading into our final game, so I was more than a little excited to be en route to Portland.

Our drive took us on winding roads through the mountains. I noticed there was not much along the road to stop a runaway car—for example a 1967 VW Bus without brakes—from going off the side of the mountain, so I began to see that Hail Mary being in Cincinnati was a good thing for everyone's safety, including hers. I still missed her and felt like I was letting her down, even though she was the one who refused to go on the last leg of the trip. Somehow, considering our propensity of living life on the edge without brakes and understanding the definite possibility of going over the side of a mountain with everyone plummeting to their deaths eased my mind about leaving her behind.

After the Raiders game, we had stayed the night in a two-star motel in southern Oregon. The motel pool was completely frozen, which made a good picture to send back to my kids but left a lot to be desired in the way of comfort. Our brief time in Oregon reminded me a lot of the lodges of Red River, New Mexico, where my family would go on ski trips—good times! Staying in a motel with a frozen pool in rural, southern Oregon, not so much. But this was our last week and my first taste of Oregon, so I was determined to enjoy it.

The next day we arrived in Portland, beginning the longest five days of the trip by far. It was a cold, overcast, depressing day when we got to the house

Grayson's cousin was renting with three other people. It was very small with a front porch where a guy was sitting taking the last few drags of his cigarette. He had long, thin, black hair that flowed from underneath his black knit hat. His beard was obviously the best he could grow since it was apparent he made no attempt to shave despite its patchy, unevenness.

Grayson's cousin was friendly enough and walked us inside to meet the others. There was a slim, blonde guy with long bangs that hung over his eyes with the sides of his hair neatly trimmed above his ears. He wore a cornflower blue button-down shirt with the sleeves rolled up revealing a rather large tattoo on his forearm.

His first question to us was to gauge our stance on cocaine. After he saw the responses on our faces, he apologetically laughed his question off, dismissing it as just needing to get that out of the way. His next question was if we wanted some "za." What the hell is za, and how crazy is it that I would rather pay for a shady motel with a frozen pool than stay for free in a house? Za, as it turns out, is short for pizza. While I still do not understand the rationale or necessity for having to abbreviate pizza, some za sounded good.

Despite at least one of them being a cocaine user who felt life was too short for two syllable words like pizza, our hosts were extremely welcoming and made us feel at home. The house itself was what you might expect from twenty-somethings living in Portland and playing in a band. The dishes may not have been done in over a week, but they were at least placed around the sink. The living room was painted a Christmas red, held a sparsely decorated Christmas tree, and was home to jam sessions we would be privy to in the coming days.

Grayson's cousin occupied the basement, and there was a small space across from his bedroom where I would stay. I looked into the bathroom to find a stand-up shower, a small sink, and a picture of a woman that had been torn out of a *Playboy* magazine taped to the wall next to the mirror. She was attractive and, as many times as I had seen her naked throughout the week, I felt like I needed to know her name. I never did get her name, nor did I use that stand-up shower. If the dishes had not been cleaned in a week or so, the shower had been an even lower priority. The more I looked around in that bathroom, the more it became obvious that the cleanest thing in there—if not the entire house—was the naked picture that stared back at me every time I stared in the mirror contemplating where life had taken me.

Over the next four days the sun remained a rumor and the temperature stayed just warm enough to be annoyingly cold. We passed the days catching up on episodes of *The League* and eating za. Suffering from cabin fever, we ventured out to VooDoo Donuts where I ate a donut topped with Cap'n Crunch. I am sure this combination has been accidentally discovered by children at countless breakfast tables around the country, but it was a first for me. Although I have not recreated this delicacy since, it was a welcomed infusion of sugar that made me question why I had not eaten more Cap'n Crunch in my lifetime.

I was excited to pass by the Rose Garden where the Portland Trail Blazers played all of those memorable games with Clyde Drexler, Terry Porter, and Jerome Kersey. The Rose Garden was electric during the playoffs and in the 1992 Finals against the Bulls. Somehow I got the impression that it was not just because it was the NBA Playoffs, but rather that the city of Portland loved the Trail Blazers. For that reason—and that reason alone—I always had a positive impression of Portland. The most redeemable quality of the city, other than its passion for the Trail Blazers, is that it had the highest per capita of VW Bus owners in the country or, at least, that was my impression.

I never took a shower while we were in Portland for fear I would emerge from the bathroom dirtier than when I went in. I never got to say goodbye to the naked girl on the wall either. The sun remained uncooperative from the day we arrived in Portland until the day we left. Although it would be great to be able to take a shower and shave, I would strangely miss the house in Portland and our za-eating friends. I guess in some weird, Stockholm syndrome way, we had bonded with our hosts in Portland. It was not perfect, just like traveling with Hail Mary had not always been perfect, but our trip would not have been the same without that experience.

Seattle meant our last game and our last motel stay. It also meant a couple more days without sunshine. Evidently the Portland weather followed us north and decided to remain with us for our stay in Seattle. There was not an overwhelming sense of sadness that our journey was coming to an end: We had too much to think about, such as getting our final interviews for the documentary, meeting NFL Films for the last time, and, if nothing else, making it home in time for Christmas.

Seattle to me had always been Steve Largent and Jim Zorn, maybe even Curt Warner in the Kingdome. Most remember the Seahawks for drafting Brian Bosworth and how he got trampled by Bo Jackson of the Raiders on *Monday Night Football*. "The Boz," as Bosworth was known at the University of Oklahoma, was a flamboyant, look-at-me type of player. I do not think it was personal between Jackson and Bosworth that Monday night, but that single play defined the career of both players in the NFL. Bosworth never materialized to be the player he was in college, and Bo Jackson offered a glimpse of the potential he had before his career was derailed with a hip injury.

Before the Monday Night Stampede, the Seahawks occasionally found their way to the late game on NBC with Dick Enberg and Merlin Olson. Never amounting to much in the American Football Conference, the Seahawks may as well have been playing in Russia because to me they were little more than a helmet on a lunch box or pennant. In recent years, the team moved to the National Football Conference and greatly improved its fortunes as a football franchise. In 2006, it lost a controversial Super Bowl to the Steelers, and I remember thinking that the Seahawks had finally joined the ranks of the haves and left the have-nots to Cleveland, Houston, Jacksonville, and Detroit as the only teams to never have played in a Super Bowl. They had redesigned their uniforms and with it came an attitude, either real or imagined, that they were a perennial contender.

Contenders are exactly where the Seahawks and their fans found themselves when we went to the game in Seattle. Known as the 12th Man in the NFL, the home of the Seahawks, CenturyLink Field, and Arrowhead Stadium in Kansas City are widely considered the loudest in the league.

The team's 12th Man designation is actually on loan from Texas A&M University, which coined the phrase "12th Man"; by coined I mean trademarked. Growing up in Texas, the Aggies will always be the 12th Man to me, but the Seahawks and their fans deserve recognition for being loud during the game and consequently having an impact on the outcome.

We went to a bar close to the stadium that is apparently the place to get a beer before the game. That is where we were introduced to "Bernie Hawk," a guy who took a job in Denver with an airline so that he could fly to Seattle for the games. "If I didn't work for the airline I would move to Washington and still be a Seahawks fan," he told us.

If we had interviewed Bernie Hawk in September I would have shaken my head in disbelief, but the countless interviews with fans around the country, and even our experiences with Hail Mary, tempered the shock value of his life decision.

The subtle, ornate texture of the Seahawks uniform was not lost on the face paint of Bernie Hawk, either. He was as complete a face-paint fan as found in the world of sports and seemed to be at peace in his hard hat, customized to resemble the helmet of the Seahawks. Bernie was not his real name, just his Seahawks fan persona. His sunglasses and black mustache bore a striking resemblance to the main character from the film *Weekend at Bernie's*.

The name caught on so he will be forever known as Bernie Hawk. He told us it was other fans and the infectious atmosphere that compelled him to develop his own character. Bernie's voice danced with excitement as he pointed out the other devoted fans in the bar, including a married couple, "Mr. and Mrs. Seahawk," and a fan known as "Cannonball," who was as reflective of a fan as we interviewed for the documentary. "If you cut me open, I would bleed blue and green. That's just the way it is," Cannonball told us.

The Seahawks were having a great season, winning their division and appearing to be a real contender, not just to go to the Super Bowl but to win it. Cannonball had made the conscious decision just to enjoy each moment as it came and not be focused so much on winning the Super Bowl. He had witnessed, in person, Seattle's loss to the Steelers in Super Bowl XL, and was determined that this season would be different. Win or lose, this season was to be enjoyed.

CenturyLink Field is a unique looking venue centered in downtown Seattle next to the baseball stadium. I would like to be able to explain where the stadium is in relation to the Space Needle, but I never saw Seattle's most iconic landmark. The clouds blanketed the sky near the top of the stadium, so what the Seattle skyline looks like is still a mystery to me.

I walked in and had a lower-level seat for the game between the Cardinals and the Seahawks. I had bought the ticket the day they went on sale, but could not figure out how to change sections when ordering. Consequently, I got a better seat than any other game except for Dallas, where our tickets were free, and maybe the Bears game. At this point, the end of our trip, I viewed it as a reward for having made it to every stadium.

From the intensity and loudness of the fans, it would have been difficult to understand how the first three quarters of the game featured a total of three field goals. It was by far the loudest stadium I had ever been to and one of the best football environments in the country.

The Seahawks lost the game 17-10, but eventually won the Super Bowl against the Denver Broncos. That win against the Broncos probably made Bernie Hawk's flight back home to Denver that much sweeter.

EPILOGUE

Austin, NFL Films, and Hail Mary

(112 Days, 32 Teams, 31 Stadiums, 26,149 miles)

Certainly, travel is more than the seeing of sights; it is a change that goes on, deep and permanent, in the ideas of living.

– Mary Ritter Beard

There are times in life that you convince yourself that after a certain event everything will be drastically different. That point in time transforms you into a different person, somehow providing a line of demarcation for your life.

For me, going to all thirty-one stadiums in sixteen weeks in Hail Mary was supposed to be that event. Almost depressingly I admit it was not, it was more of a feeling of "I cannot believe that is it." The journey was over. We had seen everything there was to see, attended thirty-two games and driven over 25,000 miles and for what?

I have never wanted to climb a mountain because I could always imagine struggling to make it to the top and looking down thinking how great the view is but how far I still had to go to get back down. For whatever reason, the mountain climbing analogy had not occurred to me until after I had climbed the NFL mountain.

By that time it was too late, and all I could think about was how far I had to drive to escape the Rocky Mountains and make it back to Austin. Doing that meant driving down to Los Angeles and picking up I-10 to Texas.

I was dejected with the experience of accomplishing my goal, but maybe this was not the pivotal, life-changing moment. Maybe that would come when I could sit with family and friends and watch what NFL Films produced about our journey. That seemed logical to me. After all, what football fan who grew up watching Steve Sabol and the great NFL Films productions would not want to be featured on a show? The more I thought about it, the more I rationalized it: That would, indeed, be the seminal moment of my life.

The feature aired on ESPN2 and the NFL Network the week of the Super Bowl. The first night my mother and I watched it together. We had patiently waited for a college basketball game to end and then, a little past midnight, it happened: Hail Mary and the entire crew were on *NFL Films Presents*. Not only that, but we were the first segment of the show.

There she was, Hail Mary in all her glory for the world to see. It was, of course, well done and perfectly encapsulated our four months of hard work in almost eight minutes. That is right, four months of time and effort neatly packaged and condensed into eight minutes!

I had just been on national television with Hail Mary, the very same VW Bus my dad thought I should have sold immediately after buying it, and yet nothing was different. It was like the feeling when you have a milestone birthday—like thirty or forty—and someone asks you if you feel any different. It is with a sense of relief that you answer in the negative, almost believing that life would be over at a certain age, yet you find yourself still alive.

The next day the same show aired on the NFL Network. This time, I watched it with my dad and his wife, my brother and his family, and my two children. The second time viewing it with my sons had to be my one shining moment because I was running out of moments. My youngest was disinterested after a few minutes of seeing dad on television, but my nephew was more into it and, for a brief period, considered me to be famous. Everyone else was rather ho-hum about the entire event. There were not any atta boys, I am proud of yous, or that was awesome. We simply returned to the table and finished the meal we were eating before the show came on.

I was monitoring Facebook with my phone just to see if anyone else had seen the show. My account had a new message that read:

> *Just watched the segment on NFL Network, and was completely amazed by you guys. The license plate for the van was great. I live here in Texas also, near San Antonio, my license plate is a Purple Heart plate that says 'LWAY', I am a life-*

> *long Broncos fan and lost both lower legs in Iraq in 2009. If someone said to me you can have your feet back...or you could go on a trip with two guys of your choice and visit all 32 stadiums...I would choose what you guys did in a heartbeat (that is not an exaggeration). Thank you for sharing it and letting those of us who cannot live that dream live vicariously through you guys, my jealousy cannot be measured. People tell me often that I am a hero or an inspiration, it always makes me uncomfortable. So I hope this doesn't make you too uncomfortable, but to me you guys are an inspiration and are my football heroes.*

I was so moved by the message that I read it aloud to everyone sitting at the table, almost as a justification of what I had accomplished, while rebuking the lack of reaction I received from my family. With a smile and tears welling up in my eyes from the touching sentiment of a stranger, I jokingly proclaimed myself a "True American Hero."

While it was not the defining moment I was looking for, it was confirmation that our journey was special and something many people could only dream of doing. I did not feel different, just more motivated to produce the documentary, write this book, and maybe help others to either vicariously live our journey or have the courage to pursue their own glory.

Maybe it is not one fleeting moment that changes us forever, maybe it is a series of moments, a journey of moments that gradually transforms us into who we are destined to become. Maybe I had looked at life all wrong—it was not a change like a light that you can turn on or off—maybe it was like a sunrise that gets more intense over time.

In the time since we completed the journey to every stadium in sixteen weeks I have relived a little bit of the trip every day. It may have something to do with producing the documentary or writing this book. What I realized in my moments of reflection was that I was looking for that one pot of gold at the end of the rainbow, but what I came to understand is that there was gold all along our journey in the most improbable places.

The map of our trip became not just crossing off teams, stadiums or cities, but making the personal connections and gaining from the experiences we shared with so many people. When we left my driveway in September, it was as if we asked the world to take care of us, and the world responded in a way that was completely unexpected and impossible to predict. Hail Mary had a lot to do with it, but some people never even got to meet her, just us, and somehow we were enough.

There were many days and nights along the way that I truly did not know how we would make it through the next day much less the next game. I just believed in myself and, after a while, I believed in the goodness of others. At first it was just the two other guys in the VW Bus with me, but slowly it became everyone we met: The people who approached us at gas stations; talked to us at motels or tailgates; who invited us to stay with them; the people at the Liberty Diner; and the poor, kind souls who stopped and helped us keep Hail Mary in place after witnessing us go through two intersections in Cincinnati. The list could go on, but I see these people, I remember them and their generosity. We entered their lives for a brief moment in time, but they will forever be with me.

Looking back on our last game and remembering what it was like to be almost disappointed in the lack of euphoria I felt when it was over, realizing that my life had not changed—it was the same as it was before I started this journey. The only difference, I thought at the time, was that I was over 2,000 miles from home.

I discovered that it was not my life that had changed; it was me. I thought I went on this tour to see every NFL stadium in one year, but why I really wanted to take this trip was to change the narrative of my life and, hopefully, those of my children. I suspect that is why anyone would do something as ambitious as *25,000 Miles to Glory*.

Evel Knievel attempted to jump the fountains at Caesars Palace in Las Vegas, and while I do not think he cared to jump over the fountains, he saw it as a way to change the story of his life. To almost anyone else, doing that jump, or even attempting to make it around the country in Hail Mary, is one step removed from needing to be in a padded room. To me it was simply what life was intended to be, and I hope that by going on this trip and seeing what can happen in life serves as proof that dreams do come true, and will encourage my sons to pursue their glory and what is in their hearts.

I am convinced this trip was planned decades before, when I lived in a small house in Austin. If I close my eyes, I can still see those small football pennants above my closet. And I remember throwing the ball left-handed because it had a Kenny Stabler (who was left-handed) signature on it, I can remember walking by and seeing the Oilers playing the Steelers thinking how crazy it was the Steelers had a logo on only one side of their helmets. I remember going through the *Sears Wish Book* every year and writing down the new NFL shirts, hats, and other items I needed to add to my Christmas list. I remember watching football on Sunday afternoons—games played in those magical shrines to sports—and feeling the electricity of *Monday Night Football* through my television.

That was a great time to grow up and an even better time to be a football fan. Looking back at myself at the age of five or six I can see that there was very little anyone could have done to prevent me from taking this trip.

The journey had cost Hail Mary her windshield wipers and horn, and replaced some of her paint with bare metal or even rust—the issues that are readily visible. But there were more issues underneath her iconic exterior, and the more I began putting the pieces back together the more I realized how bad of an idea it was to take her around the country. The engine was missing a bolt, allowing the alternator to wobble and the belt to be chewed up as we drove from stadium to stadium. The nest of wires crisscrossing underneath the dashboard leading to more fuses than were originally in a VW Bus were more of a burden than any vehicle could bear. These issues, along with the others, made our trip more miraculous than I originally thought.

Hail Mary served to force me, as a person, to actively flirt with the line between rational and what most—even in the air-cooled VW community—would call foolish. I prefer adventurous, but whatever the adjective, Hail Mary pushed my boundaries of what I thought was possible and what I knew or believed as logical, while somehow making me comfortable with discomfort.

The challenge, however, was not with Hail Mary or making it to every stadium in sixteen weeks. The real challenge was me: Could I manage the days of sleeping on the side of the road, calling on strangers for help, and finding a way out when there seemed to be an endless supply of obstacles preventing us from making it to our next destination? Could I drive from El Centro, California, to Austin in one day, or Miami to Dallas to Green Bay from Friday to Monday? Did I want what I said I wanted bad enough to ride a bus overnight from New Jersey to Buffalo just to get in Hail Mary and drive back to New Jersey? The answer was always a resounding yes.

I did not do this trip alone, though, and could not have done it alone. Grayson and Eric were as unflinching and unrelenting as I was, sometimes even more. And the thought of my sons, Chandler and Roman, kept me moving forward knowing that each day was a day closer to being with them. That, combined with the fear of failing and refusing to disappoint those who had helped us along the way and who supported me in Texas, prevented me from ever admitting defeat and surrendering to the constant struggle of completing the trip.

I was, like so many millions of other boys growing up, a huge football fan. I dreamed of being Roger Staubach or Eric Dickerson or Dan Marino, and watched countless hours of NFL Films productions. I still have the NFL Films feature about my journey on DVD, but rarely, if ever, watch it, however, the experience will be with me for the rest of my life.

Hail Mary has remained in my garage since Grayson and I drove her back from Ohio the May following our trip. At first, when I walked by her I was apologetic about what I put her through. Slowly, she began to be able to look me in the eyes as I passed. I would often give her a few pats as if to say: "That is a good girl. Love you." After a few months of this she began to talk to me again, asking when we were going to go out on the road. Although I have never promised her that she would ever see outside the city limits of Austin again, the more she talks to me the more I realize that keeping her parked would be like keeping a race horse tied to a tree. The horse longs to run just like Hail Mary longs for the open road.

I am unable to explain my irrational attachment to Hail Mary. All I can offer is the advice of own a split-window VW Bus and then you will understand. Driving in a '67 VW Bus is unlike any other experience you can imagine. It shows you how much the world needs something different from the everyday, mundane choices our typical lives so generously give us, and how little it takes to make people smile, wave, and talk to a complete stranger. The world needs more people driving VW Buses. We need more smiles, more waves, and more strangers coming together. Hail Mary is unequivocally the best money I have ever spent, and this trip was my life's greatest adventure thanks to her.

There is nothing special about me or anyone who went on the trip. We did not have any special advantages and did not know much about VW Buses, obviously. We did not have a lot of money either, leading me to believe that in life it is the things we do not have that prove we are innately resourceful and capable of creating our destiny on our own. I simply had to stop making excuses for why something was not going to happen or could not happen, and focus on how to make it happen with the limited resources I did have. I believed that no matter what came our way we were going to make it and be okay. Even though the world kept telling me no, I kept insisting that it was going to happen and eventually that belief stopped the world from saying no and helped me achieve my dream.

Anyone, regardless of circumstances, should not let doubt stifle their dreams or strangle them into silence. Our craziest dreams are worth believing in and worth living out. As someone who has been wherever you are in life and reading this book for whatever reason, I can tell you that the only chances we truly regret in life are those that we did not take. There are two types of pain in life. The pain of regret, of letting your dreams fade away and the pain of the hard work and countless hours that it takes to make your dreams a reality

Edward Abbey said: "Freedom happens between the ears," and he could not be more right. You have the freedom to create your own amazing adventure. We all have a film, a book, or a dream within us. Ask yourself these questions: Where is my glory? Where are those dreams I had as a child when anything was possible?

I implore you to find the journey that lies within you and breathe life into your dreams. Now is the time to make them happen!